THE REAL FOOD OF CHINA

Leanne Kitchen   Antony Suvalko

hardie grant books
MELBOURNE · LONDON

SBS

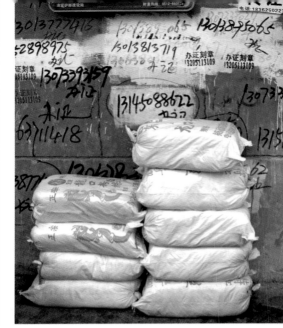

Right: Upper Xiaoqi village, Wuyuan,
Jiangxi Province

The Chinese Kitchen

Can there be a subject in the entire culinary world more vast than that of Chinese cuisine? After regularly visiting this great country for nearly twenty years, we don't think so. At once familiar and confoundingly foreign, the notions of 'China' and 'Chinese food' are not easy to define or neatly quantify. After all, we're talking about one of the world's oldest civilisations, and a nation today of over 1.3 billion people, five time zones, twenty-two provinces and five autonomous regions. It has over fifty distinct ethnic groups, dozens of languages and dialects, and fourteen direct neighbours as disparate as India, Tajikistan, North Korea, Burma (Myanmar), Laos, Russia, Mongolia and Kazakhstan. A mind-blowing diversity of plants and animals are found there and China's climatic regions span the chilling arctic blasts of the far north and the lush tropical languor of the south. In between are epic mountain ranges, deserts, fertile plateaus, river lowlands and vast lakes, plus more than 14,000 kilometres of coastline abundant with fish and seafood. To say this is one diverse country, with a rich, complex and lengthy history of culinary refinement, is as colossal an understatement as the place itself.

To travel around China today, even for a short spell, is to grasp how much there is to learn about the myriad ways this nation cooks and eats. The 'Chinese' food we're most familiar with in the West is actually Cantonese food — peoples from that one, southern province were the earliest Chinese immigrants to places such as Canada, America, Australia and New Zealand. With them, the Cantonese brought their distinctive cooking style and insinuated it marvellously into our own — their barbecued and roasted meats, their morning yum cha habit, and dishes such as sweet and sour pork, wonton noodle soup, whole steamed fish and chow mein. While Cantonese cuisine is considered the pinnacle in China, it's only part of the story; there are eight officially recognised culinary styles in all, namely Shandong, Sichuan, Guangdong (Cantonese), Fujian, Jiangsu, Zhejiang, Hunan and Anhui.

While these eight styles represent a bountiful and wide-ranging canon, they don't even begin to take into account the distinct cuisines of the many ethnic minorities, nor the rustic dishes of places such as Inner Mongolia, the sprawling northeast region of Dongbei or western parts of the country such as Xinjiang, Qinghai and Tibet, these days subsumed into China proper. Nor do they account for the specialties and styles that exist within a region — seemingly each city has its own unique dishes, ingredients or ways of cooking that differ from the next. Sometimes, as happens in other food-rich countries, this divergence even occurs at the village level.

From the sweetish grilled *rubing* (goat's milk cheese) of Yunnan and her incredible species of edible wild mushrooms; the artisanal smoked pork of Hunan; the stone-cooked flatbreads of Shandong; the fermented, 'stinky' foods of Shaoxing; and the cumin-encrusted lamb skewers of Xinjiang; to the diverse noodle culture of Shanxi; the tenderest spring bamboo shoots of Zhejiang; the extraordinary treatment of seafood in Fujian; the simple grain congees of the centre and north; and the sublime duck dishes of Nanjing ... Chinese food takes you on one hell of a tasty ride.

In all of this mind-bending gustatory variance, though, there are common strands that bind the country together. There's a saying that the Chinese people 'regard food as their heaven'. If you take that to mean, as we do, that they *adore* good food and that the preparing, cooking and enjoying of it are vitally important in their daily lives, you'll start to build a picture. Whether dining takes place on the street (China surely has one of the world's richest street-food cultures), in restaurants or in the home, there's a joy and exuberance around the act of eating that is infectious. As anywhere, people will grab a quick, solo refuel if they need to, but, generally, eating is a communal act where diners share dishes from large serving bowls or plates. The notions of 'harmony' (*he* in Chinese) and family relationships are central to life here and nowhere is this expressed more clearly than in a strong desire to eat together. Meals are composed of a careful mix of ingredients, cooking techniques and textures, where hot and cold, sweet and savoury, carbs and proteins, vegetables and meat, oily and lean, steamed and fried are kept in rigorous balance. Achieving a harmony of salty, sour, bitter, spicy and sweet notes is also key, as is an observance of the health-giving properties of many ingredients.

Take a wander down any of China's streets or tangle of small alleyways and you'll find culinary adventures galore. There, the streets are permeated not just with tantalising food smells, but also with the loud sizzle, hiss, whoosh and spit from woks, steamers and coal-fuelled grills spewing out dumplings, rice, soups, meats and flatbreads. And, in the wheat-eating northern parts, streets ring with the rhythmic thwack of hand-made noodles being belted out against tabletops and benches.

Internally, some of China's regional cooking styles are considered more refined than others. Those of Shandong, Fujian, the afore-mentioned Guangdong (Canton) and the Imperial cuisine of Beijing, for example, are lauded for their complex techniques and dainty presentation that show a highly evolved culinary aesthetic. For us, though, the real draw of Chinese food is found in its simplest expressions — in a bowl of knife-cut noodles doused in chilli and vinegar; in a plate of springy, boiled dumplings; or a shared serve of succulent roast duck with a side of just-steamed greens — and the near-religious respect Chinese people have for perfectly fresh ingredients. We love scratching around Chinese produce markets and marvelling at the enticing layers of fat on their pork, the piles of fresher-than-fresh seasonal fruits and vegetables, and the diversity of ingredients, such as the huge range of tofu or grades of dried chilli available. We love the way the Chinese insist on purchasing poultry and fish live and having it dispatched to order; perhaps over time, with growing wealth and the inevitable increase in the number of supermarkets, this may change but, for now, 'fresh' and 'seasonal' define the way the country shops. We're fascinated, too, that everything is fair dining game: frogs, duck's tongues, cock's combs, donkey, turtles, bee larvae, raw pig skin, rats, snake and every style of innards you could possibly imagine.

....

'Beneath these green mountains where spring rules the year,

the irbarbutus and loquat in season appear,

And feasting on lychee — 300 a day,

I shouldn't mind staying eternally here.'

Su Shih, 1094 AD

About the recipes

While you won't discover anything quite so exotic in this book, what you will find are recipes that celebrate what we've come to love the most about this incredible cuisine: easy cooking techniques, punchy flavours, everyday ingredients (you'll find most of what you need in a Chinese supermarket or your local Asian market) and a generous approach to the shared table. We've in no way intended to exhaustively document the depth and breadth of the country and its fare — that would require several lifetimes — and much that is so unique about Chinese food needs to be appreciated in situ. There simply is no way to experience the hand-made fermented sausages of Anchang, the catfish of Sichuan, the hams of Jinhua, the bamboo-cooked rice of Guilin, the gooey, sweet fire crystal persimmons of Xi'an, the hairy crabs of Shanghai, the raw pork skin of Dali, the unique street snacks of Chaozhou or the celebrated rice flour noodles of Nanchang unless you go there yourself ...

Failing that, your next best bet is to cook! Which is where this book comes in. We've deliberately chosen dishes that, in the main, are achievable at home; we're aware that complete proficiency in the Chinese kitchen demands mastery of the cleaver and wok plus dexterity at tasks such as filling dumplings and slapping noodles around — all skills that require practice. The majority of these recipes can be made with basic proficiency and equipment; we've actually avoided too many stir-fries, for example, as we find most domestic stoves lack the fire power to truly give good results (which isn't to say you don't need a wok; in fact, having a few different sized ones is useful). Quite a number of the dishes involve simmering, stewing and steaming, all homey cooking methods that produce the sort of no-fuss, full-flavoured food we love. Those that do get you rolling wrappers, cutting up chicken or folding lotus leaves are doable even for the novice, so rarely should you come unstuck. Neat cutting for even cooking and tidy presentation is helpful for many of the dishes, but if your knife work isn't so exact, no worries — common sense with cooking times will cover a multitude of inexact slicing sins!

For convenience, this book is parcelled up into chapters based on main ingredients — 'pork', 'noodles and rice' and 'vegetables and tofu', for example. We want you to be able to easily dip in and out of sections to build a meal, whether simple or sumptuous. Choose a few meat and/or fish dishes, throw in a good number of cold ones (many of these can conveniently be done in advance) and a vegetable option or two and you've got a banquet on your hands. Note that just about all the recipes here are designed to share, in keeping with how the Chinese dine. Select across the various cooking techniques (deep-frying, steaming, simmering) for textural interest and feel free to substitute vegetables in dishes depending on what's in season.

Many of the vegetable, rice, noodle and dumpling recipes are perfect to serve as stand-alone, easy meal ideas, and so are rustic dishes such as Xingjiang 'big bowl' chicken and Beer fish. Others such as Soy sauce chicken, Beef ribs with vinegar and honey dates or, our favourite, Crisp roast pork belly, just need a pot of steamed rice and some wok-fried greens to constitute an effortless meal. Cook as many, or as few, dishes as the occasion, available time and hunger levels dictate.

And, although the Chinese don't usually end a meal with a pudding as such, we've gone the *laowai* (foreigner) route and fashioned some of our sweet favourites from the street and the Chinese snacking repertoire into recipes that we call 'dessert'. As for drinks, we think the spicy, heavier dishes here demand beer, and Chinese Tsingtao, developed in 1904 in Shandong Province on the back of German brewing know-how, is an admirable choice. Otherwise we like tea ... as do the Chinese. 'Better to be deprived of food for three days than tea for one,' as another Chinese saying goes. *Tie guanyin* (a semi-fermented tea that's a type of oolong from Fujian) or *longjing* (the famous green 'dragon well' tea from Hangzhou) are our favourites, although for yum cha we choose pu-erh, a dark, smoky fermented tea from Yunnan that's said to aid digestion.

Left, clockwise from top left: Zhuxian, Henan Province; Xiamen, Fujian Province; Pingyao, Shanxi Province; Pingyao, Shanxi Province

Right: Near Dali, Yunnan Province

Previous page, left to right: Pingyao, Shanxi Province; Fenghuang, Hunan Province

Left: Near Dali, Yunnan Province

Right, clockwise from top left: Lushan, Sichuan Province; near Meizhou, Guangdong Province; Lake Erhai, Yunnan Province; Chengdu, Sichuan Province

24

From left to right: Chengdu, Sichuan
Province; near Yangshuo, Guangxi
Province; Guangzhou, Guangdong
Province

From left to right: Wuyuan, Jiangxi Province; Shangli village, Sichuan Province

Left, clockwise from top left: Beijing; near Meizhou, Guangdong Province; Changsha, Hunan Province; Shaoxing, Zhejiang Province

Right: Suzhou, Jiangsu Province

From left to right: Pingyao, Shanxi
Province; Qibao, Shanghai; Beihai,
Guangxi Province

From left to right: Shaoxing, Zhejiang Province; Beijing

Left: Zhuxian Zhen, Henan Province

Right, clockwise from top left: Xi'an, Shaanxi Province; Lushan, Sichuan Province; Pingyao, Shanxi Province; Xi'an, Shaanxi Province

From left to right: Hangzhou, Zhejiang Province; Xi'an, Shaanxi Province; Guangzhou, Guangdong Province

Left, clockwise from top left: Pingyao,
Shanxi Province; Shanghai, Zhejiang
Province; Guangzhou, Guangdong
Province; Chaozhou, Guangdong
Province

Right: Shanghai

From left to right: Guangzhou, Guangdong Province; Suzhou, Jiangsu Province

Following page: Fenghuang, Hunan Province

Cold Dishes & Snacks

In Chinese cuisine there's an entire repertoire of *liang cai* (cold dishes) served before the main meal event. Also called 'welcoming' dishes, these serve to spark appetites with their fragrant tastes, crisp textures, bright colours and beautiful presentation. For the Chinese, if these dishes are good, then they can relax, knowing the rest of the meal will be up to scratch too. The few hot snacks also included here can be served at any time, and with anything you fancy.

Chilli-fried dried anchovies and peanuts

Serves 6

vegetable oil, for deep-frying
100 g (3½ oz) dried anchovies
120 g (4½ oz/¾ cup) raw, skinned peanuts
2–3 long red chillies, finely sliced

3 garlic cloves, finely sliced
3 spring onions (scallions), finely sliced
1 tablespoon clear rice wine

Fill a wok one-third full of oil and heat to 180°C (350°F), or until a cube of bread dropped into the oil turns deep golden in 15 seconds. Add the anchovies and fry for 2–3 minutes, or until crisp and golden. Remove with a slotted spoon and drain on paper towel. Add the peanuts to the oil and fry for about 3 minutes, or until golden, then remove and drain on paper towel.

Pour off all but 2 tablespoons of oil from the wok. Return the wok to a medium heat, add the chillies, garlic and spring onions and stir-fry for 30 seconds, then add the rice wine. Return the anchovies and peanuts to the wok and toss to combine well. Serve hot or at room temperature.

Tea eggs

Makes 8

8 eggs
2 tablespoons light soy sauce
1 tablespoon dark soy sauce
2 star anise

1 piece cassia bark
1 piece dried tangerine peel
4 slices peeled ginger
2 tablespoons black tea leaves

Put the eggs in a small saucepan, cover with cold water and slowly bring to a simmer. Cook for 3 minutes, then drain and rinse under cold running water to cool.

Combine the remaining ingredients with 750 ml (25½ fl oz/3 cups) water in a small saucepan. Gently tap and roll the unpeeled eggs on a solid surface to crack the shells (do not peel the eggs). Add the cracked eggs to the soy sauce mixture in the pan and bring to a simmer. Cook over a low heat for 2 hours, adding extra water as necessary to keep the eggs just covered. Remove the pan from the heat and leave the eggs to cool in the liquid. Drain, peel the eggs and serve.

Fennel-flavoured broad beans

Serves 8

330 g (11½ oz/2 cups) dried, unpeeled broad (fava) beans

2½ tablespoons dark soy sauce

1½ star anise

1 piece cassia bark

2 tablespoons fennel seeds

Put the broad beans in a bowl, cover with plenty of cold water and leave to soak overnight. Drain well.

Transfer the broad beans to a saucepan, add the remaining ingredients and enough cold water to just cover, then bring to a simmer over a medium-low heat. Reduce the heat to low and cook for about 1 hour and 20 minutes, or until the beans are tender, stirring occasionally so they cook evenly, and adding a little more water to keep them covered, if necessary. Take care not to overcook the beans or they will fall apart. Remove the pan from the heat and leave the beans to cool in the liquid. Drain and serve at room temperature.

Photograph page 51

Fragrant peanuts

Serves 4 to 6

1 piece dried tangerine peel

2 star anise

1 piece cassia bark

2½ tablespoons dark soy sauce

1 tablespoon light soy sauce

½ teaspoon five-spice

55 g (2 oz/¼ cup) caster (superfine) sugar

240 g (8½ oz/1½ cups) raw, red-skinned peanuts

Combine all the ingredients and 625 ml (21 fl oz/2½ cups) water in a small saucepan. The peanuts should be covered in liquid; add a little extra water if necessary. Bring the mixture to a simmer, then partially cover the pan and cook over a low heat for 2½ hours, or until the peanuts are tender. Remove the lid and simmer for a further 30 minutes, or until the liquid has reduced and is syrupy. Cool to room temperature before serving.

Fried stuffed tofu skins

Makes 8

Strictly speaking, tofu skin is actually soy milk skin (it's made by lifting off the skin that forms on soy milk in the early stages of making tofu, then drying it). Wonderfully versatile, the skin is sometimes used to extend (or mimic) meat in braised dishes and hotpots, or it can be used as a wrapping for fried or steamed fillings.

....

600 g (1 lb 5 oz) raw king prawns (shrimp), peeled, cleaned and chopped

100 g (3½ oz) minced (ground) pork, not too lean

8 tinned water chestnuts, finely chopped

1 teaspoon sesame oil

2 teaspoons clear rice wine

2 spring onions (scallions), very finely chopped

2 teaspoons cornflour (cornstarch)

2 large sheets dried tofu skins

1 tablespoon plain (all-purpose) flour

vegetable oil, for deep-frying

chilli sauce, to serve

black rice vinegar, to serve

....

Put the prawn meat and pork in a bowl, then add the water chestnuts, sesame oil, rice wine, spring onions and cornflour. Use your hands to mix everything together, then divide into eight even portions.

Unwrap the sheets of tofu skin and cut into eight pieces measuring about 20 x 16 cm (8 x 6¼ inches) and eight pieces measuring about 8 x 5 cm (3¼ x 2 inches).

Combine the flour in a small bowl with 1½ tablespoons water and stir to form a smooth, thick paste. Work with one piece of tofu skin at a time, brushing the skins lightly with water to soften them a little. Place one of the larger pieces on the work surface with the shorter side nearest to you. Place one of the smaller pieces of skin on top of that piece, positioning it in the middle of the larger piece (this will reinforce the tofu skin under the filling).

Place one portion of filling on the smaller piece of tofu skin and use your hands to spread it evenly to cover the smaller piece. Lightly brush the furthest end of the skin with some of the flour paste. Fold the sides over the filling, then fold the tofu skin over a few times to form a rectangular parcel, pressing the pasted side gently to seal. Repeat with the remaining pieces of tofu skin and filling.

Pour enough oil into a wok to come about 5 cm (2 inches) up the side, and heat to 180°C (350°F), or until a cube of bread dropped into the oil turns deep golden in 15 seconds. Add half the stuffed tofu skins and cook, turning once, for 5–6 minutes, or until golden brown. Remove using kitchen tongs and drain on paper towel. Cook the remaining stuffed skins. Serve with small bowls of chilli sauce and black vinegar, for dipping.

Taro and peanut fritters

Makes 10

We ate these in the southern city of Meizhou, home to both a significant ethnic Hakka population and some pretty drop-dead amazing food. Taro is popular in the south, and they cook these fritters in a deep-fryer using two wire spiders. We've shaped our fritters into rounds using metal rings, but you can fry them free-form if it's easier — you'll have all the flavour and crispness, just not the nice, neat shape.

1 taro (840 g/1 lb 14 oz)
80 g (2¾ oz/½ cup) small raw, red-skinned
   peanuts

175 g (6 oz/1 cup) rice flour
vegetable oil, for shallow-frying
sea salt, to serve

Peel the taro using a large, sharp knife, then cut it crosswise into 3 mm (⅛ inch) thick slices. Stack the slices on top of each other, then cut into 3 mm (⅛ inch) thick shreds.

Put the taro and peanuts in a large bowl, add the rice flour and toss to coat. Add 170 ml (5½ fl oz/⅔ cup) water and use your hands to combine well, until the taro and peanuts are lightly coated in the mixture.

Pour enough oil into a large, heavy-based frying pan to come halfway up the side of the pan, then heat over a medium–high heat. Lightly grease the inside of two or three 9 cm (3½ inch) non-stick metal crumpet rings or similar (as many as will fit in the pan), then place the rings in the pan. Fill each ring with about 185 g (6½ oz/¾ cup) of taro mixture, using kitchen tongs to push it down evenly. Cook for 8 minutes, or until the underside is golden and crisp, then remove the rings and turn the fritters over. Cook for another 8 minutes, or until golden, then remove and drain on paper towel. Repeat with the remaining taro mixture. Sprinkle with sea salt and serve.

Salt and pepper school prawns

Serves 4 to 6

Sweet and intensely prawny-flavoured, school prawns (shrimp) are a great gift to the cook. They are inexpensive, don't need peeling and there's no waste because you eat the lot: heads, legs, tails and shells — everything! You might just want to trim the super-long feelers, though, before you cook them, as these can cause an annoying tangle in the fryer.

1 tablespoon sichuan peppercorns
1½ tablespoons sea salt
500 g (1 lb 2 oz) raw school prawns (shrimp)

vegetable oil, for deep-frying
90 g (3 oz/½ cup) rice flour

Dry-roast the peppercorns in a small, heavy-based frying pan over a medium–low heat, shaking the pan often, for 3–4 minutes, or until fragrant. Cool, then transfer to a mortar (or an electric spice grinder) and pound with the pestle to form a coarse powder. Combine with the salt in a small bowl and set aside.

Line a large tray with a few layers of paper towel, then spread the school prawns over the tray. Using more paper towel, pat the prawns to dry them as best you can. Divide the prawns between two large bowls.

Fill a wok one-third full of oil and heat to 190°C (375°F), or until a cube of bread dropped into the oil turns deep golden in 10 seconds. Add half the rice flour to each bowl of prawns and toss to coat the prawns. Working with one batch at a time, add the prawns to the hot oil, stirring gently with a large metal spoon to ensure the prawns don't stick to each other. Fry for 2–3 minutes, or until the prawns are light golden, crisp and cooked through. Drain briefly on paper towel, then transfer to a serving bowl and serve immediately with the salt and pepper mixture, to sprinkle over as desired. Cook the next batch in the same way, and serve immediately.

Salt and pepper school prawns; Deep-fried pig's ears (page 58)

Deep-fried pig's ears

Serves 4

We make a big deal in the West about 'nose to tail' eating, but this is something the Chinese have practised for millennia. When you deep-fry pig's ears, they become chewy, gelatinous and crisp all at the same time, which makes them the ultimate beer food in our book.

2 pig's ears
1 tablespoon shaoxing rice wine
2 tablespoons potato starch
500 ml (17 fl oz/2 cups) vegetable oil

2 garlic cloves, finely chopped
2 spring onions (scallions), finely sliced
1 red chilli, finely sliced
sea salt and freshly ground black pepper

Use a knife to scrape any hairs off the pig's ears, then rinse the ears under cold water. Put the ears in a saucepan with the rice wine, add enough cold water to cover, then invert a plate over the ears to keep them submerged. Bring to the boil over a high heat, then reduce the heat to medium–low and simmer for 1 hour, or until tender. Remove the pan from the heat, drain the ears and cool to room temperature.

Cut the pig's ears into 5 mm (¼ inch) slices, put in a bowl and toss with the potato starch. Pour the oil into a large wok and heat to 180°C (350°F), or until a cube of bread dropped into the oil turns deep golden in 15 seconds. Add the pig's ears, in two batches if necessary, and deep-fry for 4–5 minutes, or until crisp. Remove with a slotted spoon and drain on paper towel.

Pour off all but 2 tablespoons of oil from the wok. Return the wok to a medium heat, add the garlic, spring onions and chilli and stir-fry for 1 minute, or until fragrant. Add the crisp pig's ears and toss to combine, then season with sea salt and pepper before serving.

Photograph page 57

Garlic cucumbers

Serves 4 to 6 as part of a shared meal

....

4 Lebanese (short) cucumbers, peeled

2 teaspoons salt

3 teaspoons caster (superfine) sugar

2½ tablespoons clear rice vinegar

2½ tablespoons peanut oil

4 large garlic cloves, finely chopped

....

Cut the cucumbers in half lengthwise, then cut them crosswise into 2–3 cm (¾–1¼ inch) thick slices. Put the cucumbers in a colander and toss with the salt, then place the colander in the sink for 1 hour for the liquid to drain. Place the cucumbers on a tea towel (dish towel) and pat dry.

In a large bowl, combine the sugar, vinegar and oil, stirring until the sugar has dissolved. Add the cucumbers and toss well. Pile the mixture onto a serving platter and scatter over the garlic.

Photograph page 267

Chilli–peanut cucumbers

Serves 4 to 6 as part of a shared meal

....

4 Lebanese (short) cucumbers, peeled

2 tablespoons peanut oil

3 garlic cloves, finely chopped

1½ tablespoons sichuan chilli bean paste, or to taste

2 teaspoons finely chopped ginger

2 tablespoons clear rice wine

3 teaspoons black rice vinegar

1½ teaspoons sugar

50 g (1¾ oz/⅓ cup) raw, skinned peanuts, roasted (page 413) and coarsely chopped

....

Cut the cucumbers in half widthwise, then cut them lengthwise into 1 cm (½ inch) thick slices. Place the cucumbers in a single layer on a tea towel (dish towel) to absorb the excess liquid.

Heat the oil in a wok over a medium heat, add the garlic and cook for 1–2 minutes, then add the chilli bean paste and cook, stirring, for 1 minute. Add the remaining ingredients and toss to combine well. Cool slightly. Arrange the cucumbers on a platter and pour over the chilli mixture.

Photograph page 238

Beef shin with jellied dressing

Serves 6 to 8 as part of a shared meal

Shin meat contains a large amount of the connective tissues that make stock turn miraculously to jelly when it's cold — hence there's no gelatine in this recipe. The combination of tender meat, salty soy sauce, a clear, meaty jelly and the zingy hit of garlic and chilli is a winner.

2 boneless beef shins (about 1 kg/2 lb 3 oz), trimmed

Dressing
2 garlic cloves, very finely chopped
2 long green chillies, seeded and very finely chopped

1 tablespoon sesame oil
2 tablespoons light soy sauce
2 teaspoons sugar
1½ tablespoons red rice vinegar
2½ tablespoons finely chopped coriander (cilantro) leaves

Place the beef shins in a saucepan, then add about 1 litre (34 fl oz/4 cups) water or enough to just cover. Invert a small plate over the shins to keep them submerged, then bring to a gentle simmer. Cook the shins over a low heat for 3–3½ hours, or until very tender, adding a little more water as necessary — the beef should remain just submerged. Remove the pan from the heat and leave the beef to cool in the liquid, then remove the meat and drain well, reserving the cooking liquid in the pan. Wrap the beef tightly in plastic wrap and refrigerate.

Remove any fat from the surface of the cooking liquid, then return the pan to the stovetop and bring the liquid to the boil. Boil for 20–30 minutes, or until reduced to about 250 ml (8½ fl oz/1 cup). Cool, then pour the liquid into a small bowl, cover and refrigerate; the liquid will quickly set to a jelly.

To make the dressing, put all the ingredients in a bowl and whisk to combine well. To serve, slice the beef shins very thinly using a cleaver or large, sharp knife and arrange the meat, overlapping neatly, on a platter. Spoon the dressing over the top. Turn out the jelly and chop it into small pieces, then scatter the jelly over the beef and serve immediately. Alternatively, you can gently stir the jelly to break it up a little, then spoon it over the beef.

Photograph page 63

Drunken chicken

Serves 4 as part of a shared meal

This elegant dish from Zhejiang makes a feature of the region's wonderful shaoxing wine. There are many grades and types of this and it's best to use a good-quality drinking one here (experts say to use hua diao, *a mellow, yellow, smooth example). Prepare the chicken the day before so it can steep overnight in all that luscious alcohol.*

· ·

2 teaspoons sea salt

¼ teaspoon freshly ground black pepper

1 x 1.6 kg (3½ lb) chicken

5 cm (2 inch) piece ginger, peeled and finely sliced

4 spring onions (scallions), white part only

250 ml (8½ fl oz/1 cup) shaoxing table wine

1 teaspoon sugar

· ·

Combine the sea salt and pepper in a small bowl, rub the mixture all over the chicken, then cover the chicken and place in the fridge to marinate for 1 hour.

Bring 3 litres (101 fl oz/12 cups) water to the boil in a large, heavy-based saucepan over a high heat. Add the ginger, spring onions and chicken, making sure the chicken is totally covered in the water (invert a plate over the chicken to keep it submerged). Return to the boil, then reduce the heat to medium–low and simmer for 20 minutes. Cover the pan, remove it from the heat and set aside until the chicken cools to room temperature.

Remove the chicken from the pan, reserving the stock. Using a cleaver, cut the chicken through the bone into neat 2 cm (1 inch) pieces. Put the chicken pieces in a large bowl.

Combine 250 ml (8½ fl oz/1 cup) of the reserved stock (use the remaining stock for other purposes), the wine and sugar in a bowl, stirring until the sugar has dissolved. Season to taste with sea salt and pepper. Pour the stock mixture over the chicken pieces, cover and refrigerate overnight. Serve the chicken in the liquid at room temperature.

Photograph page 63

From left to right: Jade mountain (page 65); Pigs' ear salad (page 64);
Drunken chicken (page 61); Beef shin with jellied dressing (page 60)

Pigs' ear salad

Serves 4 to 6 as part of a shared meal

The Chinese, like the people of any great food culture, like to eat almost every part of an animal, even the ears. Snouts, tails, feet and every offaly bit imaginable are common fixtures in wet markets (these aren't places for the squeamish). While eating pigs' ears might be a foreign concept to us, the Chinese have long appreciated them for their pleasing, chewy texture. This salad is one popular way to serve them.

4 pigs' ears

½ large leek, white part only, cut into long shreds

2 large red chillies, seeded and finely shredded

1 handful coriander (cilantro) leaves

Cooking liquid

2 dried red chillies

½ piece cassia bark

2 star anise

2 teaspoons sichuan peppercorns

80 ml (2½ fl oz/⅓ cup) shaoxing rice wine

60 ml (2 fl oz/¼ cup) dark soy sauce

80 g (2¾ oz/⅓ cup) caster (superfine) sugar

6 slices unpeeled ginger

Dressing

2 tablespoons chicken stock (page 405)

1 teaspoon sugar

60 ml (2 fl oz/¼ cup) clear rice vinegar

80 ml (2½ fl oz/⅓ cup) peanut oil

Use a knife to scrape any hairs off the pigs' ears, then rinse the ears under cold water. Put all the cooking liquid ingredients in a saucepan with 750 ml (25½ fl oz/3 cups) water. Add the pigs' ears, then invert a plate over the ears to keep them submerged. Slowly bring the mixture to a simmer, then cook over a low heat for about 1¼ hours, or until the ears are tender. Remove from the heat and leave the ears to cool in the liquid. Drain the ears well, reserving the liquid for another use.

Meanwhile, to make the dressing, put all the ingredients in a bowl and whisk to dissolve the sugar, adding more vinegar to taste, if desired.

Using a large, sharp knife, very finely slice the pigs' ears widthwise. Combine in a large bowl with the leek, chillies and coriander. Pour the dressing over the salad, toss to coat and serve immediately.

Photograph page 63

Jade mountain

Serves 4 to 6 as part of a shared meal

This recipe was inspired by a vegetable dish we ate in Suzhou, a beautiful place near Shanghai, famed for its classical gardens and the subtlety of its food. There they use sugar and vinegar, in judicious amounts, as a seasoning to bring out the bright flavours of ingredients — even green vegetables.

....

700 g (1 lb 9 oz) English spinach (2 bunches) or chrysanthemum leaves

150 g (5½ oz) pressed tofu shreds or fresh, firm tofu, finely chopped

1 teaspoon caster (superfine) sugar

3 teaspoons sesame oil

sea salt and freshly ground black pepper

....

Trim the root ends off the spinach. If using chrysanthemum leaves, trim off the tough stems. Wash well, shaking off the excess water.

Heat a large saucepan over a medium–high heat, add the spinach, then cover the pan tightly and cook for 5 minutes, or until the spinach and stems are just tender. Transfer immediately to a sink full of cold water to refresh, then drain well in a colander. Squeeze out as much water as possible, then place the spinach in a tea towel (dish towel), roll it up and gently squeeze to remove any remaining water.

Using a large, sharp knife, finely chop the spinach and place in a large bowl. Add the tofu shreds, sugar and sesame oil and season to taste with sea salt and pepper. Toss well to combine, then place in a mound on a platter to serve. Alternatively, transfer to a 625 ml (21 fl oz/2½ cup) bowl, press the mixture down tightly, then turn out onto a serving plate.

Photograph page 62

Salt-cured duck

Serves 4 to 6 as part of a shared meal

We were lured to the old Chinese capital of Nanjing by tales of its refined cuisine — and we weren't disappointed. Nanjingers have a special place in their culinary hearts for duck and this dish is a local specialty. They say it's best made in mid-autumn during the osmanthus blooming season, but we say it's great any time. And don't be alarmed by the amount of salt used here — the salt draws out the moisture in the duck, then the salty liquid is drained off. If you prefer, you can lightly rinse the duck under cold water before steaming.

1 tablespoon sichuan peppercorns

75 g (2¾ oz/¼ cup) salt

1 x 2 kg (4 lb 6 oz) duck

10 cm (4 inch) piece ginger, peeled and cut into 1 cm (½ inch) thick slices

4 spring onions (scallions), cut into quarters

chilli sauce, to serve

light soy sauce, to serve

Dry-roast the peppercorns and salt in a small, heavy-based frying pan over a low heat, shaking the pan often, for 5–6 minutes, or until the salt has turned light brown and the peppercorns are fragrant. Cool, then transfer to a mortar (or an electric spice grinder) and pound with the pestle to form a coarse powder.

Prepare the duck by removing the excess fat and skin around the neck and cavity, then rinse under cold water and dry well with paper towel. Rub the salt and pepper mixture all over the duck and inside the cavity, then put the duck in a large bowl, cover with plastic wrap and place in the fridge for 2 days to cure, turning the duck over after the first day.

Fill a large saucepan one-third full of water and bring to the boil. Drain the duck well, then place the ginger and spring onions in the cavity. Place the duck in a heatproof bowl that will snugly fit into the saucepan, then put the bowl into the pan (you may need to adjust the water level in the pan; the water needs to come halfway up the side of the bowl). Cover the pan and steam the duck over a medium heat for 1½ hours, or until cooked through, adding more water to the pan as necessary.

Remove the duck from the bowl and place on a plate to cool. Using a cleaver, chop the duck through the bone into bite-sized pieces. Serve with small bowls of chilli sauce and soy sauce.

Salt-cured duck; Bitter melon with goji berries (page 68); Stir-fried snow pea sprouts (page 113)

Bitter melon with goji berries

Serves 4 to 6 as part of a shared meal

The world is divided squarely into two camps: those who loathe, and those who love, bitter melon. Prized by the Chinese for its medicinal qualities, it's said to prevent illnesses such as diabetes and cancer … and everything in between. Bitter melon is related to the cucumber, but that's where any similarity ends. It's really bitter.

425 g (15 oz) bitter melons (about 2 large)
60 ml (2 fl oz/¼ cup) vegetable oil
4 garlic cloves, finely sliced
4 small red chillies, halved lengthwise

2 teaspoons sugar
60 ml (2 fl oz/¼ cup) clear rice vinegar
60 ml (2 fl oz/¼ cup) chicken stock (page 405)
sea salt and freshly ground black pepper

Cut the bitter melons in half lengthwise, then use a teaspoon to remove the seeds and soft pith, and discard. Cut each half into thin slices on a slight diagonal. Bring a saucepan of salted water to the boil, add the melon and cook for 2 minutes, or until just tender. Drain, then transfer to a bowl of iced water to cool. Drain well.

Heat the oil in a small saucepan over a medium–low heat, then add the garlic and chillies and cook for 2 minutes, or until the garlic has softened. Add the sugar, vinegar and stock, swirling the pan to combine well. Remove from the heat and cool.

Just before serving, put the melon and cooled vinegar mixture in a bowl and toss to coat the melon well. Season to taste with sea salt and pepper.

Photograph page 67

Vinegared cabbage salad

Serves 6 as part of a shared meal

500 g (1 lb 2 oz) Chinese cabbage (wombok), tough outer leaves and hard core removed
1 teaspoon salt
80 ml (2½ fl oz/⅓ cup) clear rice vinegar

2 tablespoons caster (superfine) sugar
2 small red chillies, finely sliced
2 teaspoons sesame oil

Using a large, sharp knife, finely slice the cabbage. Place the cabbage in a large bowl, add the salt, vinegar and sugar and toss to combine well. Cover the bowl and set aside for 1–2 hours, or until the cabbage has softened slightly. Add the chillies and sesame oil, toss to combine and serve.

Tofu shred salad

Serves 4 to 6 as part of a shared meal

½ large red capsicum (pepper), seeded and cut into long shreds
1 carrot, cut into long shreds
200 g (7 oz) pressed tofu shreds
2 spring onions (scallions), finely shredded
1 handful coriander (cilantro) sprigs
2 tablespoons sesame seeds, toasted (page 413)

Dressing
1 garlic clove, crushed
large pinch of caster (superfine) sugar
1½ tablespoons clear rice vinegar
1½ tablespoons light soy sauce
1½ tablespoons sesame oil

To make the dressing, put all the ingredients in a bowl and whisk to combine well.

Bring a saucepan of salted water to the boil, then add the capsicum, carrot and tofu shreds and cook for 1 minute. Drain well in a colander and leave to cool. Place the cooled ingredients in a large bowl and combine with the spring onions, coriander and sesame seeds. Add the dressing, toss to combine and serve.

Photograph page 96

Squid and Chinese celery salad

Serves 6 as part of a shared meal

Chinese celery has a much stronger taste than regular celery, but if you can't find it, substitute the normal stuff by all means. The flavours here are very typical of a simple eastern Chinese cold dish, although we've taken a few liberties with the presentation — it's decidedly Western!

800 g (1 lb 12 oz) fresh squid

3 Chinese celery stalks, cut into thin strips, plus 1 small handful celery leaves, to serve

3 spring onions (scallions), very finely sliced on the diagonal

Dressing

2 garlic cloves, finely chopped

1 teaspoon caster (superfine) sugar

2½ tablespoons clear rice vinegar

2 tablespoons light soy sauce

2 tablespoons peanut oil

3 teaspoons sesame oil

To clean the squid, gently pull the tentacles away from the tube (the intestines should come away at the same time). Remove the intestines from the tentacles by cutting under the eyes, then remove the beak if it remains in the centre of the tentacles by using your fingers to push up the centre. Reserve the tentacles. Pull the transparent cartilage from inside the body and remove. Clean out the inside of the tube. Hold the tube under running water and peel the skin off; the wings can also be used. Place the cleaned squid tubes on a chopping board and use a sharp knife to cut each tube all the way down one side to open it out. Using the knife, score the inside of each tube in a fine crisscross pattern (be careful you don't cut all the way through), then cut the tubes into 4 cm (1½ inch) pieces.

Bring a large saucepan of water to the boil. Add the squid pieces and tentacles and cook for 1½–2 minutes, or until the squid pieces are tender and have curled — take care not to overcook them. Drain, then transfer the squid to a large bowl of iced water to cool. Drain well.

To make the dressing, put all the ingredients in a large bowl and whisk to combine well. Add the squid, celery strips and spring onions to the bowl and toss to coat well. Transfer to a platter or bowl, scatter over the celery leaves and serve immediately.

Cold spicy sichuan chicken

Serves 4 to 6 as part of a shared meal

This is based on a famous Sichuan dish called 'strange flavour chicken', and is also known as 'bang bang' chicken after the wooden implement street vendors once used to help bang a cleaver through the chicken to cut it into pieces. The sauce is a seductive blend of sour, hot, numbing, sweet and salty flavours and you can vary these to taste as you like.

1 x 1.6 kg (3½ lb) chicken, cooked and cooled (pages 196–7), meat picked, bones and skin removed

3 spring onions (scallions), finely shredded

½ bunch (about 200 g/7 oz) watercress, sprigs picked (optional)

50 g (1¾ oz/⅓ cup) sesame seeds, toasted (page 413)

Sauce

3 teaspoons sichuan peppercorns

2 tablespoons caster (superfine) sugar

2 tablespoons black rice vinegar

2 tablespoons light soy sauce

80 ml (2½ fl oz/⅓ cup) Chinese sesame paste

1½ tablespoons sesame oil

60 ml (2 fl oz/¼ cup) chilli oil (page 407), or ready-made

To make the sauce, dry-roast the peppercorns in a small, heavy-based frying pan over a medium–low heat, shaking the pan often, for 3–4 minutes, or until fragrant. Cool, then transfer to a mortar (or an electric spice grinder) and pound with the pestle to form a coarse powder. Place the ground peppercorns and the remaining sauce ingredients in a food processor and process until smooth. Add 2–3 tablespoons hot water to thin the sauce if necessary — it should be thick and creamy.

Using your fingers, shred the chicken into large pieces and place in a bowl with the spring onions and watercress, if using, and toss to combine. Divide the chicken mixture among plates, or pile onto a platter, and drizzle with the sauce. Scatter the sesame seeds over the top and serve.

English spinach with glass noodles

Serves 4 to 6 as part of a shared meal

Here's a light, refreshing dish that is easy to make and one that works well in all sorts of scenarios. Serve it with soy sauce chicken or roast quails and steamed rice for a quick and easy meal, or include it as part of a more elaborate spread containing a mix of hot and cold dishes.

75 g (2¾ oz) bean thread (glass) vermicelli noodles
700 g (1 lb 9 oz) English spinach (2 bunches)
40 g (1½ oz/¼ cup) sesame seeds, toasted (page 413)

Dressing
3 garlic cloves, finely chopped
60 ml (2 fl oz/¼ cup) black rice vinegar
1½ tablespoons light soy sauce
1 tablespoon caster (superfine) sugar
2 tablespoons sesame oil
1 tablespoon peanut oil

To make the dressing, put all the ingredients in a small bowl and whisk to combine well.

Put the noodles in a small heatproof bowl, cover with boiling water and soak for 15 minutes, or until softened, then drain. Using kitchen scissors, cut the noodles into smaller pieces. Cook the noodles in a saucepan of boiling water for 2 minutes, then drain in a sieve and cool under running water. Leave to drain while you prepare the spinach.

Cut about 4 cm (1½ inches) off the ends of the spinach stems, then cut each bunch widthwise into thirds, including the stems. Wash well. Cook the spinach in a saucepan of boiling salted water for 2 minutes, or until wilted, then transfer immediately to a sink full of ice-cold water to refresh. Drain well, then gently squeeze out as much water as possible. Transfer to a tea towel (dish towel), wrap the spinach up and wring out any remaining water.

Put the spinach in a bowl and use your hands to separate the pieces. Add the noodles and sesame seeds, reserving some of the seeds for garnish, and toss well. Pour the dressing over the spinach salad and toss to combine. Transfer to a serving bowl or platter and sprinkle the remaining sesame seeds over the top.

Photograph page 213

Sichuan radish salad

Serves 4 to 6 as part of a shared meal

½ small daikon (white radish) (about 250 g/9 oz), peeled

1 small bunch red radishes (about 250 g/9 oz), washed and trimmed

1 bunch coriander (cilantro), sprigs picked

Dressing

1 tablespoon caster (superfine) sugar

1 tablespoon black rice vinegar

1 tablespoon sichuan chilli bean paste

2 garlic cloves, finely chopped

2 tablespoons chilli oil (page 407), or ready-made

2 tablespoons peanut oil

To make the dressing, put all the ingredients in a food processor and process until the mixture is smooth.

Cut the daikon into 5 cm (2 inch) matchsticks and very finely slice the red radishes into rounds. Pat the radishes dry using paper towel, then combine the radishes and daikon in a bowl with three-quarters of the coriander sprigs. Toss to combine well, then add the dressing and toss to coat. Transfer the salad to a platter, scatter over the remaining coriander and serve immediately.

Photograph page 239

Wood ear fungus salad

Serves 4 to 6 as part of a shared meal

30 g (1 oz/1 slightly heaped cup) dried wood ear fungus

1–2 small red chillies, finely sliced

2 spring onions (scallions), finely shredded

1 bunch coriander (cilantro), sprigs picked (optional)

Dressing

2½ tablespoons light soy sauce

2 tablespoons black rice vinegar

1 teaspoon caster (superfine) sugar

3 teaspoons sesame oil

2 garlic cloves, crushed

Put the wood ear fungus in a heatproof bowl, cover with boiling water and soak for 30–40 minutes, or until softened, then drain. Meanwhile, to make the dressing, put all the ingredients in a bowl and whisk to combine well.

Bring a large saucepan of water to the boil, add the wood ears and cook for 3–4 minutes, then drain well and cool. Using your hands, tear each wood ear into two or three pieces, discarding any hard pieces. Place in a bowl with the chillies, spring onions and coriander sprigs, if using. Add the dressing and gently toss to combine well, then transfer to a serving bowl.

Photograph page 233

Tofu skin salad

Serves 6 as part of a shared meal

Technically, tofu skin isn't made from tofu but from the dried skin of soy milk. The skins are packaged in flat, dried sheets or sold in long, wrinkled brittle sticks, and usually labelled as tofu or bean curd sticks. They are highly nutritious and are used to great effect in a variety of dishes, especially vegetarian ones. Tofu sticks are simple to prepare and take on other flavours rather well, making them an excellent blank canvas in braises, stir-fries or salads, such as this incredibly simple one.

....

200 g (7 oz) dried tofu skin sticks
vegetable oil, for deep-frying
sea salt and freshly ground black pepper
5 spring onions (scallions), finely sliced

Dressing
125 ml (4 fl oz/½ cup) chicken stock (page 405)
3 teaspoons sugar
2 garlic cloves, finely chopped
80 ml (2½ fl oz/⅓ cup) clear rice vinegar
80 ml (2½ fl oz/⅓ cup) light soy sauce
1 tablespoon sesame oil
2½ tablespoons peanut oil

....

Break the tofu skin sticks into pieces about 3 cm (1¼ inches) long. Fill a large bowl with cold water.

Fill a wok one-third full of oil and heat to 180°C (350°F), or until a cube of bread dropped into the oil turns deep golden in 15 seconds. Add the pieces of tofu sticks in two batches and cook for about 1 minute, or until they have expanded slightly and are light golden. Transfer immediately to the bowl of water and leave to soak for 2–3 hours, or until softened, then drain well. Gently squeeze out the excess water, then place on a tea towel (dish towel) to absorb as much remaining water as possible. Place in a bowl.

To make the dressing, combine all the ingredients in a bowl, stirring until the sugar has dissolved. Pour over the tofu sticks in the bowl, toss to coat well, then season to taste with sea salt and pepper. Transfer the tofu to a serving bowl or platter and scatter the spring onions over the top.

Marinated spicy carrot

Serves 4 to 6 as part of a shared meal

400 g (14 oz) carrots (about 4), finely shredded

2 garlic cloves, very finely sliced

2–3 teaspoons chilli oil (page 407), or ready-made, to taste

3 teaspoons sesame oil

1 tablespoon caster (superfine) sugar

60 ml (2 fl oz/¼ cup) red rice vinegar

3 spring onions (scallions), finely shredded

1 large handful coriander (cilantro) leaves, chopped

sea salt

Bring a saucepan of salted water to the boil. Add the carrots and cook for about 2 minutes, or until very slightly softened. Transfer to a colander and rinse under cold running water to cool. Drain well and place in a tea towel (dish towel), wrap it up and gently wring out as much water as possible.

Put the garlic, chilli oil, sesame oil, sugar and vinegar in a large bowl and stir until the sugar has dissolved. Add the carrots, toss to combine, then cover the bowl with plastic wrap and leave for 20 minutes for the flavours to develop. Add the spring onions and coriander and toss to combine. Season to taste with sea salt, then transfer to a platter and serve.

Sweet vinegared lotus

Serves 4 to 6 as part of a shared meal

600 g (1 lb 5 oz) lotus root

2½ tablespoons peanut oil

2 teaspoons finely chopped ginger

3 spring onions (scallions), very finely chopped

6 dried red chillies, each cut into 3 or 4 pieces

1 tablespoon sugar, or to taste

70 ml (2¼ fl oz) clear rice vinegar, or to taste

sea salt and freshly ground black pepper

Cut the lotus root into pieces where they naturally link, then peel each piece. Using a large, sharp knife, cut the lotus into thin slices. Bring a large saucepan of salted water to the boil, add the lotus and boil for 4–5 minutes, or until tender. Drain in a large colander and set aside until cooled. Transfer to a large bowl.

Heat the oil in a small saucepan over a medium heat, then add the ginger, spring onions and chillies and cook, stirring often, for 3 minutes, or until the ginger and spring onions have softened. Add the sugar and vinegar, bring to the boil, then pour over the lotus in the bowl. Season to taste with sea salt and pepper, then gently toss the lotus to coat in the sweet vinegar, adding more sugar and a dash of vinegar if desired.

Photograph page 193

Braised red capsicums with century eggs

Serves 4 as part of a shared meal

The ingenious preservation method that turns eggs translucent, gooey and unnervingly black is originally from Hunan and we ate a dish similar to this in Changsha. The eggs are cured in a mix of lime ash, clay and rice husks, which alters their texture almost beyond recognition — and gives them quite an odorous whiff. Some find all this off-putting but the Chinese love them and refer to them variously as century eggs or thousand-year eggs, or pine-patterned eggs because of the spidery effect that emerges on their surface after preservation.

3 large red capsicums (peppers) (about 1 kg/ 2 lb 3 oz)
3 garlic cloves, finely sliced
60 ml (2 fl oz/¼ cup) light soy sauce

2 teaspoons black rice vinegar
1½ teaspoons sesame oil
sea salt
4 preserved duck eggs

Preheat the oven to 180°C (350°F/Gas 4). Cut the capsicums in half lengthwise and remove the seeds, then cut each piece in half lengthwise again, so you have four pieces per capsicum. Remove the membranes. Place the capsicums in a large baking dish in a single layer. Combine the garlic, soy sauce, vinegar and 60 ml (2 fl oz/¼ cup) water in a bowl, then pour over the capsicums in the dish. Cover tightly with foil and bake for 1 hour, then remove the dish from the oven and cool to room temperature. Carefully pull the skin off the capsicums.

Arrange the capsicums in a shallow bowl, reserving the braising liquid. Add the sesame oil to the braising liquid, season with sea salt and mix well, then taste and adjust the seasoning if required.

Peel the preserved eggs and rinse under cold running water, then cut each egg into wedges and place around the capsicums. Pour over the reserved braising liquid and serve.

Chicken and jellyfish salad

Serves 4 to 6 as part of a shared meal

The Chinese have a great appreciation for texture in food as well as flavour, and the relatively bland salted jellyfish provides a wonderfully toothsome point of interest in this salad. Use watercress instead of the snow pea sprouts if you like and substitute fresh podded broad (fava) beans, snow peas (mangetout) or even asparagus for the sugar snaps if you prefer.

375 g (13 oz) salted jellyfish

about 1 litre (34 fl oz/4 cups) chicken stock
(page 405)

2 boneless, skinless chicken breasts

250 g (9 oz) sugar-snap peas

1 small red onion, halved and very finely sliced

100 g (3½ oz/2 cups) snow pea (mangetout)
sprouts

40 g (1½ oz/¼ cup) sesame seeds, toasted
(page 413)

Dressing

60 ml (2 fl oz/¼ cup) light soy sauce

2½ tablespoons clear rice vinegar

1½ tablespoons sesame oil

1 tablespoon peanut oil

2½ teaspoons caster (superfine) sugar

ground white pepper, to taste

Rinse the jellyfish in cold water and drain. Place in a large bowl, cover with plenty of cold water and leave to soak for 1 hour, then drain well. Squeeze out the excess liquid and use a tea towel (dish towel) to pat dry. Very finely slice the jellyfish, then place in a large bowl.

Meanwhile, pour the stock into a saucepan (just large enough to hold the chicken) and bring to a gentle simmer, add the chicken, then add a little extra stock or water to just cover if necessary. Cover and cook over a low heat for 15 minutes — the stock should be just murmuring; do not allow it to simmer hard or the chicken will be tough. Remove the pan from the heat and leave the chicken for about 20 minutes to cool in the liquid. Drain, reserving the cooking liquid for another use. Use your hands to finely shred the chicken, then place in the bowl with the jellyfish.

Bring a small saucepan of water to the boil, then add the sugar-snap peas and cook over a high heat for 1–2 minutes, or until just tender. Drain and refresh under cold water, drain well and pat dry. Slice in half lengthwise and add to the bowl, along with the onion and snow pea sprouts.

To make the dressing, combine all the ingredients in a small bowl, stirring until the sugar has dissolved. Pour the dressing over the chicken and jellyfish salad and toss to coat well. Transfer to a platter, sprinkle the sesame seeds over the top and serve immediately.

Vegetables
&
Tofu

To fully understand how important vegetables are to the Chinese,
you need two things: a rudimentary understanding of the
language (the word *cai* means both 'vegetable' and 'dish') and
just five minutes in a Chinese produce market. Only there can you
fully grasp the variety and pristine freshness of what's on offer
and how simply mind-blowing it all is.

Stir-fried tofu sticks with green vegetables

Serves 4 to 6 as part of a shared meal

If there's one thing we miss when we're not in China it's the variety of tofu available there. It comes in pressed sheets, rounds and shreds, and is variously firm, silky-soft, smoked and sometimes even stinky. Shaoxing is famed for its fermented tofu, which is often fried street-side — its aroma literally permeates whole neighbourhoods. Back home we have to be satisfied with the local fresh selection and products such as these dried tofu sticks. Here they bring excellent texture to a simple stir-fry of green vegetables.

100 g (3½ oz) dried tofu skin sticks, broken into 5 cm (2 inch) pieces

2 tablespoons vegetable oil

1 large garlic clove, finely chopped

2 cm (¾ inch) piece ginger, peeled and finely chopped

200 g (7 oz) sugar-snap peas, trimmed

1 bunch asparagus (about 12 spears), trimmed and cut into 5 cm (2 inch) pieces

400 g (14 oz) peas, podded, or 200 g (7 oz) frozen peas

2 tablespoons light soy sauce

2 teaspoons sesame oil

sea salt

Put the pieces of tofu sticks in a heatproof bowl, cover with boiling water and soak for 1 hour, or until soft, then drain well.

Heat the vegetable oil in a large wok over a medium–high heat until just smoking, then add the garlic and ginger and stir-fry for 30 seconds, or until fragrant. Add the tofu sticks and stir-fry for 2 minutes, then add the sugar-snap peas, asparagus and peas and stir-fry for another 4 minutes — the vegetables should still be a little crisp. Add the soy sauce and sesame oil and toss to combine. Season with sea salt, transfer to a platter and serve.

Fried radish cakes

Makes 16 pieces

You might know these from the yum cha trolley — this is a favourite Cantonese dim sum. Although technically morning food, these wouldn't be out of place at dinner served with other southern-inspired dishes (steamed fish, roast pork or soy sauce chicken, for example). You can make these in advance, keep them in the fridge and then fry as needed.

35 g (1¼ oz/⅓ cup) dried shrimp

3 Chinese pork sausages (lap cheong), very finely chopped

2½ tablespoons lard or vegetable oil, plus extra for greasing

1.2 kg (2 lb 10 oz) daikon (white radish) (about 2), peeled and grated

250 ml (8½ fl oz/1 cup) chicken stock (page 405) or water

350 g (12½ oz/2 cups) rice flour

2 teaspoons sugar

1 tablespoon light soy sauce

vegetable oil, for frying

Put the dried shrimp in a small heatproof bowl, cover with boiling water and soak for 30 minutes. Drain well, then combine the shrimp in a bowl with the chopped sausage.

Heat the lard in a wok over a medium–high heat, add the sausage mixture and stir-fry for 2 minutes, then add the grated daikon radish and stir-fry for another 2 minutes. Add the stock and bring the mixture to a simmer, then cover the wok, reduce the heat to medium and cook for 7–8 minutes, or until the daikon has softened. Remove from the heat, add the rice flour, sugar and soy sauce and stir until the mixture is smooth.

Grease the base and sides of a 20 cm (8 inch) square cake tin. Place the daikon mixture in the tin, using your hands to smooth the surface. Cover the tin tightly with foil, then place the tin in a large steamer over a wok or saucepan of boiling water. Cover and steam for 1 hour, or until firm. Remove the tin from the steamer and set aside until cool, then refrigerate overnight.

Cut the daikon cake into eight pieces, then carefully cut each piece in half horizontally. Pour enough oil into a large non-stick frying pan to cover the base, then place over a medium heat. Cook the cakes in batches for about 4 minutes on each side, or until golden. Drain on paper towel and serve hot.

Photograph page 241

Stir-fried sprouts with omelette, dried fish and chilli

Serves 4 to 6 as part of a shared meal

Dried fish lends that unmistakable umami edge (the flavour that everyone in food circles is so fond of talking abut these days) to this stir-fried dish. The Chinese have been umami-fying their dishes long before the notion became so fashionable in the West.

50 g (1¾ oz) dried salted fish

4 large eggs

sea salt and freshly ground black pepper

80 ml (2½ fl oz/⅓ cup) vegetable oil

2 garlic cloves, finely chopped

400 g (14 oz) mung bean sprouts

2 tablespoons clear rice wine

1 tablespoon light soy sauce

1 teaspoon caster (superfine) sugar

2 large red chillies, seeded and finely shredded

Soak the dried fish in water for 30 minutes, or until softened, then drain well and pat dry with paper towel.

Put the eggs in a bowl with 2 tablespoons water and whisk to combine well, then season with sea salt and pepper. Heat 3 teaspoons of the oil in a 20 cm (8 inch) heavy-based frying pan over a medium–high heat. Add half the egg mixture, swirling the pan to evenly coat the base with the egg, and cook for 2 minutes, or until the egg is firm on the base. Lift up the sides as the omelette cooks to allow uncooked egg to run underneath and cook. Carefully remove the omelette to a plate, cooked side down, then invert it back into the pan and cook for another 30 seconds, or until firm. Remove to a plate. Repeat with another 3 teaspoons of oil and the remaining egg mixture. When the omelettes have cooled slightly, transfer to a chopping board and slice into very thin strips.

Heat the remaining oil in a wok over a medium heat, add the fish and cook for 2–3 minutes, or until golden, then remove using a slotted spoon.

Increase the heat to medium–high, then add the garlic and bean sprouts and cook, tossing the wok often, for 2–3 minutes, or until the sprouts have softened. Add the rice wine, soy sauce, sugar, fish and omelette strips and toss to combine well. Season to taste with sea salt and pepper, then transfer to a platter. Scatter over the chilli and serve immediately.

Hot and numbing eggplant

Serves 4 to 6 as part of a shared meal

We've never eaten anything as spicy as Sichuanese food. This large, populous province in the southwest of China has a damp and humid climate and the logic goes that chilli combats the ill effects of this ... we just think the Sichuanese are addicted to capsaicin. Beware, this is a spicy dish, so tone down the chilli if you prefer.

....

1 kg (2 lb 3 oz) Lebanese (long, thin) eggplants (aubergines) (about 10), peeled

2 teaspoons sichuan peppercorns

1 tablespoon chilli oil (page 407), or ready-made

2 teaspoons vegetable oil

2 garlic cloves, crushed

1 tablespoon finely chopped ginger

1½–2 tablespoons sichuan chilli bean paste, to taste

1 tablespoon light soy sauce

1 tablespoon clear rice vinegar

1–1½ tablespoons sugar, to taste

1 tablespoon sesame oil

3 spring onions (scallions), finely sliced

....

Cut the eggplants in half lengthwise, then cut each piece in half widthwise, then in half lengthwise again, so each eggplant gives eight pieces. Put the eggplants in a large steamer and place over a wok or saucepan of boiling water, then cover and steam for 25 minutes, or until very soft. Transfer to a colander and leave to cool, allowing any excess liquid to drain off.

Meanwhile, dry-roast the peppercorns in a small, heavy-based frying pan over a medium–low heat, shaking the pan often, for 3–4 minutes, or until fragrant. Cool, then transfer to a mortar (or an electric spice grinder) and pound with the pestle to form a coarse powder. Set aside.

Heat the chilli and vegetable oils in a small saucepan over a medium heat, then add the garlic and ginger and cook, stirring, for 2 minutes, or until fragrant. Add the chilli bean paste and cook, stirring, for another 1–2 minutes. Add the soy sauce, vinegar, sugar, sesame oil and ground peppercorns and stir to combine well. Bring the mixture to a simmer and cook for 2–3 minutes, then pour over the eggplant in the bowl and gently toss to combine well. Leave to cool to room temperature, then transfer to a serving dish and scatter over the spring onions.

Mapo doufu

Serves 4

A few years ago, on our first trip to Chengdu, we taxied with great excitement to the old mapo doufu *restaurant near Qingyang Temple, only to find it destroyed by fire. This is so often the story in China, although generally it's the wrecking ball that claims most old buildings. Luckily, iconic dishes such as this don't depend on bricks and mortar for survival; it's an entrenched Sichuanese favourite.*

1 teaspoon sichuan peppercorns

60 ml (2 fl oz/¼ cup) vegetable oil

2 teaspoons finely chopped ginger

2 garlic cloves, crushed

4 small dried red chillies

250 g (9 oz) minced (ground) beef

300 ml (10 fl oz) chicken stock (page 405)

500 g (1 lb 2 oz) silken tofu, drained well and
   cut into 1.5 cm (½ inch) squares

1½ tablespoons potato starch

2 spring onions (scallions), finely sliced on
   the diagonal

Sauce

2½ tablespoons sichuan chilli bean paste

1 tablespoon light soy sauce

2 teaspoons caster (superfine) sugar

1 tablespoon fermented black beans, rinsed

1 tablespoon clear rice wine

2 teaspoons red rice vinegar

½ teaspoon chilli powder

To make the sauce, put all the ingredients in a small bowl and stir to combine well. Set aside.

Dry-roast the peppercorns in a small, heavy-based frying pan over a medium–low heat, shaking the pan often, for 3–4 minutes, or until fragrant. Cool, then transfer to a mortar (or an electric spice grinder) and pound with the pestle to form a fine powder.

Heat the oil in a wok over a high heat. Add the ginger, garlic and chillies and cook, stirring, for 10 seconds, or until fragrant, then add the beef and cook, stirring to break up the meat, for about 3 minutes, or until cooked through. Add the sauce mixture and cook, stirring, for 1 minute, or until fragrant. Stir in the stock, reduce the heat to medium, then add the tofu and stir gently to combine; take care not to break up the tofu.

Combine the potato starch in a small bowl with 60 ml (2 fl oz/¼ cup) water and stir until smooth. Add the starch mixture to the wok and cook, stirring gently, for 1–2 minutes, or until the mixture simmers and thickens. Sprinkle over the ground peppercorns. Divide the tofu among four bowls, scatter over the spring onions and serve with rice.

Tofu with prawns, tomato and ham

Serves 4 to 6 as part of a shared meal

This recipe is based on one found in a great cookbook called Chinese Home-Style Cooking, *purchased some years ago at the Foreign Languages Bookstore in Beijing. The combination of soothingly bland tofu, salty ham, rich prawns (shrimp) and juicy, bright tomatoes is a winner.*

600 g (1 lb 5 oz) raw tiger prawns (shrimp),
  peeled, cleaned and halved lengthwise
60 ml (2 fl oz/¼ cup) clear rice wine
2 firm, ripe tomatoes (about 300 g/10½ oz)
500 g (1 lb 2 oz) firm silken tofu
1 tablespoon vegetable oil
2 garlic cloves, crushed

75 g (2¾ oz) Chinese cured ham, finely chopped
2 spring onions (scallions), finely chopped
625 ml (21 fl oz/2½ cups) chicken stock
  (page 405)
2½ teaspoons cornflour (cornstarch)

Combine the prawns and half the rice wine in a bowl. Stir to combine well, then set aside for 30 minutes.

Meanwhile, bring a large saucepan of water to the boil. Cut the stem end off each tomato and use a sharp knife to score a small cross in the base of each tomato. Plunge the tomatoes into the boiling water for about 30 seconds, then remove using a slotted spoon and transfer to a bowl of iced water. Drain the tomatoes, then peel off the skins. Cut into quarters, remove the seeds, then cut the tomatoes into neat pieces about 1 cm (½ inch) square. Set aside.

Cut the tofu into 1.5 cm (½ inch) squares and place in a heatproof bowl. Pour boiling water over the tofu, set aside for 2 minutes, then drain.

Meanwhile, heat the oil in a large wok over a medium–high heat, then add the garlic, ham and spring onions and stir-fry for 1–2 minutes, or until fragrant. Add the undrained prawns and remaining rice wine and cook for 1 minute, then add the tofu and tomatoes and toss the wok to combine well. Add the stock, bring the mixture to a simmer and cook for 2–3 minutes, or until the prawns are cooked through.

Combine the cornflour with about 1 tablespoon water and stir to make a smooth paste, then add to the simmering mixture in the wok. Stir gently to combine well, then cook for another minute, or until the mixture has thickened slightly. Transfer to a platter and serve immediately.

Vinegared potato shreds

Serves 4 to 6 as part of a shared meal

We first ate potatoes cooked this way in Beijing years ago and back then we were convinced they were raw — crunchy potatoes are somewhat counterintuitive — but they weren't, as we soon discovered. The secret here is to soak the shreds to remove some of the starch, and then to lightly cook the potato in a wok. You can serve them hot or cold but, either way, be warned — they are incredibly addictive.

2 teaspoons salt

500 g (1 lb 2 oz) waxy or all-purpose potatoes, such as desiree, peeled

2½ tablespoons clear rice vinegar

1 tablespoon light soy sauce

2 teaspoons sugar

2 teaspoons sichuan pepper oil, or to taste (page 408)

60 ml (2 fl oz/¼ cup) vegetable oil

6 small dried red chillies

2 garlic cloves, finely chopped

2 spring onions (scallions), white part only, finely shredded

Combine 1 litre (34 fl oz/4 cups) cold water and the salt in a large bowl and stir to dissolve the salt. Using a large, sharp knife, cut the potatoes into even slices about 2 mm (⅛ inch) thick. Stack the slices on top of each other, then cut the potato slices into 2 mm (⅛ inch) thick matchsticks, placing the potatoes in the salted water as you cut them. Leave the potatoes to soak for 15 minutes to get rid of some of the starch, then tip into a colander and rinse well. Shake the excess water from the potatoes, then place on a tea towel (dish towel), loosely roll the towel up and gently squeeze to get rid of the excess water.

Put the vinegar, soy sauce, sugar and pepper oil in a large bowl and stir to combine well. Set aside.

Heat the vegetable oil in a wok over a medium heat, then add the chillies and garlic and stir-fry for 30 seconds. Add the potatoes and stir-fry for about 3 minutes, or until the potatoes no longer look raw but are still crunchy (the potatoes will change colour only slightly). Remove with a slotted spoon and place in the bowl with the vinegar mixture. Add the spring onions and toss to coat well. Transfer to a platter and serve hot or at room temperature.

Photograph page 259

Stir-fried spinach with peanuts

Serves 4 to 6 as part of a shared meal

700 g (1 lb 9 oz) English spinach (2 bunches)
2 tablespoons vegetable oil
2 garlic cloves, finely chopped

50 g (1¾ oz/⅓ cup) salted, roasted red-skinned peanuts
1 tablespoon black rice vinegar

Wash the spinach thoroughly in cold water and dry well with a tea towel (dish towel). Discard the stems and roughly chop the leaves.

Heat a wok over a medium heat, then add the oil and garlic and stir-fry for 30 seconds, or until fragrant. Increase the heat to medium–high, add the spinach and stir-fry for 2–3 minutes, or until the spinach just begins to wilt. Add the peanuts and vinegar and toss well. Transfer to a platter and serve.

Photograph page 177

Carrots stir-fried with ginger and gingko nuts

Serves 4 to 6 as part of a shared meal

110 g (4 oz/⅔ cup) gingko nuts
500 g (1 lb 2 oz) carrots (about 5), peeled
2½ tablespoons peanut oil
2 tablespoons finely shredded ginger

2½ tablespoons chicken stock (page 405)
1½ tablespoons shaoxing rice wine
1 tablespoon light soy sauce
large pinch of sugar

Put the gingko nuts in a heatproof bowl, cover with boiling water and soak for 30 minutes, then drain well.

Thinly slice the carrots into rounds. Heat the oil in a wok over a medium–high heat, then add the carrots and ginger and stir-fry for about 4 minutes, or until the carrots are cooked but still a little crisp. Add the gingko nuts, stock, rice wine, soy sauce and sugar and stir-fry for about 3 minutes, or until the liquid has reduced by about half and the gingko nuts are heated through. Transfer to a bowl and serve.

Photograph page 213

Edamame and salted mustard greens

Serves 4 to 6 as part of a shared meal

400 g (14 oz) packet frozen, salted mustard greens, thawed and rinsed

1½ tablespoons vegetable oil

350 g (12½ oz) frozen, peeled edamame (soybeans), thawed

250 ml (8½ fl oz/1 cup) chicken stock (page 405) or water

1 teaspoon sugar

Squeeze the salted mustard greens to remove as much liquid as possible, then set aside.

Heat the oil in a wok over a medium–high heat, then add the edamame and stir-fry for 2–3 minutes, or until starting to soften. Add the vegetables, stock and sugar and stir-fry for 3–4 minutes, or until most of the liquid has evaporated — the edamame will remain a little firm. Serve hot or at room temperature.

Photograph pages 96–7

Braised pumpkin with Chinese cured pork

Serves 4 to 6 as part of a shared meal

650 g (1 lb 7 oz) jap or kent pumpkin (winter squash) in one piece, peeled and seeded

2 pieces red fermented tofu, plus 2 teaspoons of the tofu liquid

185 ml (6 fl oz/¾ cup) chicken and pork stock (page 405)

1 tablespoon vegetable oil

100 g (3½ oz) Chinese-style cured (dried) pork, finely sliced

1 teaspoon sugar

Cut the wedge of pumpkin in half widthwise, then cut each piece lengthwise into wedges about 5 mm (¼ inch) thick. Put the tofu and liquid in a small bowl and mash together with a fork, then stir in the stock.

Heat the oil in a wok over a medium–high heat, add the dried pork and stir-fry for 2–3 minutes, or until fragrant. Add the pumpkin and stir-fry for 2 minutes, then add the sugar and the tofu and stock mixture. Bring to a simmer, then cook over a medium–high heat for 5 minutes, or until the pumpkin is tender but not falling apart. Transfer to a warmed platter and serve immediately.

Photograph page 97

Mixed mushrooms in chilli oil

Serves 4 to 6 as part of a shared meal

150 g (5½ oz) each oyster, shiitake, chestnut, wood ear, king oyster and shimeji mushrooms
200 g (7 oz) enoki mushrooms
60 ml (2 fl oz/¼ cup) vegetable oil

3 garlic cloves, finely chopped
1½ tablespoons light soy sauce
1 handful garlic chives, chopped
chilli oil (page 407), or ready-made, to taste

If the oyster and shiitake mushrooms are large, cut them in half, otherwise leave whole. Trim the stems of the chestnut mushrooms and leave whole. Tear the wood ears in half, discarding any hard pieces. Slice the king oyster mushrooms lengthwise and trim the shimeji mushrooms at the base to separate them. Trim the ends of the enoki and separate the mushrooms into small bundles. Keep all the mushrooms separate.

Heat the oil in a large wok over a medium–high heat, then add the garlic, shiitake, chestnut, king oyster and oyster mushrooms and stir-fry for 2 minutes, or until the mushrooms start to soften. Add the wood ears, shimeji and enoki mushrooms and stir-fry for another 2–3 minutes, or until all the mushrooms are tender. Add the soy sauce and garlic chives and cook for 30 seconds, tossing to combine. Drizzle with chilli oil and serve.

Photograph page 96

Red capsicum with black beans

Serves 4 to 6 as part of a shared meal

1½ tablespoons fermented black beans, rinsed
2 tablespoons clear rice wine
3 large red capsicums (peppers)
2 tablespoons vegetable oil

3 spring onions (scallions), finely sliced
2 garlic cloves, crushed
1 tablespoon light soy sauce
1 tablespoon clear rice vinegar

Combine the black beans and rice wine in a small bowl and set aside for 30–40 minutes for the beans to soften. Meanwhile, cut the capsicums in half lengthwise, discard the seeds and the tough stem ends, then cut the capsicums into 3 cm (1¼ inch) pieces. Put the capsicum pieces in a bowl and toss with half the oil.

Heat a large, heavy-based frying pan or chargrill pan over a medium–high heat, then add the capsicums in batches (and in a single layer) and cook for 5–6 minutes on each side, or until slightly charred and softened. Remove from the pan and place in a bowl.

Heat the remaining oil in a wok over a medium heat, then add the spring onions and garlic and stir-fry for 2–3 minutes, or until softened and fragrant. Add the capsicums, soy sauce, vinegar and the black bean mixture and stir-fry for 3–4 minutes, or until the liquid has boiled and reduced a little. Serve immediately.

Photograph page 96

From left to right: Edamame and salted mustard greens (page 94); Mixed mushrooms in chilli oil (page 95); Tofu shred salad (page 69); Red capsicum with black beans (page 95); Braised pumpkin with Chinese cured pork (page 94)

Spicy black bean tofu

Serves 4 to 6 as part of a shared meal

This is an easy, quickly made home-style meal to serve with rice and maybe a simple green vegetable stir-fry. The mix of chilli, black beans, garlic and dark soy sauce makes for a flavoursome combo that lifts tofu from the ordinary to the sublime. Vegetarians can swap the chicken stock for vegetable and ditch the pork; its inclusion here isn't make-or-break.

600 g (1 lb 5 oz) firm tofu
750 ml (25½ fl oz/3 cups) vegetable oil
cornflour (cornstarch), for dusting
150 g (5½ oz) minced (ground) pork
4 garlic cloves, crushed
6 spring onions (scallions), cut into 1 cm (½ inch) pieces

3 large red chillies, finely sliced
2½ tablespoons fermented black beans, rinsed
250 ml (8½ fl oz/1 cup) chicken stock (page 405)
1 tablespoon shaoxing rice wine
3 teaspoons dark soy sauce
chilli oil (page 407), or ready-made, to serve (optional)

Drain the tofu well, then cut into 8.5 x 3 cm (3¼ x 1¼ inch) rectangles, about 1 cm (½ inch) thick.

Pour the oil into a large wok and heat to 180°C (350°F), or until a cube of bread dropped into the oil turns deep golden in 15 seconds. Dust the tofu slices in cornflour to coat well, shaking off the excess. Add the tofu to the hot oil in three batches and deep-fry for 5–6 minutes, or until light golden, then remove and drain on paper towel.

Pour off all but 2 tablespoons of oil from the wok. Return the wok to a high heat, then add the pork and stir-fry for 2 minutes, or until it changes colour, stirring constantly to break up the meat. Add the garlic and spring onions and cook, stirring, for 1 minute, or until the spring onions have softened slightly. Add the chillies, black beans, stock, rice wine and soy sauce and bring to the boil.

Add the fried tofu to the wok and cook, gently tossing the tofu to coat well, for about 4 minutes, or until the tofu is heated through and the sauce has thickened slightly. Serve the tofu immediately, drizzled with chilli oil to taste, if desired.

Wheat gluten braised with mushrooms, fungus and lily buds

Serves 4 to 6 as part of a shared meal

This dish is a classic from Shanghai where it's called sixi kaofu *or 'four happiness gluten'. Wheat gluten may not sound like the sexiest ingredient but it's highly prized in China, especially in the Buddhist vegetarian kitchen. It has an intriguingly spongy texture and earthy flavour and this dish is a brilliant introduction to its charms.*

300 g (10½ oz) frozen wheat gluten, thawed

6 dried shiitake mushrooms

10–12 dried wood ear fungus

20 g (¾ oz/½ cup) dried lily buds

500 ml (17 fl oz/2 cups) vegetable oil

1 star anise

80 ml (2½ fl oz/⅓ cup) dark soy sauce

2 tablespoons shaoxing rice wine

1½ tablespoons sugar

80 g (2¾ oz/½ cup) raw, skinned peanuts

Cut the wheat gluten into 1 cm (½ inch) pieces, then place between layers of paper towel and press firmly to remove the excess liquid. Set aside.

Put the shiitake mushrooms, wood ear fungus and lily buds in separate heatproof bowls, cover each with boiling water and soak for 30 minutes, or until softened. Drain the shiitake mushrooms, reserving the soaking liquid, trim the stalks and cut each mushroom into four pieces. Drain the wood ears and the lily buds, discarding the liquid. Remove any hard bits from the wood ears and tear into large pieces. Cut any hard tips off the lily buds and discard.

Pour the oil into a large wok and heat to 180°C (350°F), or until a cube of bread dropped into the oil turns deep golden in 15 seconds. Add half the wheat gluten and fry for 5–6 minutes, or until golden brown. Remove using a slotted spoon and place in a bowl lined with paper towel to drain the excess oil. Repeat with the remaining wheat gluten.

Pour the reserved mushroom liquid into a measuring jug, taking care not to include any grit that has sunk to the bottom, then add enough water to make up to 500 ml (17 fl oz/2 cups). Pour the liquid into a saucepan and add the shiitake, wood ears, lily buds and wheat gluten, then add the star anise, soy sauce, rice wine, sugar and peanuts. Stir to combine, then bring the mixture to a simmer, cover and cook over a low heat, stirring occasionally, for about 1 hour, or until the liquid has been absorbed. Serve hot or warm.

Steamed eggplant

Serves 4 as part of a shared meal

Steaming renders eggplants (aubergines) super soft. Don't skip the salting part as this process really does help achieve a great texture (despite what you might read, salting eggplant has little to do with expelling bitterness; these days, eggplants aren't especially 'bitter'). This is one of those easy recipes where you can make the sauce well ahead of time and then simply pour it over the eggplants once they are tender.

2 large eggplants (aubergines) (about 900 g/2 lb)

1 tablespoon salt

60 ml (2 fl oz/¼ cup) light soy sauce

2 tablespoons clear rice vinegar

2 tablespoons clear rice wine

1 teaspoon sesame oil

1 tablespoon sugar

1 tablespoon Chinese sesame paste

1 red chilli, or to taste, finely chopped

3 garlic cloves, finely chopped

5 cm (2 inch) piece ginger, peeled and finely chopped

1 small handful coriander (cilantro) leaves, roughly chopped

Cut the eggplants in half lengthwise, then in half crosswise. Place the eggplant quarters in a colander and sprinkle with the salt, then leave to drain for 25–30 minutes. Rinse well and pat dry with paper towel.

Put the eggplant on a rimmed plate and place in a steamer over a wok or saucepan of boiling water, then cover and steam for 25 minutes, or until the eggplant is tender when pierced with a skewer. Carefully remove the eggplant from the steamer, then cover with foil to keep warm.

Combine the soy sauce, vinegar, rice wine, sesame oil, sugar, sesame paste, chilli, garlic and ginger in a small saucepan. Place over a medium–high heat and bring to the boil, then reduce the heat to medium and simmer for about 10 minutes, or until the sauce has reduced and thickened. Carefully place the steamed eggplant on a platter, then pour over the sauce. Sprinkle with the coriander before serving.

Crisp fried tofu squares

Serves 4 to 6 as part of a shared meal

This dish was inspired by the spicy fried tofu we ate at the incredible night market in Kaifeng in northern China. With its slightly shambolic air and huge selection of interesting regional snacks, this market is a favourite of ours. There, the tofu is cooked on the back of a mobile cart and topped with grated carrot and coriander (cilantro), but we've made an even easier version.

500 g (1 lb 2 oz) firm tofu

3 teaspoons ground cumin

3 teaspoons chilli flakes

3 garlic cloves, crushed

100 ml (3½ fl oz) peanut oil

1 tablespoon light soy sauce

1 large handful coriander (cilantro) leaves, chopped

chilli oil (page 407), or ready-made, to serve (optional)

Cut the tofu into pieces about 3 cm (1¼ inches) square, then pat dry using paper towel. Combine the cumin, chilli flakes and garlic in a small bowl and set aside.

Heat the oil in a large frying pan over a medium–high heat, then add the tofu and cook for 3 minutes, or until golden. Turn the tofu over and cook for another 3–4 minutes, or until golden. Sprinkle the cumin mixture over the tofu, turn over and cook for 2 minutes on each side, or until deep golden, crisp and fragrant. Add the soy sauce and scatter over the coriander, then turn the tofu again to coat in the sauce. Transfer to a platter, pour any oil in the pan over the tofu and drizzle with chilli oil to taste, if desired. Serve immediately.

Wok-fried broccoli with ginger and mushrooms

Serves 4 to 6 as part of a shared meal

4 dried shiitake mushrooms

2 heads broccoli (about 600 g/1 lb 5 oz)

1 tablespoon vegetable oil

1½ teaspoons finely chopped ginger

1 tablespoon shaoxing rice wine

Put the shiitake mushrooms in a small heatproof bowl, cover with boiling water and soak for 30 minutes, or until softened. Drain, reserving 60 ml (2 fl oz/¼ cup) of the soaking water. Squeeze the mushrooms dry, then finely slice. Wash the broccoli and cut the heads into florets. Trim off the base of the stalks, and cut the stalks into 1.5 cm (½ inch) slices.

Heat a wok over a medium–high heat, add the oil and then the ginger and stir-fry for 20–30 seconds, or until fragrant. Add the broccoli stalks and stir-fry for 1–2 minutes, then add the florets and mushrooms and stir-fry for another 1–2 minutes. Add the reserved mushroom liquid and rice wine and bring to a simmer; continue simmering for 2–3 minutes, or until the broccoli is just tender (be careful you don't overcook the broccoli or it will lose its bright green colour). Serve hot or at room temperature.

Coriander salad

Serves 6 as part of a shared meal

250 ml (8½ fl oz/1 cup) vegetable oil

5 garlic cloves, very finely sliced

3 bunches coriander (cilantro), sprigs picked

3 spring onions (scallions), finely sliced on the
    diagonal

1½ tablespoons black rice vinegar

1 tablespoon sesame oil

2½ tablespoons light soy sauce

5 cm (2 inch) piece ginger, peeled and shredded

1 long red chilli, finely sliced (optional)

Heat the oil in a small saucepan over a medium heat. Add the garlic and cook, stirring occasionally, for about 2 minutes, or until golden, then remove using a slotted spoon and drain on paper towel. Reserve the oil for another use. Toss the coriander and spring onions together in a bowl. Put the vinegar, sesame oil, soy sauce, ginger and chilli, if using, in a bowl and whisk to combine well. Drizzle the dressing over the salad and gently toss to coat, then scatter over the fried garlic.

Photograph page 266

Dry-fried green beans

Serves 4 to 6 as part of a shared meal

1 teaspoon sichuan peppercorns

2½ tablespoons peanut oil

400 g (14 oz) green beans, trimmed and cut into 5 cm (2 inch) pieces

2 spring onions (scallions), white part only, finely sliced on the diagonal

10 small dried red chillies, halved lengthwise

4 garlic cloves, very finely chopped

2 cm (¾ inch) piece ginger, peeled and finely shredded

sea salt, to taste

Dry-roast the peppercorns in a small, heavy-based frying pan over a medium–low heat, shaking the pan often, for 3–4 minutes, or until fragrant. Cool, then transfer to a mortar (or an electric spice grinder) and pound with the pestle to form a coarse powder. Set aside.

Heat the oil in a large wok over a medium–high heat, then add the beans and stir-fry for 5 minutes, or until almost tender and the skins look slightly shrivelled — it is important to keep the beans moving as they cook. Add the spring onions, chillies, ground peppercorns, garlic and ginger and cook, stirring constantly, for another 2 minutes, or until fragrant. Season to taste with sea salt and serve immediately.

Smashed radish

Serves 4 to 6 as part of a shared meal

2 bunches red radishes (about 600 g/1 lb 5 oz)

1 teaspoon salt

2 tablespoons clear rice vinegar

2 teaspoons sugar

2 tablespoons light soy sauce

2 tablespoons peanut oil

2 garlic cloves, crushed

Trim the radishes and wash them. Using the side of a heavy knife or cleaver, press hard on each radish to crack it open. Don't press too hard — you only want the radish to just crack open. Place the radishes in a bowl, sprinkle over the salt and set aside for 40 minutes to soften slightly.

Put the remaining ingredients in a large bowl and whisk to combine well. Add the radishes and toss to coat, then transfer to a serving bowl or plate.

Photograph page 343

Zucchini pancakes

Makes 6

This is our version of a snack from Beijing, a city with a rich tradition of street food. You might not think of zucchini (courgettes) as particularly 'Chinese' but, really, they cook practically every vegetable there — kohlrabi, cauliflower, asparagus ... With its diverse range of climatic regions, almost everything grows in some part of China or another.

500 g (1 lb 2 oz) zucchini (courgettes) (about 3), finely grated

3 eggs, lightly beaten

1 tablespoon light soy sauce

75 g (2¾ oz/½ cup) plain (all-purpose) flour

ground white pepper

vegetable oil, for cooking

Dipping sauce

80 ml (2½ fl oz/⅓ cup) black rice vinegar

1½ tablespoons light soy sauce

2 garlic cloves, crushed

3 cm (1¼ inch) piece ginger, peeled and finely shredded

2½ teaspoons caster (superfine) sugar

1½ teaspoons sesame oil

To make the dipping sauce, put all the ingredients in a bowl and stir to combine well.

Put the grated zucchini in a tea towel (dish towel), then gather the towel around the zucchini into a tight bundle. Holding the bundle over a bowl to collect the juices, wring the zucchini to extract as much liquid as possible. Place the zucchini in a large bowl. Measure the zucchini juice, then add enough water to make it up to 200 ml (7 fl oz). Add the liquid to the zucchini, then add the eggs and soy sauce and stir to combine well. Add the flour and stir until a smooth batter forms. Add a little more water if necessary — the mixture should have a light batter consistency. Season with white pepper.

Brush the base of a 20 cm (8 inch) non-stick frying pan with oil, then place over a medium heat. When the pan is hot, add about 80 ml (2½ fl oz/⅓ cup) of the zucchini mixture, then use a spatula to spread the mixture out to cover the base of the pan. Cook for 2–3 minutes, or until the pancake is dry on top, then carefully turn it over using the spatula and cook the other side for 1–2 minutes, or until light golden. Remove to a large plate lined with baking paper. Cook the remaining mixture. Serve the pancakes, folded into quarters, with the dipping sauce.

Scrambled egg with tomato

Serves 4 to 6 as part of a shared meal

This isn't necessarily a breakfast dish — in Beijing you eat this with boiled dumplings or plates of noodles as a lunch or light dinner. It's one of those simple meals that can go horribly wrong with watery tomatoes and sub-par eggs, so make sure you use the best of each you can find.

2 tablespoons tomato sauce (ketchup)

1½ tablespoons light soy sauce

2 teaspoons black rice vinegar

2 teaspoons sugar

3 teaspoons cornflour (cornstarch)

8 eggs

1 tablespoon shaoxing rice wine

2½ tablespoons vegetable oil

5 large firm, ripe tomatoes (about 700 g/ 1 lb 9 oz), cut into 2.5 cm (1 inch) pieces

2 garlic cloves, finely chopped

Put the tomato sauce, soy sauce, vinegar and sugar in a bowl and stir to combine. Mix half the cornflour with 2 tablespoons water and add to the mixture, stir to combine well, then set aside. Break the eggs into a bowl, whisk well, then stir in the rice wine and remaining cornflour.

Heat 1 tablespoon of the oil in a wok over a medium–high heat. Add the tomatoes and garlic and stir-fry for 2 minutes, or until the tomatoes just start to soften. Add the tomato sauce mixture and cook, stirring, for 1–2 minutes, or until the mixture boils and thickens.

Working quickly, heat the remaining oil in a large non-stick frying pan or another wok over a medium–high heat. Add the egg mixture and cook just until the eggs start to set around the edges, then use a spatula to push the edges into the centre of the pan. Continue cooking the eggs, pushing them into the middle as they cook, for another 2 minutes, or until just set. Add the tomatoes and gently stir to combine, then transfer to a bowl and serve immediately.

Photograph page 107

Chinese cabbage with mustard

Serves 4 as part of a shared meal

This dish is another specialty from Beijing and Dongbei, often enjoyed after Lunar New Year feasting when something a bit lighter and palate-cleansing is required. This is a simplified version of the original, where the cabbage is partially fermented for an extra kick. Even without the fermentation, this still packs quite a punch.

3½ tablespoons hot English mustard powder

1½ teaspoons caster (superfine) sugar

2½ teaspoons clear rice vinegar

2 teaspoons sesame oil

1 Chinese cabbage (wombok)

Combine the mustard powder, sugar, vinegar and sesame oil with 80 ml (2½ fl oz/⅓ cup) water in a small bowl and whisk until smooth.

Trim the base off the cabbage, then remove and discard the large, tough outer leaves. Separate out the remaining leaves. Bring a large saucepan of salted water to the boil. Add the cabbage in three batches and cook for 3 minutes, or until the white stems are just tender. Use kitchen tongs to transfer each batch to a colander and leave to drain and cool to room temperature. Working in batches, spread the cooled leaves on tea towels (dish towels), then roll up and gently squeeze to remove as much water as possible.

Divide the mustard sauce among four 250 ml (8½ fl oz/1 cup) bowls. Use some of the leaves to line each bowl, opening the leaves and allowing any excess to hang over the edge of the bowls. Fill the bowls with the remaining cabbage, then bring the overhanging leaves over the top, to cover. Wrap each bowl in plastic wrap and refrigerate for 3 hours, or overnight. To serve, turn the cabbage out onto plates, making sure you remove as much of the mustard sauce from the bowls as possible.

Photograph page 278

Brussels sprouts and dried shrimp stir-fry

Serves 4 to 6 as part of a shared meal

This dish couldn't be more simple — but like all simple things it does rely on a few crucial details. The first lies in cutting the brussels sprouts very, very finely, and the second is in using the variety of dried shrimp so tiny they are practically krill (the Chinese call these tiny dried shrimp 'shrimp skin').

80 ml (2½ fl oz/⅓ cup) vegetable oil

20 g (¾ oz/½ cup) very small dried shrimp

600 g (1 lb 5 oz) brussels sprouts, very finely sliced

3 garlic cloves, finely chopped

2½ tablespoons light soy sauce

3 spring onions (scallions), finely sliced

Heat the oil in a wok over a medium–high heat, then add the shrimp and stir-fry for 2–3 minutes, or until light golden and fragrant. Using a slotted spoon, remove the shrimp to a bowl.

Add the brussels sprouts and garlic to the wok and stir-fry over a medium–high heat for 4–5 minutes, or until the sprouts are just tender. Return the shrimp to the wok, then add the soy sauce and spring onions and stir to combine well. Cook for another minute to heat through, then transfer to a large bowl and serve.

Lettuce cooked with garlic

Serves 4 to 6 as part of a shared meal

1 iceberg lettuce
60 ml (2 fl oz/¼ cup) peanut oil
4 garlic cloves, finely chopped

2 tablespoons light soy sauce
1 teaspoon caster (superfine) sugar

Remove and discard the tough outer leaves of the lettuce. Remove the leaves, discarding the core, and tear the leaves into large pieces.

Heat the oil in a wok over a medium–high heat, then add the garlic and stir-fry for 1 minute, or until fragrant. Add the lettuce leaves and toss to combine well, then add the soy sauce and sugar. Cover the wok and cook, tossing the wok occasionally, for 3–4 minutes, or until the lettuce is wilted but still has some crunch. Transfer to a large bowl and serve immediately.

Snake beans with pork and Chinese olives

Serves 4 to 6 as part of a shared meal

175 g (6 oz) pork neck, in one piece
2 bunches snake (long) beans (about 400 g/ 14 oz), trimmed
2 tablespoons vegetable oil

2 garlic cloves, finely chopped
40 g (1½ oz/⅓ cup) sliced Chinese olives
1 tablespoon clear rice wine
60 ml (2 fl oz/¼ cup) chicken stock (page 405)

Finely slice the pork neck. Using a large knife, finely chop the pork and set aside. Cut the snake beans into 5 mm (¼ inch) pieces and set aside.

Heat the oil in a wok over a medium–high heat, then add the garlic, pork and snake beans and stir-fry for 3 minutes, or until the meat changes colour. Add the remaining ingredients, bring the liquid to a simmer, then cook, stirring occasionally, for another 3 minutes, or until the beans are tender, the pork is cooked through and most of the liquid has evaporated. Transfer to a bowl and serve.

Watercress and fermented tofu stir-fry

Serves 4 to 6 as part of a shared meal

1 tablespoon vegetable oil

2 teaspoons finely chopped ginger

1 bunch watercress (about 400 g/14 oz), washed, ends trimmed and cut into 6 cm (2½ inch) lengths

3 pieces red fermented tofu, mashed with 1 tablespoon of the tofu liquid

1 tablespoon tofu liquid

1 teaspoon sesame oil

Heat the vegetable oil in a wok over a medium–high heat. Add the ginger and stir-fry for 30 seconds, or until fragrant, then add the watercress and stir-fry for 2–3 minutes, or until the cress has wilted. Add the mashed fermented tofu, tofu liquid and sesame oil and toss to combine well. Serve immediately.

Stir-fried snow pea sprouts

Serves 4 as part of a shared meal

1 tablespoon vegetable oil

2 garlic cloves, finely chopped

1 tablespoon finely chopped ginger

300 g (10½ oz) snow pea (mangetout) sprouts

60 ml (2 fl oz/¼ cup) chicken stock (page 405)

Heat the oil in a wok over a medium–high heat. Add the garlic and ginger and stir-fry for 30 seconds, or until fragrant. Add the snow pea sprouts and stir-fry for another minute, or until the sprouts start to wilt. Add the stock and bring to the boil, then reduce the heat to medium and simmer for 2–3 minutes, or until the liquid has reduced and coats the sprouts. Cool to room temperature and serve.

Photograph page 67

Enoki mushrooms with egg tofu

Serves 4 to 6 as part of a shared meal

Egg tofu is tofu that's had egg added to it before being cooked, usually directly in the packaging it's sold in (look for it in plastic tubes). The egg gives the tofu a slightly richer flavour than ordinary tofu and it marries perfectly with the delicate flavour of enoki mushrooms, although you could use any mushroom, or even a variety of them, here.

400 g (14 oz) enoki mushrooms
150 g (5½ oz) tube of egg tofu
60 ml (2 fl oz/¼ cup) peanut oil

1 tablespoon finely shredded ginger
1½ tablespoons light soy sauce
1½ tablespoons shaoxing rice wine

Trim the ends of the enoki, separate the mushrooms into very small bundles and set aside. Cut the tofu into 1 cm (½ inch) thick slices.

Heat half of the oil in a heavy-based frying pan over a medium heat, then add the tofu and cook, turning once, for 5–6 minutes, or until light golden.

Meanwhile, heat the remaining oil in a wok over a medium–high heat, then add the ginger and stir-fry for 1 minute, or until fragrant. Add the mushrooms and stir-fry for 3 minutes, or until tender. Add the soy sauce and rice wine, bring to a simmer, then add the tofu and gently toss to combine. Cook for another minute to heat the tofu through, then serve immediately.

Photograph page 185

Garlic stems with speck

Serves 4 to 6 as part of a shared meal

Oh Hunan, how we loved your smoked ham. Pitch black on the outside from the smoking chamber and smoky and sweet on the inside, we ate it in many guises and in all sorts of dishes. One of our favourites is this one, paired with thick, juicy garlic stems. We find good-quality speck to be a respectable stand-in for the real Hunan deal although, truthfully, nothing else really comes close.

250 g (9 oz) piece speck

500 g (1 lb 2 oz) garlic stems (2 bunches)

2½ tablespoons vegetable oil

2 tablespoons light soy sauce

1 tablespoon shaoxing rice wine

½ teaspoon sugar

Cut the speck widthwise into thin slices and set aside. Cut the garlic stems into 4 cm (1½ inch) pieces.

Heat the oil in a wok over a medium–high heat, then add the speck and stir-fry for 4–5 minutes, or until light golden. Using a slotted spoon, transfer the speck to a bowl. Add the garlic stems to the wok and stir-fry for 2 minutes, or until they start to soften. Add the soy sauce, rice wine and sugar and cook for another 3 minutes. Add the garlic stems to the bowl with the speck and toss to combine. Serve immediately.

Photograph page 269

Tofu and chrysanthemum leaf rolls with pork sauce

Makes 8

Muttering darkly on one trip that we weren't going to make it to Dongbei in China's extreme northeast, we consoled ourselves with a meaty feast from the region at a branch of Dongbei Ren, a restaurant in Shanghai. This is our version of a most intriguing dish that we ate there. We've used frozen tofu sheets here, although it's way better made with fresh pressed tofu sheets, if you can find them.

1 bunch chrysanthemum leaves

2 frozen large tofu sheets, about 48 x 24 cm (19 x 9½ inches), thawed

24 spring onions (scallions), green parts only, about 23 cm (9 inches) in length, for tying

Pork sauce

1½ tablespoons vegetable oil

½ onion, finely chopped

2 garlic cloves, finely chopped

300 g (10½ oz) minced (ground) pork, not too lean

150 ml (5 fl oz) yellow bean sauce

2 teaspoons sugar

2 teaspoons clear rice vinegar

3 teaspoons clear rice wine

200 ml (7 fl oz) chicken stock (page 405)

1½ teaspoons cornflour (cornstarch)

To make the pork sauce, heat the oil in a small saucepan over a medium heat. Add the onion, garlic and pork and cook, stirring to break up the meat, for 4–5 minutes, or until the onion has softened slightly and the pork has changed colour. Add the remaining ingredients, except the cornflour, and bring the mixture to a simmer. Reduce the heat to low, cover and cook for 15 minutes. Combine the cornflour with 1 tablespoon water in a small bowl and mix to form a smooth paste. Stirring the pork sauce constantly, add the cornflour paste to the sauce and cook for 1–2 minutes, or until it simmers and thickens.

Meanwhile, pick the chrysanthemum leaves from the long, thick stems, discarding any thick stems. Gently wash the leaves and spin dry. Divide the leaves into eight even piles. Cut each tofu sheet into four pieces widthwise, to give you eight pieces that measure around 24 x 12 cm (9½ x 4¾ inches).

Bring a small saucepan of water to the boil, add the spring onion lengths and blanch for 1 minute, or until softened, then drain well. Working with one piece of tofu at a time, place a portion of chrysanthemum leaves along the middle of the sheet, arranging them so that half the leaves (and not the stems) are hanging out a little at one end and half are hanging out the other end. Roll the tofu sheets up quite firmly around the chrysanthemum leaves. Using a blanched spring onion stem, tie each end of the roll to secure it. Continue until all the tofu sheet pieces and leaves are used — you probably won't need all the spring onion stems, but some may break. Place the rolls on a platter and serve immediately with the hot or warm pork sauce.

Roasted cumin and chilli potatoes

Serves 4 to 6 as part of a shared meal

We snacked ourselves stupid on our last visit to Chengdu, the capital of Sichuan Province. One of our favourite fast foods there was a paper tub of tiny peeled potatoes, roasted and slathered in chilli flakes, salt and the freshest of ground cumin seeds. We couldn't have been happier.

800 g (1 lb 12 oz) new potatoes or other small potatoes, peeled

2½ teaspoons cumin seeds

2 teaspoons sichuan peppercorns

2 teaspoons chilli powder or chilli flakes

2 garlic cloves, crushed

1½ teaspoons sea salt

80 ml (2½ fl oz/⅓ cup) vegetable oil

Cook the potatoes in a saucepan of boiling water for 10 minutes, or until just tender. Drain well, then place in a roasting tin in a single layer. Preheat the oven to 200°C (400°F/Gas 6).

Meanwhile, dry-roast the cumin seeds and peppercorns separately in a small, heavy-based frying pan over a medium–low heat, shaking the pan often, for 3–4 minutes, or until fragrant. Cool, then transfer to a mortar (or an electric spice grinder) and pound with the pestle to form a coarse powder.

Combine the ground cumin and peppercorns in a bowl with the chilli powder, garlic, sea salt and oil. Pour over the potatoes and toss to coat well. Roast the potatoes, turning them occasionally, for 30 minutes, or until golden. Serve immediately.

Photograph page 275

Dongbei cabbage salad

Serves 6 as part of a shared meal

In Dongbei, a collection of three provinces (including the old 'Manchuria') in the country's northeast, cabbage is a staple. The climate is harsh, the winters are long and not a lot grows, so people have learned all kinds of ways to prepare and preserve cabbage. This salad is popular when the vegetable is available fresh — we like to think of it as a kind of Chinese coleslaw.

500 g (1 lb 2 oz) Chinese cabbage (wombok), hard core trimmed

2 carrots, peeled and cut into thin matchsticks

2 Lebanese (short) cucumbers, cut into thin matchsticks

1 large handful coriander (cilantro) leaves

80 g (2¾ oz/½ cup) small raw, red-skinned peanuts, roasted (page 413)

Dressing

3 garlic cloves, finely chopped

1 tablespoon caster (superfine) sugar

60 ml (2 fl oz/¼ cup) black rice vinegar

60 ml (2 fl oz/¼ cup) peanut oil

2 teaspoons sesame oil

To make the dressing, combine all the ingredients in a small bowl, stirring until the sugar has dissolved.

Finely slice the cabbage and combine with the carrots and cucumbers in a large bowl. Add the dressing and toss to combine well. Add the coriander and peanuts, toss lightly to combine, then transfer to a large platter or bowl and serve immediately.

Photograph page 275

Hot and sour soup

Serves 4 as a light meal

There are versions of this soup made throughout China and, like many soups there, it's thought to possess healing properties. Wood ear and lily buds are believed to be good for circulation; vinegar (the 'sour' part) is thought to have antiseptic properties; and good chicken stock is, as we all know, nature's penicillin. Sometimes slivers of pork are added, so feel welcome to do that (fillet would work well, added at the last minute), and the soup is often seasoned with extra pepper for added heat.

6 dried shiitake mushrooms

6 dried wood ear fungus

20 dried lily buds

250 g (9 oz) firm tofu, cut into thick matchsticks

1 tablespoon dark soy sauce

1 egg, lightly beaten

2 teaspoons sesame oil

1 litre (34 fl oz/4 cups) chicken stock (page 405)

125 g (4½ oz/½ cup) drained, tinned bamboo shoots, cut into thick matchsticks

2 cm (¾ inch) piece ginger, peeled and finely chopped

2 tablespoons black rice vinegar

2 teaspoons chilli oil (page 407), or ready-made, or to taste

2 tablespoons cornflour (cornstarch)

sea salt and freshly ground black pepper

3 spring onions (scallions), green part only, finely shredded

1 small handful coriander (cilantro) leaves

Put the shiitake mushrooms and wood ear fungus in a heatproof bowl and the lily buds in another bowl. Cover each with boiling water and soak for 30 minutes, or until softened. Combine the tofu and soy sauce in a bowl, gently toss the tofu to coat, then set aside to marinate for 15 minutes. Combine the egg and sesame oil in a small bowl, mix well and set aside.

Drain the mushrooms, reserving 250 ml (8½ fl oz/1 cup) of the soaking liquid. Finely slice the shiitakes. Remove any hard bits from the wood ears and tear or cut into small pieces. Drain the lily buds, discarding the water, and cut any hard tips off the lily buds.

In a large saucepan, combine the stock, mushroom soaking liquid, shiitakes, wood ears, lily buds, marinated tofu, bamboo shoots, ginger, vinegar and chilli oil. Bring to the boil over a high heat, then reduce the heat to medium–low and simmer for 10 minutes.

Combine the cornflour with 60 ml (2 fl oz/¼ cup) water in a small bowl and stir to form a smooth paste, then add to the soup and simmer for 1 minute, or until the soup thickens. Remove the pan from the heat. While stirring the soup continuously, slowly pour the egg mixture in a steady stream into the soup. Season to taste with sea salt and pepper. Divide the soup among large bowls, scatter over the spring onions and coriander and serve immediately.

Chrysanthemum leaf salad

Serves 4 to 6 as part of a shared meal

1 bunch chrysanthemum leaves, trimmed
60 ml (2 fl oz/¼ cup) vegetable oil
3 garlic cloves, chopped
2 tablespoons black rice vinegar

1 tablespoon shaoxing rice wine
2 tablespoons chicken stock (page 405)
1 teaspoon sugar
1 tablespoon sesame seeds, toasted (page 413)

Wash the chrysanthemum leaves well, shake or spin dry, then cut into 3 cm (1¼ inch) pieces. Place the leaves in a bowl.

Heat the oil in a wok over a medium heat, then add the garlic and cook, stirring often, for about 4 minutes, or until the garlic turns golden, taking care that it doesn't burn. Add the vinegar, rice wine, stock and sugar and bring to the boil, then pour the hot dressing over the leaves in the bowl, tossing to coat. Transfer to a platter, sprinkle with the sesame seeds and serve immediately.

Tofu with sesame dressing

Serves 4 to 6 as part of a shared meal

500 g (1 lb 2 oz) silken tofu, cut into 1 cm (½ inch) squares
1 large handful coriander (cilantro) leaves, roughly chopped
chilli oil (page 407), or ready-made, to serve
2 tablespoons sesame seeds, toasted (page 413)

Sesame dressing
60 ml (2 fl oz/¼ cup) Chinese sesame paste, plus 1½ tablespoons oil from the jar
1½ tablespoons clear rice vinegar
2 garlic cloves, very finely chopped
sea salt and ground white pepper

To make the sesame dressing, combine the sesame paste, oil and 60 ml (2 fl oz/¼ cup) warm water in a small bowl and whisk until smooth. Stir in the vinegar and garlic and season to taste with sea salt and white pepper.

Place the tofu in a large heatproof bowl, then carefully pour boiling water over the tofu to cover it. Set aside for 3 minutes, or until heated through, then drain well, taking care that the tofu doesn't break up. Place the tofu on a serving platter and scatter the coriander over the top. Drizzle the sesame dressing over the tofu, then drizzle with a little chilli oil, to taste. Sprinkle with the sesame seeds and serve.

Spicy Xi'an carrot and daikon

Serves 6 as part of a shared meal

We adore the Muslim Quarter of Xi'an so much that we've never bothered to venture beyond it to see anything else around town (such as the Terracotta Army ... oops). It's a true enclave with mosques, narrow laneways, atmospheric old low-rise buildings and some very unique food. This simple dish, with its gutsy, fiery, satisfying flavours is just one we loved — there were dozens more!

500 g (1 lb 2 oz) carrots (about 5)

500 g (1 lb 2 oz) daikon (white radish) (about 1)

2½ tablespoons vegetable oil

3 garlic cloves, finely chopped

2 tablespoons finely chopped ginger

1 piece cassia bark, broken into smaller pieces

6 dried red chillies

3 teaspoons chilli flakes, or to taste

1 teaspoon cumin seeds

1 teaspoon fennel seeds

60 ml (2 fl oz/¼ cup) light soy sauce

2 teaspoons dark soy sauce

60 ml (2 fl oz/¼ cup) black rice vinegar

1 tablespoon sugar

1 tablespoon sesame oil

Peel the carrots and daikon, then cut them into strips about 5 cm (2 inches) long and 5 mm (¼ inch) wide.

Heat the vegetable oil in a large wok over a medium heat, then add the garlic, ginger and dried spices and cook, stirring, for 2 minutes, or until fragrant. Add the carrot and daikon and toss to combine well. Add the soy sauces, vinegar, sugar, sesame oil and 60 ml (2 fl oz/¼ cup) water. Bring to a simmer, then cover the wok and cook for 3–4 minutes, or until the vegetables just start to soften. Remove the lid, toss the carrots and daikon well, then cook for another minute to allow some of the liquid to evaporate — the vegetables should still be a little crisp. Transfer to a bowl and cool to room temperature before serving.

Photograph page 263

Stir-fry of celery and five-spice tofu

Serves 4 to 6 as part of a shared meal

This is a quick and easy stir-fry, with celery at centre stage. The tender heart of the vegetable is an excellent foil for the fragrant five-spice tofu, which has a firm texture pleasantly reminiscent of a slightly rubbery cheese.

1 x 300 g (10½ oz) celery heart
60 ml (2 fl oz/¼ cup) peanut oil
3 garlic cloves, finely chopped
150 g (5½ oz) five-spice tofu, finely sliced

1½ teaspoons sugar
2½ tablespoons clear rice vinegar
1 tablespoon clear rice wine
sea salt and freshly ground black pepper

Trim the celery heart, reserving some of the leaves. Finely slice the celery on the diagonal. Roughly chop the leaves and set aside.

Heat the oil in a wok over a medium–high heat, then add the garlic and celery and stir-fry for 2–3 minutes, or until the celery has softened slightly. Add the tofu, sugar, vinegar and rice wine and toss together. Cook, tossing the wok often, for about 1 minute, or until the liquid boils and the tofu is heated through — the celery should be cooked through but still a little crisp. Toss in the reserved celery leaves, season to taste with sea salt and pepper and serve immediately.

Stir-fried bamboo with speck

Serves 4 to 6 as part of a shared meal

We were lucky enough to be in Zhejiang Province in spring, when thin, tender bamboo shoots were in season. Staying in the picturesque village of Guodong, we ordered them at every meal, even breakfast — they really were that good. Unhappily, fresh young bamboo isn't readily available, so we make do with frozen bamboo; it's not the same but still good nonetheless.

600 g (1 lb 5 oz) frozen winter bamboo shoots, thawed

100 g (3½ oz) speck

1 tablespoon vegetable oil

2 garlic cloves, finely chopped

1½ tablespoons light soy sauce

1 tablespoon clear rice wine

about 250 ml (8½ fl oz/1 cup) chicken stock

Thinly slice the bamboo lengthwise on the diagonal and set aside. Cut the speck into thin slices. Heat the oil in a wok over a medium heat, then add the speck and cook for 3 minutes on each side, or until golden. Remove to a plate.

Reheat the oil over a medium heat, add the garlic and bamboo and stir-fry for 3 minutes, then add the soy sauce, rice wine and stock and bring to a simmer. Cook the bamboo, tossing the wok often, for 5–6 minutes, or until the bamboo is tender, adding a little more stock or water if the liquid evaporates (there should still be liquid in the wok when the bamboo is cooked). Transfer the bamboo and cooking liquid to a serving bowl, scatter over the speck and serve.

Hot and sour cabbage

Serves 4 to 6 as part of a shared meal

1 tablespoon clear rice vinegar

3 teaspoons black rice vinegar

3 teaspoons sugar

2 teaspoons light soy sauce

60 ml (2 fl oz/¼ cup) peanut oil

4 garlic cloves, finely chopped

4 dried red chillies, finely chopped

500 g (1 lb 2 oz) Chinese cabbage (wombok) stems (use the green leaves in a stir-fry), cut on the diagonal into 3 cm (1¼ inch) pieces

Combine the vinegars, sugar and soy sauce in a small bowl and set aside.

Heat the oil in a wok over a medium–high heat, then add the garlic and chillies and stir-fry for 1 minute, or until fragrant. Add the cabbage stems and stir-fry for about 4 minutes, or until the stems start to soften — do not let them brown. Add the vinegar mixture, increase the heat to high and stir-fry for another 2 minutes, or until the cabbage stems are just tender and the liquid has boiled and reduced. Transfer to a bowl or platter and serve.

Oil-braised bamboo

Serves 4 to 6 as part of a shared meal

600 g (1 lb 5 oz) frozen winter bamboo shoots, thawed

vegetable oil, for deep-frying

1 teaspoon sichuan peppercorns

1 teaspoon finely chopped ginger

1 tablespoon caster (superfine) sugar

1 tablespoon light soy sauce

1 tablespoon dark soy sauce

2½ tablespoons shaoxing rice wine

300 ml (10 fl oz) chicken stock (page 405)

Cut the bamboo into 2 cm (¾ inch) pieces and pat dry with paper towel. Fill a wok one-third full of oil and heat to 180°C (350°F), or until a cube of bread dropped into the oil turns deep golden in 15 seconds. Add the bamboo in two batches and cook for 3–4 minutes, or until golden. Remove using a slotted spoon and drain on paper towel.

Pour off all but 2 tablespoons of oil from the wok. Add the peppercorns and ginger and cook for 30 seconds, or until fragrant. Add the remaining ingredients and return the bamboo to the wok. Bring to a simmer, then cook, tossing the wok occasionally, for 25 minutes, or until the bamboo is very tender and the liquid has reduced and thickened. Transfer to a plate and serve.

Photograph page 231

Silken tofu with spicy sauce and peanuts

Serves 4 as a light meal

We have fond memories of eating soft, hot tofu like this in Sheng Li, an historic village in the Sichuan backblocks. In the mornings an elderly fellow would go from alley to alley, selling ladlefuls of his home-made tofu, steaming and hot from a large wooden tub. It tasted smoky and comforting ... until we got to the sediment at the base of the bowl — a fiery sludge of oil, chilli and mouth-numbing sichuan peppercorns.

750 ml (25½ fl oz/3 cups) vegetable oil, or enough for deep-frying

8 fresh egg wrappers, sliced into thin strips

1 kg (2 lb 3 oz) silken tofu

110 g (4 oz/⅔ cup) raw, red-skinned peanuts, roasted (page 413)

2 spring onions (scallions), finely sliced

ready-made sichuan preserved vegetables, to serve (optional)

Sauce

60 ml (2 fl oz/¼ cup) peanut oil

60 ml (2 fl oz/¼ cup) sichuan chilli bean paste, or to taste

80 ml (2½ fl oz/⅓ cup) black rice vinegar

2 tablespoons light soy sauce

250 ml (8½ fl oz/1 cup) chicken stock (page 405)

3 garlic cloves, finely chopped

1½ tablespoons sesame oil

2½ tablespoons caster (superfine) sugar

1½ tablespoons chilli oil (page 406), or ready-made (optional)

To make the sauce, heat the peanut oil in a small saucepan over a medium heat, then add the chilli bean paste and cook, stirring, for 2–3 minutes, or until fragrant. Remove from the heat, then add the remaining sauce ingredients, stirring until the sugar has dissolved.

Pour the vegetable oil into a large wok and heat to 180°C (350°F), or until a cube of bread dropped into the oil turns deep golden in 15 seconds. Add the strips of egg wrapper and fry for 3–4 minutes, or until puffed, golden and crisp. Remove using a slotted spoon and drain on paper towel.

Using a metal spoon, scoop off pieces from the tofu block, dividing them carefully between two large heatproof bowls. Carefully pour over enough boiling water to cover the tofu, leave for 6–7 minutes to heat through, then drain. Divide among four warmed bowls. Pour the sauce over the tofu, then scatter some of the fried wrappers, peanuts and spring onions over the top. Serve the remaining wrappers, peanuts and spring onions separately, with the preserved vegetables, if using.

Dry-fried vegetables with sesame seeds

Serves 6 as part of a shared meal

The key ingredient in this easy dish is the sichuan preserved vegetables, or zha cai, *made using the stems of mustard greens, which have been rubbed with salt and chilli powder and left to ferment. A pantry staple in most Chinese kitchens, these are readily found in jars or plastic sachets in Asian grocery stores.*

300 g (10½ oz/3⅓ cups) mung bean sprouts

60 ml (2 fl oz/¼ cup) vegetable oil

300 g (10½ oz/1¼ cups) drained, tinned bamboo shoots

300 g (10½ oz) long white Chinese turnip, peeled and cut into thick matchsticks

1 onion, finely sliced

1 teaspoon sesame oil

2 tablespoons sesame seeds, toasted (page 413)

Sauce

3 cm (1¼ inch) piece ginger, peeled and finely chopped

2 tablespoons clear rice wine

2 tablespoons light soy sauce

120 g (4½ oz/½ cup) ready-made sichuan preserved vegetables, roughly chopped

To make the sauce, combine all the ingredients in a small bowl and set aside.

Wash the bean sprouts and dry well with paper towel. Heat the oil in a large wok over a medium–high heat until the oil is just starting to smoke, then add the bean sprouts, bamboo shoots, turnip and onion and stir-fry for 2 minutes. Add the sauce mixture and cook for another minute, then add the sesame oil and toss to combine. Transfer to a platter, sprinkle with the sesame seeds and serve.

Beans in cumin and salt batter

Serves 6 as part of a shared meal

225 g (8 oz/1½ cups) plain (all-purpose) flour
1 egg
1 tablespoon sugar
1 teaspoon sea salt, plus extra to serve

2 tablespoons cumin seeds
500 g (1 lb 2 oz) green beans, trimmed
1 litre (34 fl oz/4 cups) vegetable oil

In a large bowl, whisk together the flour, egg and 375 ml (12½ fl oz/1½ cups) water to form a smooth batter that has the consistency of thick pouring cream. Add a little more water if necessary. Stir in the sugar, sea salt and cumin seeds. Add the green beans and stir to coat well.

Preheat the oven to 150°C (300°F/Gas 2). Heat the oil in a wok over a high heat until just smoking. Taking care, add the beans to the hot oil in batches and cook for 5–7 minutes, or until the batter is golden and crisp and the beans are tender. Drain on paper towel and place in the warm oven until all the beans are cooked. Transfer to a platter and season with sea salt before serving.

Mashed sesame eggplant

Serves 4 to 6 as part of a shared meal

800 g (1 lb 12 oz) Lebanese (long, thin) eggplants (aubergines) (about 8), peeled
2 teaspoons sesame oil, plus extra to serve
2 tablespoons Chinese sesame paste

2 garlic cloves, crushed
sea salt, to taste
1 tablespoon sesame seeds, toasted (page 413)
1 small handful coriander (cilantro) sprigs

Cut the eggplants in halves lengthwise. Put the eggplants in a steamer and place over a wok or saucepan of boiling water, then cover and steam for 25 minutes, or until very soft. Transfer the eggplants to a bowl and cool to room temperature, then drain off any liquid that has accumulated.

Add the sesame oil, sesame paste and garlic to the eggplant in the bowl, then use your hands to work the sesame paste into the eggplant. Season to taste with sea salt, then transfer to a serving bowl. Sprinkle with the sesame seeds, drizzle with a little sesame oil and scatter over the coriander. Serve immediately.

Seafood

Lao Tzu, the philosopher considered the father of Chinese Taosim, famously said that 'governing a great nation is like cooking a small fish — too much handling will spoil it'. Nowhere is the simplicity of Chinese cooking techniques and the reverence for the freshest of raw materials more evident than in their approach to seafood.

Steamed fish with ginger and orange

Serves 4 to 6 as part of a shared meal

Steaming is best reserved for the freshest, sweetest, white-fleshed fish you can find. We've used snapper here, but this works just as well with bream, barramundi or even coral trout. Whatever fish you choose, don't wimp out of cooking it whole, head and all — it has a much better flavour when cooked on the bone. You will need a large steamer for this dish, or alternatively cook two smaller fish.

1 orange

6 spring onions (scallions), trimmed

60 ml (2 fl oz/¼ cup) light soy sauce

1 tablespoon oyster sauce

60 ml (2 fl oz/¼ cup) clear rice wine

1 teaspoon caster (superfine) sugar

2 kg (4 lb 6 oz) whole snapper, cleaned

6 cm (2½ inch) piece young ginger, peeled and finely shredded

80 ml (2½ fl oz/⅓ cup) peanut oil

coriander (cilantro) leaves, to serve (optional)

Using a small, sharp knife, remove the peel from the orange in wide strips — you will need six strips. Use a knife to slice off all the white pith, then cut the strips into very fine shreds. Bring a small saucepan of water to the boil, add the shredded orange zest and bring to the boil, then drain into a fine sieve and rinse under cold water. Set aside.

Cut the green stems from the spring onions and place on a plate large enough to hold the fish. Cut the white stems into fine shreds and set aside. Put the soy sauce, oyster sauce, rice wine and sugar in a bowl and whisk to combine well.

Cut three diagonal slashes in each side of the fish, taking care not to cut through to the bone. Put half the ginger and half the green onion stems in the fish cavity, then place the fish on the plate, on top of the remaining green onion. Pour the soy sauce mixture over the fish. Put the fish in a large steamer over a wok or saucepan of boiling water, then cover and steam for 20–25 minutes, or until cooked through (if using two smaller fish, check after about 15 minutes). Scatter the remaining ginger and white spring onion over the fish, then scatter over the orange zest. Heat the oil in a small saucepan; when hot, pour the oil over the fish. Scatter over the coriander, if using, and serve immediately.

Seafood san choy bau

Serves 4 to 6 as part of a shared meal

This is a dish you'd be more likely to find in any major city's Chinatown restaurants rather than anything you'd hope to find on the Mainland, but we love it nonetheless. We love the crunch of water chestnuts, and eating the fresh ones during a Chinese summer is a wonderful revelation. The tinned ones are a perfectly fine substitute.

6 small dried shiitake mushrooms

2 tablespoons pine nuts

1 egg white, beaten

2 teaspoons cornflour (cornstarch)

600 g (1 lb 5 oz) raw king prawns (shrimp), peeled, cleaned and chopped

350 g (12½ oz) skinless ocean trout fillet, pin bones removed, chopped

2 tablespoons light soy sauce

2 tablespoons oyster sauce

2 tablespoons shaoxing rice wine

2 teaspoons finely shredded ginger

2 garlic cloves, crushed

225 g (8 oz) tin water chestnuts, drained and finely chopped

3 spring onions (scallions), finely shredded

1 teaspoon sesame oil

2 tablespoons vegetable oil

coriander (cilantro) leaves, to garnish (optional)

iceberg lettuce leaves, thick ribs removed, to serve

Put the dried mushrooms in a small heatproof bowl, cover with boiling water and soak for 30 minutes, or until softened. Drain, reserving 2 tablespoons of the soaking liquid. Finely chop the mushrooms.

While the mushrooms are soaking, toast the pine nuts in a small, heavy-based frying pan over a medium–low heat, shaking the pan often, for 2–3 minutes, or until lightly golden, taking care as they can burn easily. Transfer to a plate to cool.

Put the egg white, cornflour, prawn meat and fish in a bowl and mix with a fork to combine well. Add the soy sauce, oyster sauce and rice wine and stir to combine. Put the mushrooms in a bowl with the ginger, garlic, water chestnuts, spring onions and sesame oil and toss to combine.

Heat a wok over a high heat, add the vegetable oil, then the mushroom mixture and stir-fry for 3 minutes, or until the mixture is fragrant and the spring onions have just started to soften. Add the fish mixture and cook, stirring often, for about 3 minutes, or until the prawns and fish are just cooked through. Add a little of the reserved mushroom liquid if the mixture is too dry.

Place the fish mixture on a warmed platter and sprinkle with the pine nuts and coriander, if using. Each guest takes a lettuce leaf, fills it with the fish mixture, then wraps it up in the leaf to eat. Serve with steamed rice (page 412) on the side.

Cold tofu with prawns and hot-sour dressing

Serves 4 to 6 as part of a shared meal

This pretty dish is very easy to make and requires minimal preparation. It can largely be done in advance so this is perfect for casual entertaining. The combination of sweet prawns (shrimp), smooth tofu and the mellow, vinegary dressing is sublime.

600 g (1 lb 5 oz) cooked medium–small tiger prawns (shrimp), peeled, leaving tails intact, and cleaned

600 g (1 lb 5 oz) block silken tofu

1 small handful coriander (cilantro) sprigs, to serve

Hot–sour dressing

60 ml (2 fl oz/¼ cup) light soy sauce

80 ml (2½ fl oz/⅓ cup) black rice vinegar

2 tablespoons sesame oil

2 tablespoons peanut oil

1 teaspoon chilli oil (page 407), or ready-made, or to taste

1 tablespoon caster (superfine) sugar

1 tablespoon shaoxing rice wine

185 ml (6 fl oz/¾ cup) chicken stock (page 405)

3 cm (1¼ inch) piece ginger, peeled and finely shredded

2 garlic cloves, finely shredded or very finely sliced

1–2 teaspoons chilli flakes, to taste

To make the hot–sour dressing, combine the soy sauce, vinegar, oils, sugar, rice wine and stock in a bowl and whisk until the sugar has dissolved. Stir in the ginger, garlic and chilli flakes. Set aside.

Cut the prawns in half lengthwise. Drain the tofu well, taking care not to break it. Carefully cut the tofu into 1 cm (½ inch) thick slices and lay them neatly in a large bowl. Scatter the prawns over the tofu, then pour over the dressing. Garnish with the coriander and serve immediately.

Tomato, chilli and coriander fish soup

Serves 6

This dish was inspired by one we ate in the southwestern province of Yunnan. Fresh, light flavours predominate there, with herbs such as mint, dill and coriander (cilantro) used widely, and influences from local ethnic groups as well as the neighbouring nations of Laos and Vietnam making themselves heard. All these make for a wildly different culinary proposition to 'mainstream' Chinese fare.

....

2 tablespoons finely shredded ginger

4 garlic cloves, finely sliced

4 small red chillies, halved lengthwise

1 tablespoon sugar

60 ml (2 fl oz/¼ cup) clear rice vinegar, or to taste

2½ tablespoons light soy sauce, or to taste

850 g (1 lb 14 oz) firm ripe tomatoes, coarsely chopped

6 x 150 g (5½ oz) salmon cutlets

3 spring onions (scallions), cut into 1 cm (½ inch) pieces

2 bunches coriander (cilantro), leaves picked

chilli oil (page 407), or ready-made, to serve (optional)

Fish and tomato stock

1.2 kg (2 lb 10 oz) very ripe tomatoes, coarsely chopped

1.2 kg (2 lb 10 oz) white fish bones

4 spring onions (scallions), chopped

....

To make the stock, put all the ingredients in a saucepan and add 2 litres (68 fl oz/8 cups) water, or enough to just cover. Bring slowly to a simmer, then simmer gently over a low heat for 1 hour, skimming off any impurities as they rise to the surface. Strain well without pressing on the solids — the stock should be clear. Let the stock settle for 30 minutes, then pour it into a bowl, discarding any cloudy solids at the bottom of the stock.

Combine the stock, ginger, garlic, chillies, sugar, vinegar and soy sauce in a large saucepan and bring to a simmer. Cook over a low heat for 10 minutes to allow the flavours to develop, adding extra vinegar or soy sauce to taste. Add the tomatoes and salmon and cook over a low heat for 6 minutes — the liquid should be barely murmuring.

Remove the pan from the heat, cover and set aside for 3–4 minutes, or until the salmon is just cooked through (the cooking time will depend on the thickness of the cutlets). Add the spring onions and coriander and stand until the coriander has wilted. Divide the soup and salmon among six large bowls. Serve with chilli oil, if using.

Fish cooked with sweet wine and lettuce

Serves 4 to 6 as part of a shared meal

This soupy, stewy dish utilises an interesting ingredient that comes from Shanghai — sweet glutinous rice wine. Cooks there make it at home (although you can easily buy it in Chinese grocery stores) by adding a special starter yeast 'pill' to jars of cooked rice and water, which is then left to ferment for about 30 hours. The rice is usually used for sweet dishes but its boozy 'punch' is interesting when teamed with delicate white fish and lettuce.

---

700 g (1 lb 9 oz) red snapper or firm, white fish fillets, skinned

2 heads baby cos (romaine) lettuce, tough outer leaves removed

2 large garlic cloves, very finely chopped

2.5 cm (1 inch) piece ginger, peeled and very finely chopped

300 ml (10 fl oz) glutinous rice wine

170 ml (5½ fl oz/⅔ cup) chicken stock (page 405)

1 teaspoon sugar

5 teaspoons cornflour (cornstarch)

1 tablespoon vegetable oil

ground white pepper, to taste

Velveting mixture

1 egg white, beaten well

1½ tablespoons clear rice wine

2 tablespoons cornflour (cornstarch)

1 teaspoon salt

1½ tablespoons vegetable oil

To make the velveting mixture, put all the ingredients in a large bowl and whisk to combine well. Cut the fish fillets into 3 x 2 cm (1¼ x ¾ inch) pieces and add to the velveting mixture, then use your hands to turn the fish in the mixture, coating well. Cover with plastic wrap and refrigerate for 2 hours.

Trim the bottom 2 cm (¾ inch) off the cos lettuce and remove the leaves. Finely chop the stems and place in a bowl along with the garlic and ginger. Coarsely chop the leaves and set aside.

Combine the glutinous rice wine, stock and sugar in a bowl, stirring to dissolve the sugar. Put the cornflour in a small bowl, then add enough of the rice wine mixture to make a smooth, thin paste.

Bring a saucepan of water to the boil. Carefully add the fish, stirring gently with a large slotted spoon to keep the pieces separated. Reduce the heat to low and gently simmer the fish for 1 minute, then drain into a colander.

Heat the oil in a wok over a medium heat, then add the chopped lettuce stems and garlic mixture and stir-fry for 1 minute, or until softened slightly. Add the leaves and stir-fry for a further 2 minutes, or until wilted. Add the remaining rice wine mixture and bring to a simmer, then add the fish and cook, tossing the wok occasionally, for 2–3 minutes, or until the fish is cooked through. Add the cornflour mixture and bring the sauce to the boil, swirling the wok to incorporate the cornflour mixture. Cook for 1 minute, or until thickened slightly, then season to taste with white pepper and serve immediately.

Stuffed red-cooked trout

Serves 4 to 6 as part of a shared meal

Red cooking is usually reserved for pork or other meats, but oily river trout stands up well to the robust flavours of this ingredient combination, especially when said fish are stuffed to the gills with our favourite meat — pork. The sauce here is a simplified version of hong shao *(red cooked), which calls for either caramelised sugar or bean paste as a starting point. Soy sauce, shaoxing wine and ginger are also used in the mix, as well as other aromatics such as five-spice, cassia, fennel and black cardamom. This dish is unashamedly rich and delicious.*

2 whole baby trout (about 460 g/1 lb each)

2½ tablespoons peanut oil

Stuffing

125 g (4½ oz) minced (ground) pork

50 g (1¾ oz) chopped raw prawn (shrimp) meat

2 tablespoons chopped, tinned water chestnuts

2 spring onions (scallions), trimmed

2 teaspoons finely chopped ginger

1 garlic clove, finely chopped

2 teaspoons light soy sauce

sea salt and freshly ground black pepper

Red-cooking mixture

6 thin slices unpeeled ginger

185 ml (6 fl oz/¾ cup) chicken stock (page 405)

2 tablespoons dark soy sauce

2 tablespoons light soy sauce

60 ml (2 fl oz/¼ cup) shaoxing rice wine

large pinch of five-spice

1½ tablespoons sugar

To make the stuffing, combine the pork, prawn meat and water chestnuts in a bowl. Finely chop the white part of the spring onions and add them to the bowl, reserving the green stems. Mix in the ginger, garlic and soy sauce and season with sea salt and pepper. Divide the mixture between the fish cavities, spreading it evenly. Tie each fish securely at 3 cm (1¼ inch) intervals with kitchen string. Using paper towel, thoroughly dry the skin of each fish.

Heat the oil in a large wok over a medium–high heat, then add the fish and cook for 1 minute on each side. Remove from the wok.

To make the red-cooking mixture, put the reserved spring onion stems and the ginger in the wok and stir to combine. Return the fish to the wok, then add the stock, soy sauces, rice wine, five-spice and sugar. Bring the mixture to a simmer, then reduce the heat to medium–low, cover the wok and cook the fish for 10 minutes on each side, or until the fish and the stuffing are cooked through. Remove the strings from the fish, then place the fish on a platter. Spoon some of the cooking liquid over the fish, discarding the ginger and spring onion stems.

Oyster omelette

Serves 2 to 4 as part of a shared meal

Here's the ultimate street snack — but ours, which is a simplified version, only modestly emulates the full glory of what's cooked kerb-side in Xiamen. There they start by frying a slurry made from sweet potato flour, then magically incorporate eggs and oysters using some cooking sorcery. The results are a scorched, slightly crisp exterior and a bouncy interior studded with nuggets of juicy oysters.

12 small oysters, on the half shell (or use bottled)

1 tablespoon sweet potato flour

4 large eggs, lightly beaten

2 teaspoons light soy sauce

½ teaspoon sugar

sea salt and freshly ground black pepper

2 tablespoons vegetable oil

1 spring onion (scallion), finely sliced

Sauce

1 tablespoon hoisin sauce

1 tablespoon tomato sauce (ketchup)

2 teaspoons chilli sauce

½ teaspoon clear rice vinegar

To make the sauce, put all the ingredients in a small bowl, add 2 tablespoons boiling water and stir to combine well. Add a little more water if the sauce is too thick — it should have a thick, pouring consistency.

Drain the oysters well, reserving any liquid in the shells. Combine the sweet potato flour in a bowl with 2 tablespoons of the oyster liquid (or water) and stir until smooth. Add the eggs, soy sauce and sugar, season with sea salt and pepper and mix well.

Heat the oil in a heavy-based, non-stick 17 cm (6¾ inch) frying pan over a high heat. When the oil starts to smoke, add the egg mixture, swirling the pan to evenly coat the base with the egg, and cook for 1 minute, then carefully lift up the edge of the omelette using a spatula, to allow the uncooked egg to run underneath. Cook for about 2 minutes, or until the base of the omelette is deep golden but still quite runny on the top. Scatter the oysters and spring onion over the top, then flip the omelette over and cook for 30–60 seconds, or until light golden and cooked through, but still a little soft and runny in the middle. Transfer to a plate, drizzle with the sauce and serve.

Pumpkin and scallop soup

Serves 4

Occasionally, we are rather partial to a grand-scale, historic hotel and the Lujiang, overlooking the water in Xiamen, ticks a few of our boxes. Its seventh-floor restaurant serves some excellent local food and it was there we ate this refined pumpkin soup, as well as popiah, *the gossamer-fine, filled savoury crepes that are a regional specialty. Their soup was made with baby abalone, perfectly scored into the finest grid pattern. We've used scallops but use abalone by all means, if you can find some fresh.*

600 g (1 lb 5 oz) jap or kent pumpkin (winter squash)
2 tablespoons vegetable oil
2 garlic cloves, finely sliced

1 litre (34 fl oz/4 cups) chicken stock (page 405)
16 scallops, roe on
sea salt and ground white pepper

Peel the pumpkin, then cut into 5 cm (2 inch) pieces. Heat the oil in a heavy-based saucepan over a medium–low heat, then add the pumpkin and garlic, cover and cook, stirring occasionally, for 20–25 minutes, or until the pumpkin is soft. Remove from the heat and leave to cool a little, then transfer to a food processor and process until smooth. Add the stock to the pumpkin purée and process again, adjusting the consistency with a little extra water if required. Return the pumpkin soup to the cleaned saucepan over a medium–low heat and bring to just below simmering.

Using a sharp knife, score the scallops with a shallow crisscross pattern on one side only. Add the scallops to the soup and cook for 2–3 minutes, or until just cooked through. Remove from the heat and season to taste with sea salt and white pepper. To serve, divide the soup and scallops among four bowls, placing the scallops scored side up in the soup.

Yusheng

Serves 4 to 6

We're cheating a little here, as this dish is popular mainly in Chinese communities in Southeast Asia, although it's thought to have originated with the Chiuchow people in southern China. It's eaten at Lunar New Year with a great deal of fanfare. The ingredients are mixed one by one, to the uttering of auspicious wishes by the server. When all the ingredients are served, diners use their chopsticks to toss everything enthusiastically in the air — the higher they toss, the greater their coming fortune in the new year.

50 g (1¾ oz/⅓ cup) sesame seeds, toasted (page 413)
¾ teaspoon five-spice
2 carrots, peeled
1 small daikon (white radish), peeled
2 Lebanese (short) cucumbers
1 jicama (yam bean), peeled
4 spring onions (scallions), cut into 5 cm (2 inch) lengths
2 pomelos, peeled
160 g (5½ oz/1 cup) raw, skinned peanuts, roasted (page 413) and coarsely chopped

1½ tablespoons finely shredded ginger
1 bunch coriander (cilantro) (optional)
1 x 750 g (1 lb 11 oz) salmon fillet, with skin on
vegetable oil, for cooking wrappers
10 wonton wrappers

Dressing
300 ml (10 fl oz) plum sauce (Ayam brand)
2½ tablespoons honey
80 ml (2½ fl oz/⅓ cup) lime juice, or to taste
1½ tablespoons sesame oil

To make the dressing, combine the plum sauce and honey in a small saucepan over a medium–low heat, and cook, stirring often, for 3–4 minutes, or until smooth. Remove from the heat, add the lime juice and sesame oil, then set aside at room temperature. Taste and stir in a little extra lime juice, if necessary, to cut the sweetness, and 1–2 tablespoons water, or enough to thin the dressing to a heavy coating consistency.

Put the sesame seeds and five-spice into a mortar and coarsely grind using the pestle. Cut all the vegetables into thin matchsticks and place in separate bowls. Remove the membrane from the pomelo segments, then tear the pomelo into pieces. Prepare the peanuts and ginger, and pick small sprigs off the coriander, if using.

Using tweezers, remove the pin bones from the salmon. Then, using a long, sharp knife and holding it at an angle against the salmon fillet, cut the salmon into very thin, wide slices, starting from the thin, tail end of the fillet and working your way up towards the head end (leaving the skin behind). Set aside.

Fill a saucepan one-third full of oil and heat to 180°C (350°F), or until a cube of bread dropped into the oil turns deep golden in 15 seconds. Add the wrappers, a few at a time, and cook for 2–3 minutes, or until they are golden and crisp. Remove with tongs and drain on paper towel. To serve, place all the prepared ingredients on a large platter or in bowls, and allow everyone to help themselves. Pour the dressing over the top and toss everything together.

Lobster poached in rice wine

Serves 4 as part of a shared meal

The clear, sweet flavours of steamed seafood remind us of eating at Beidaihe, east of Beijing and once a beach reserved for Communist Party officials, unionists and the like. These days it's way more egalitarian and the seafood there is sensational. When we cook lobster or crab, we prefer to steam or gently poach it, taking care not to overcook it, which toughens all that succulent (and expensive) flesh. We serve it simply, with just a few sauces, like our fabulous XO and a slightly sweetened soy and ginger sauce.

1 kg (2 lb 3 oz) live lobster

100 g (3½ oz/⅓ cup) salt

5 cm (2 inch) piece ginger, unpeeled and sliced

4 spring onions (scallions), chopped

500 ml (17 fl oz/2 cups) clear rice wine

Place the lobster in a large plastic bag, then place the lobster in the freezer for 30–40 minutes to put it to sleep. Using a sharp knife, spike the lobster between the tail and the head to humanely dispatch it.

Put the salt, ginger, spring onions and rice wine in a large saucepan. Add about 2 litres (68 fl oz/8 cups) water, then put the lobster in the pan — add more water if needed, so the lobster is covered. Bring to a simmer over a medium heat and cook for 20–25 minutes, or until the tail is firmly curled. Remove the lobster and cool.

To serve, cut the lobster in half lengthwise and remove the digestive tract. Use a knife to loosen the flesh from the tail, removing the meat to cut it into small pieces (you can then return the meat to the shell if desired). Serve with XO sauce and Sweet soy–ginger sauce (recipes opposite) and/or the Spring onion and ginger dipping sauce (pages 196–7).

Variations

Other seafood can be prepared and served at the same time. To cook live mud crabs or blue swimmer crabs, follow the same procedure as above for freezing the lobsters, to send them to sleep. Mud crabs weigh about 1 kg (2 lb 3 oz) each and take 20 minutes to cook; blue swimmer crabs weigh about 300 g (10½ oz) each and take 7–8 minutes to cook. Allow 1 mud crab for 2–3 people, as part of a shared meal, and 1 blue swimmer crab for 1–2 people, as part of a shared meal.

To cook prawns (shrimp), choose raw jumbo king prawns and don't peel them. Cook for about 5 minutes, or just until they are firm — take care not to overcook them or they will be tough.

Photograph pages 152–3

XO sauce

Makes about 625 ml (21 fl oz/2½ cups)

25 g (1 oz/¼ cup) dried shrimp
40 g (1½ oz/¼ cup) small dried scallops
1 Chinese pork sausage (lap cheong), chopped
45 g (1½ oz) jinhua cured ham or prosciutto, very finely chopped
185 ml (6 fl oz/¾ cup) vegetable oil, plus extra
8 garlic cloves, very finely chopped

2 tablespoons very finely chopped ginger
50 g (1¾ oz) red Asian shallots, very finely chopped
1 tablespoon very finely chopped red chilli
1½ tablespoons chilli flakes
2 tablespoons light soy sauce
3 teaspoons sugar

Put the dried shrimp and scallops in separate heatproof bowls, cover each with boiling water and soak for 30 minutes, then drain well.

Put the shrimp in a small food processor and process until finely chopped, then transfer to a bowl. Put the scallops in the processor and process until finely chopped. Add to the shrimp in the bowl, then repeat with the chopped sausage. Add the chopped ham to the mixture in the bowl and set aside.

Heat the oil in a saucepan over a medium heat, then add the garlic, ginger, shallots, fresh chilli and chilli flakes. Cook for 2–3 minutes, or until fragrant, then add the shrimp and scallop mixture and stir to combine well. Cook over a low heat for 30 minutes, then add the soy sauce and sugar and stir until the sugar has dissolved. Remove from the heat and cool. Transfer to sterilised jars, then pour in enough extra oil to cover the sauce. The XO sauce will keep, stored in the fridge, for up to 2 months.

Photograph page 153

Sweet soy-ginger sauce

Makes about 250 ml (8½ fl oz/1 cup)

125 ml (4 fl oz/½ cup) light soy sauce
60 ml (2 fl oz/¼ cup) clear rice vinegar

2 tablespoons caster (superfine) sugar
1½ tablespoons finely shredded ginger

Combine the soy sauce, vinegar and sugar in a bowl, stirring until the sugar has dissolved. Add the ginger and stir to combine, then cover and set aside for 30 minutes for the flavours to develop.

Photograph page 152

From left to right: Seafood poached in rice wine (page 150), served with Sweet soy-ginger sauce (page 151), XO sauce (page 151) and Spring onion and ginger dipping sauce (pages 196–7)

XO scallop and sugar-snap stir-fry

Serves 6 as part of a shared meal

XO sauce is a relatively recent invention. It was created during the 1960s in Hong Kong and today is used there and in neighbouring Guangdong. Recipes for it abound, but it is essentially a mix of chopped and dried seafoods, cured pork, chilli, garlic and oil. Ours takes a bit of effort to make, but it is utterly delicious. Add it to noodle dishes and stir-fries, as here, or serve it with simply cooked seafood as a condiment on the side.

500 g (1 lb 2 oz) scallops, roe on
125 ml (4 fl oz/½ cup) XO sauce (page 151)
1 tablespoon light soy sauce
2½ tablespoons shaoxing rice wine

80 ml (2½ fl oz/⅓ cup) peanut oil
400 g (14 oz) sugar-snap peas, trimmed
2 garlic cloves, crushed

Place the scallops in a single layer on several layers of paper towel, then place several layers of paper towel on top and gently press to absorb the excess liquid.

Put the XO sauce, soy sauce and rice wine in a small bowl and stir to combine well. Set aside.

Heat half of the oil in a wok over a medium heat, then add the sugar-snap peas and stir-fry for 2–3 minutes, or until tender but still a little crisp. Remove to a plate. Return the wok to a high heat, add the remaining oil, then add the scallops and garlic and stir-fry for about 3 minutes, or until the scallops are nearly cooked through. Add the XO sauce mixture, return the sugar-snap peas to the wok, then toss for 30 seconds, or until everything is heated through and the scallops are cooked. Serve immediately.

XO scallop and sugar-snap stir-fry: Fried noodle cake (page 297)

Steamed mussel custards

Serves 4 as part of a shared meal

We ate a wonderful version of this silky egg dish in Changsha, where it was a soothing foil for the heavy, smoky Hunanese flavours and dishes laced with chilli. That version was plain (the mussels are our addition), but you could also make this using cooked crabmeat or chopped prawns (shrimp). A little care needs to be taken when making this. Whisk the eggs gently so you don't generate too many bubbles and then strain the custard to get rid of any that do form, plus any lumpy bits of egg. And have your water at a constant simmer — don't let it boil hard or the custard will overcook and be studded with unsightly holes.

1 kg (2 lb 3 oz) small black mussels

6 eggs, beaten

1 tablespoon shaoxing rice wine

2 teaspoons sesame oil

1 tablespoon light soy sauce

1 spring onion (scallion), finely sliced

2 tablespoons peanut oil

Scrub the mussels and pull out the hairy beards, then rinse well. Discard any broken mussels.

Bring 250 ml (8½ fl oz/1 cup) water to the boil in a large saucepan. Add the mussels, then cover and cook for about 4 minutes, or until they open — do not overcook. Remove the mussels to a colander set over a bowl to catch the juices as they drain. Reserve the cooking liquid in the pan. Measure the drained juices and the cooking liquid to make 375 ml (12½ fl oz/1½ cups), taking care not to take any gritty sediment when you pour it off to measure. Discard any remaining liquid.

Combine the reserved cooking liquid, eggs, rice wine, sesame oil and soy sauce in a bowl and gently whisk to combine well. Strain through a sieve.

Remove the mussels from the shells and cut in half. Divide the mussels among four 300 ml (10 fl oz) heatproof ceramic bowls, then place in a large steamer over a wok or saucepan of simmering water. Pour the custard mixture into the bowls, then cover the steamer and cook the custards over a medium–low heat for about 20 minutes, or until just set — the middle of the custards should still jiggle slightly when you shake them. Do not cook the custards too fast or they will be tough.

Remove the custards from the steamer and sprinkle with the spring onion. Heat the peanut oil in a small saucepan until it starts to sizzle, then carefully pour the hot oil over the custards. Serve immediately.

Steamed garlic prawns

Serves 4 to 6 as part of a shared meal

We first tried this southern dish with mantis prawns (shrimp), a curious crustacean that resembles both a praying mantis and a large prawn. Their sweet flesh, held in broad, meaty tails, is more delicate than king, tiger or banana prawns and we love them split, deep-fried and lightly salted, or steamed with plenty of garlic, as here. You probably won't find mantis prawns outside of Asia, but you'll still be happy campers if you make this with any fresh, large raw prawn.

2 tablespoons peanut oil

12 large garlic cloves, finely chopped

4 spring onions (scallions), white part only, finely chopped

2 tablespoons clear rice wine

large pinch of sugar

3 teaspoons light soy sauce

½ teaspoon sesame oil

16 jumbo or 20 raw, extra large king prawns (shrimp), unpeeled

Heat the peanut oil in a small saucepan over a low heat, then add the garlic and spring onions and cook, stirring often, for 4 minutes, or until the garlic has softened slightly. Do not allow the garlic to colour. Add 1 tablespoon of the rice wine, the sugar, 1 teaspoon of the soy sauce and the sesame oil. Cook, stirring, for 2 minutes, or until most of the liquid has evaporated. Remove from the heat and cool to room temperature.

Using kitchen scissors, trim the feelers and all legs from the prawns. Using the scissors, or a very sharp knife, cut through the top of each prawn, starting from just behind the head and working down towards the tail, to form a pocket in the top of each prawn. Remove the digestive tracts.

Neatly stuff each prawn cavity with the cooled garlic mixture, then place the prawns, stuffed side up, in a tight row on a plate large enough to fit inside your steamer (you may need to steam the prawns in two batches). Place the plate in the steamer and drizzle the remaining rice wine and soy sauce over the prawns. Place the steamer over a wok or saucepan of boiling water, then cover and steam for about 15 minutes, or until the prawns are just cooked through. Serve immediately.

Photograph page 167

Stir-fried pipis with spring onion, sa cha and basil

Serves 4 to 6 as part of a shared meal

60 ml (2 fl oz/¼ cup) vegetable oil

6 spring onions (scallions), cut into 1 cm (½ inch) pieces

4 garlic cloves, finely chopped

100 ml (3½ fl oz) sa cha sauce (page 408)

60 ml (2 fl oz/¼ cup) clear rice wine

60 ml (2 fl oz/¼ cup) light soy sauce

1.5 kg (3 lb 5 oz) live pipis, purged of sand

1 large handful Thai basil leaves

Heat the oil in a wok over a medium–high heat. Add the spring onions and garlic and stir-fry for 1 minute, or until fragrant. Add the sa cha sauce, rice wine, soy sauce and pipis. Cover, then cook, shaking the wok often, for 4–5 minutes, just until the pipis have opened. Toss in half the basil, then transfer the mixture to a warm platter. Scatter over the remaining basil and serve immediately.

Photograph page 166

Steamed oysters

Serves 4 to 6 as part of a shared meal

2 tablespoons very finely chopped young ginger

1 teaspoon sesame oil

3 teaspoons peanut oil

12 extra large fresh oysters, on the half shell

Dressing

1½ teaspoons caster (superfine) sugar

2 garlic cloves, crushed

3 teaspoons clear rice vinegar

1 tablespoon clear rice wine

2½ tablespoons light soy sauce

2½ tablespoons chicken stock (page 405)

To make the dressing, combine all the ingredients in a bowl and whisk until the sugar has dissolved.

Combine the ginger, sesame oil and peanut oil in a bowl and mix well. Put the oysters in a large steamer over a wok or saucepan of boiling water. Spoon a little of the ginger mixture over each oyster, then cover and steam for 2 minutes, or until just warmed in the middle — be careful you don't overcook the oysters. Transfer the oysters to a platter, taking care so the juices in the shells don't spill, then spoon some dressing over each oyster and serve immediately.

Photograph page 166

From left to right: Stir-fried pipis with spring onion, sa cha and basil
(page 165); Steamed oysters (page 165); Fried whiting with ginger
(page 168); Steamed garlic prawns (page 164)

Fried whiting with ginger

Serves 6 as part of a shared meal

Like many Chinese fish dishes, this isn't so much about what's in the recipe, but more about how you cook the fish. Go to any good Chinese restaurant and your fish will come live from the tank, be weighed for your bill, then killed to order and cooked how you like. The point of Chinese seafood cookery is to highlight the taste and fine texture of fresh seafood, not to dazzle the diner with culinary science, fancy ingredients and tricky garniture.

6 sand whiting (about 750 g/1 lb 11 oz), cleaned

2 tablespoons shaoxing rice wine

1 tablespoon light soy sauce

vegetable oil, for deep-frying

8 cm (3¼ inch) piece young ginger, peeled and finely shredded

potato flour, for dusting

Dipping sauce

1 teaspoon caster (superfine) sugar

60 ml (2 fl oz/¼ cup) light soy sauce

60 ml (2 fl oz/¼ cup) shaoxing rice wine

2½ tablespoons chicken stock (page 405)

½ teaspoon ground white pepper

To make the dipping sauce, combine all the ingredients in a bowl, stirring until the sugar has dissolved.

Place the whiting in a large bowl, then add the rice wine and soy sauce and turn to coat. Cover the bowl with plastic wrap and refrigerate for 4 hours, turning the fish occasionally.

Fill a wok one-third full of oil and heat to 180°C (350°F), or until a cube of bread dropped into the oil turns deep golden in 15 seconds. Add the ginger, stirring with a large metal spoon to keep the shreds separated, and cook for 3–4 minutes, or until light golden and crisp. Using a slotted spoon, remove the ginger and drain on paper towel.

Remove the fish from the marinade and shake the fish dry. Lightly dust the fish with potato flour, shaking off the excess. Add the fish to the oil in two batches and deep-fry for 8 minutes, or until crisp and golden and cooked through. Drain on paper towel. Place the fish on a platter, scatter over the fried ginger and serve with the dipping sauce.

Photograph page 167

Beer fish

Serves 6

Yangshuo, in Guangxi Province, has the most dreamy karst vistas, shrouded in mist and achingly beautiful. But with its endless tourist hordes, the place has never really been our gig, although we do have a fondness for this particular dish, a hallmark of the area. It's honest home-style cooking, traditionally made using carp pulled from the Li River, beer brewed in nearby Guilin and capsicum (peppers) and tomatoes grown in fields that dot the moody landscape.

6 x 150 g (5½ oz) salmon cutlets

100 ml (3½ fl oz) peanut oil

4 garlic cloves, finely sliced

1 tablespoon finely shredded ginger

1 large red or orange capsicum (pepper), seeded and cut into 2 cm (¾ inch) pieces

4 tomatoes, cut into 2 cm (¾ inch) pieces

2½ tablespoons guilin chilli sauce

1½ tablespoons oyster sauce

2½ tablespoons light soy sauce

about 300 ml (10 fl oz) beer

2 teaspoons sesame oil

3 spring onions (scallions), finely chopped

pickled chillies, to serve (page 410)

Pat the salmon dry using paper towel, and set aside. Heat 2 tablespoons of the peanut oil in a wok over a medium–high heat, then add the garlic, ginger and capsicum and stir-fry for 3 minutes, or until the capsicum starts to soften. Remove to a bowl and set aside.

Heat the remaining peanut oil in the wok, then add the salmon cutlets and cook over a medium heat for 1–2 minutes on each side. Return the capsicum mixture to the wok along with the tomatoes, chilli sauce, oyster sauce, soy sauce and beer — adding a little more beer to just cover the fish, if necessary. Bring to a simmer and cook for 8–10 minutes, or until the fish is cooked through and the liquid has reduced. Transfer the fish to a large bowl, drizzle with the sesame oil, scatter with spring onions and serve immediately with the pickled chillies.

Cumin and chilli barbecued perch

Serves 4

We asked to be taken to a 'wild' part of the Great Wall, far from the crazy crowds and cable-car frenzy. We were guests of a posh hotel and they'd packed a special lunch for us to take. The driver was horrified when we opted instead to eat river trout with locals at a nearby restaurant in the middle of nowhere, right by a stream. The fish was slathered in spices and cooked simply, over coals, and was completely divine.

4 x 400 g (14 oz) silver perch, trevally or other whole, small fish

3 teaspoons black peppercorns

1 tablespoon sichuan peppercorns

1 tablespoon cumin seeds

1 teaspoon chilli flakes

1 teaspoon chilli powder

1 tablespoon sea salt

vegetable oil, for cooking

1 handful coriander (cilantro) sprigs, to serve

Using a sharp knife, carefully cut a few crisscrosses through the skin on each side of the fish, taking care not to cut through to the bone.

Combine the black and sichuan peppercorns, cumin seeds and chilli flakes in an electric spice grinder and grind until reasonably fine. Alternatively, use a mortar and pestle. Transfer to a bowl and stir in the chilli powder and sea salt.

Preheat a barbecue to high. Liberally brush the fish all over with the oil, then sprinkle the spice mixture on both sides. Place the fish inside a grill fish cage and cook, skin side down, for 5 minutes, or until the skin is crisp. Turn the fish over and cook for another 3 minutes, or until cooked through. Place the fish on a platter, garnish with the coriander and serve.

Soy sauce prawns

Serves 4 to 6 as part of a shared meal

We love the relaxed, untouristy vibe of Beihai, a coastal city on the southern edge of Guangxi Province. It's got a good number of historic buildings, streets fragrant with osmanthus flowers, some excellent food markets and a coastal river choked with creaky wooden fishing boats — and brilliant seafood. We love fish-feasting in places like this. The sea critters are live in tanks and cooked how you like: steamed, salt-and-peppered, stir-fried with soy sauce, or grilled with nothing but ginger and a few wisps of spring onion (scallion).

1 kg (2 lb 3 oz) raw large king or tiger prawns (shrimp)

1½ tablespoons light soy sauce

2½ teaspoons dark soy sauce

3 garlic cloves, finely chopped

1 tablespoon sugar

2 tablespoons tomato sauce (ketchup)

2 tablespoons shaoxing rice wine

2 teaspoons clear rice vinegar

1½ teaspoons cornflour (cornstarch)

2 tablespoons chicken stock (page 405)

125 ml (4 fl oz/½ cup) peanut oil

1 small handful coriander (cilantro) sprigs, to serve

Remove the heads from the prawns. Using kitchen scissors, cut off the legs, then cut through the back of the shell down to the tail. Use a small knife to make a slightly deeper incision at the tail end, then open up each prawn and flatten it gently. Remove the digestive tracts.

Put the soy sauces, garlic, sugar, tomato sauce, rice wine and vinegar in a bowl, and stir to mix well. Combine the cornflour and stock in a small bowl and stir until smooth.

Heat the oil in a wok over a high heat, then add the prawns and stir-fry for 2–3 minutes, or until the prawns just turn pink. Quickly pour most of the oil out of the wok, return the wok and prawns to the heat, then add the soy sauce mixture. Cook, tossing the wok, for 2–3 minutes, or until the prawns are cooked through. Add the cornflour mixture and cook until the sauce boils and thickens. Serve immediately.

Soy sauce prawns; Grilled squid (page 174)

Grilled squid

Serves 4 to 6 as part of a shared meal

This is a classic seafood dish from the coastal city of Xiamen, where they cook it on the street from mobile grill stands shrouded in swirls of delicious-smelling smoke. Use ready-made sa cha sauce if you like and do as the locals do — sprinkle the squid with a little chilli powder as it cooks. Don't even try this with anything less than the freshest of squid and don't be afraid of gutting the squid yourself — it's easier than you think.

3 fresh whole squid
1 tablespoon vegetable oil

Glaze
2½ tablespoons sa cha sauce (page 408)
1½ tablespoons light soy sauce
1½ tablespoons clear rice wine
1½ tablespoons sugar
2 garlic cloves, finely crushed

To clean the squid, gently pull the tentacles away from the tube (the intestines should come away at the same time). Remove the intestines from the tentacles by cutting under the eyes, then remove the beak if it remains in the centre of the tentacles by using your fingers to push up the centre. Reserve the tentacles. Pull the transparent cartilage from inside the body and remove. Clean out the inside of the tube. Hold the tube under running water and peel the skin off. Place the cleaned squid tubes on a chopping board and use a sharp knife to score horizontal cuts on one side only, reserving the tentacles. Place on a plate and set aside.

To make the glaze, combine all the ingredients in a bowl. Brush the squid tubes and tentacles all over with some of the mixture.

Heat a chargrill pan or cast-iron pan over a medium–high heat, add the oil and then place the tentacles and the squid, scored side down, in the pan. Brush more glaze over the tentacles and squid, using tongs to press down on the squid tubes to help them sear, and cook for 2–3 minutes, then turn them over, brush with more glaze, and cook for another 2–3 minutes, or until cooked through. Take the squid and tentacles off the heat and brush with more glaze. To serve, put the squid tubes on a platter and arrange the tentacles inside the squid tubes, placing them so they are just hanging out a little.

Photograph page 173

Fish steamed in sweet potato flour with pickled radish

Serves 4

1½ tablespoons light soy sauce

1½ tablespoons clear rice wine

2 garlic cloves, crushed

1 teaspoon caster (superfine) sugar

2 teaspoons sesame oil

4 x 175 g (6 oz) snapper fillets or other firm, white fish fillets

sweet potato flour, for coating

8 tablespoons pickled radish, drained (page 411)

Combine the soy sauce, rice wine, garlic, sugar and sesame oil in a bowl large enough to hold the fish, and stir to combine well. Cut each fish fillet in half widthwise, then place in the bowl and toss to coat well in the marinade. Cover and refrigerate for 3 hours, or overnight.

Remove the fish from the marinade. Dust each piece well in sweet potato flour. Put the fish in a single layer in a large steamer over a wok or saucepan of boiling water, then scatter about 1 tablespoon of pickled radish over each fish piece. Cover and steam for 5–6 minutes, depending on the thickness, or until the fish is cooked through. Serve immediately with steamed rice (page 412).

Stir-fried gherkin cucumbers and school prawns

Serves 4 to 6 as part of a shared meal

1 teaspoon sugar

3 teaspoons light soy sauce

2 teaspoons shaoxing rice wine

2 teaspoons sesame oil

1 tablespoon vegetable oil

2 garlic cloves, crushed

500 g (1 lb 2 oz) gherkin cucumbers, peeled and finely sliced

500 g (1 lb 2 oz) raw school prawns (shrimp), heads removed

Combine the sugar, soy sauce, rice wine and sesame oil in a small bowl and set aside.

Heat the vegetable oil in a large wok over a medium–high heat. Add the garlic and cook for 30 seconds, then add the cucumbers and prawns and cook, tossing the wok often, for 4–5 minutes, or until the cucumbers have softened slightly and the prawns are just cooked through. Add the soy sauce mixture to the wok, bring to the boil, then toss to combine well. Serve immediately.

Sweet and sour fish

Serves 4 to 6 as part of a shared meal

Sweet and sour flavours are popular in many parts of China and are not just applied to pork. When visiting Hangzhou it's essential to eat the famous 'West Lake vinegar fish' at least once. Grass carp from the West Lake, starved for two days to purge any muddy tastes, are first poached, then slathered in a thick, brown, sweet vinegar sauce that's made pleasantly sharp by the addition of local Zhejiang black vinegar. Here's a far less grand interpretation of those sweet and sour flavours using deep-fried fillets of tender john dory.

vegetable oil, for deep-frying

750 g (1 lb 11 oz) john dory, snapper or
  barramundi fillets

cornflour (cornstarch), for dusting

1 small red capsicum (pepper), seeded and
  finely shredded

2 spring onions (scallions), finely shredded

Sauce

2½ tablespoons aged black rice vinegar

1½ tablespoons light soy sauce

1½ tablespoons clear rice wine

2½ tablespoons chicken stock (page 405)
  or water

1½ tablespoons caster (superfine) sugar

1 tablespoon lard or vegetable oil

2 tablespoons finely shredded ginger

2 teaspoons cornflour (cornstarch)

To make the sauce, put the vinegar, soy sauce, rice wine, stock and sugar in a small bowl and stir to combine well. Heat the lard in a small saucepan over a medium–low heat, add the ginger and cook, stirring often, for 2–3 minutes, or until fragrant. Add the vinegar mixture and bring to a simmer. Combine the cornflour with 1 tablespoon water in a small bowl and stir to form a smooth paste. Stirring constantly, add the cornflour mixture to the sauce and cook for 1–2 minutes, or until the sauce is simmering and has thickened. Cover and remove the pan from the heat.

Fill a wok one-third full of oil and heat to 180°C (350°F), or until a cube of bread dropped into the oil turns deep golden in 15 seconds. While the oil is heating, cut the fish into 5 cm (2 inch) pieces. Dust each piece well with cornflour, shaking off the excess. Add the fish to the oil in two batches and cook for 3–4 minutes, or until light golden and cooked through. Drain well on paper towel and transfer to a warmed platter.

Gently reheat the sauce, then spoon the sauce over the fish pieces. Serve immediately with the capsicum and spring onions scattered over the top.

Leatherjacket with spicy braised bamboo and tofu skins

Serves 4

You could happily serve the tofu skin 'stew' here on its own — and if you're vegetarian feel free — but throw deep-fried leatherjacket into the equation and you've got the best kind of quick meal ever. Steam some rice, toss some green leafy vegetables in a hot wok and you've got a great casual (and spicy) meal on your hands. Leatherjackets tend to be a bit underrated, but they have a lovely firm texture that holds its shape and stands up to robust flavours, they are usually sold cleaned, with their heads and tough skins removed, and are listed as a sustainable seafood choice.

200 g (7 oz) dried tofu skins

4 leatherjackets, with heads removed

1 egg white, beaten

60 ml (2 fl oz/¼ cup) shaoxing rice wine

1 teaspoon salt

1½ tablespoons cornflour (cornstarch)

2 tablespoons vegetable oil, plus extra for deep-frying

2 garlic cloves, finely chopped

1 tablespoon finely chopped ginger

2 teaspoons sichuan peppercorns

300 g (10½ oz) frozen bamboo shoots, thawed and cut into matchsticks

2½ tablespoons sichuan chilli bean paste

1½ tablespoons fermented black beans, rinsed

2 tablespoons dark soy sauce

1 tablespoon black rice vinegar

625 ml (21 fl oz/2½ cups) chicken stock (page 405)

potato flour, for dusting

Put the tofu skins in a large bowl, cover with water and soak for about 1 hour, or until softened, weighting the skins down with an inverted plate to keep them submerged. Drain well, then squeeze out as much water as possible. Cut the skins into 1 cm (½ inch) wide strips and set aside.

Using a large, sharp knife, cut three or four diagonal slashes on both sides of each leatherjacket, taking care not to cut through to the bone. Put the egg white, half of the rice wine, the salt and cornflour in a large bowl and whisk to combine well. Add the fish and turn to coat, then cover the bowl and refrigerate for 1 hour.

Heat the oil in a wok over a medium heat, then add the garlic, ginger, peppercorns and bamboo shoots and cook, stirring, for 2 minutes, or until fragrant and the bamboo has softened slightly. Add the chilli bean paste and black beans and cook, stirring, for another minute. Add the remaining rice wine, the soy sauce, vinegar and stock and bring to a simmer. Reduce the heat to low and cook for about 5 minutes, or until the bamboo is tender, then stir in the strips of tofu skin.

Fill a wok one-third full of oil and heat to 180°C (350°F), or until a cube of bread dropped into the oil turns deep golden in 15 seconds. Put the potato flour on a plate, then dust each fish in the flour, shaking off the excess. Deep-fry the fish, two at a time, for about 7 minutes, or until cooked through. Divide the bamboo and tofu skin mixture among four deep bowls and place a leatherjacket on top of each. Serve immediately.

Poultry

Ubiquitous, but by no means boring, poultry holds an important part in the Chinese diet — and symbology. Duck represents fidelity, a whole chicken stands for family unity, quails mean courage, a goose resourcefulness and the pheasant is emblematic of beauty and fortune. The bottom line, however, is they're simply birds that are all good to eat.

Yunnan grilled spatchcocks

Serves 4

We will never forget the first time we landed in Dali in Yunnan Province. The doors of the aeroplane opened and we were greeted by a vista of wonderful open spaces and clean, fresh air — such a welcome relief after spending time in China's hectic and relentless cities. We ate a version of this simple dish at one of the many restaurants dotted around the incredibly beautiful Erhai Lake.

1½ teaspoons sichuan peppercorns

4 x 500 g (1 lb 2 oz) spatchcocks (poussin)

6 garlic cloves, finely chopped

1 tablespoon sea salt

1 tablespoon vegetable oil

1½ teaspoons coarsely ground black pepper

1 lime, halved, to serve

fresh chilli paste (page 406), to serve (optional)

Mint salad

50 g (1¾ oz/2 cups lightly packed) mint leaves

1 garlic clove, finely chopped

1 tablespoon clear rice vinegar, or to taste

2 tablespoons lime juice, or to taste

large pinch of sugar

2 teaspoons sesame oil

1 tablespoon peanut oil

Dry-roast the peppercorns in a small, heavy-based frying pan over a medium–low heat, shaking the pan often, for 3–4 minutes, or until fragrant. Cool, then transfer to a mortar (or an electric spice grinder) and pound with the pestle to form a coarse powder.

Using poultry shears or a large kitchen knife, cut down either side of the backbone of each spatchcock (reserve the backbones for a stock) then open each one out and firmly press down on the breastbone to flatten it. Trim any excess skin or fat from the spatchcocks. Place in a large bowl and add the garlic, sea salt, oil and ground sichuan and black peppers. Rub thoroughly over the spatchcocks and leave to marinate for at least 30 minutes or up to 2 hours (refrigerate the spatchcocks if you intend to marinate them for the longer time).

Heat a chargrill pan or barbecue grill plate to medium–high. Cook the spatchcocks for 25 minutes, turning occasionally. Check to see if the spatchcocks are cooked by piercing the thigh through the thickest part — if the juices run clear the birds are cooked; if not, continue cooking for a few more minutes.

While the spatchcocks are cooking, make the mint salad. Wash and dry the mint leaves. Pick the leaves off the harder stems, but leave the mint and tender stems together. Combine the garlic, vinegar, lime juice, sugar and oils and mix well, then taste and adjust the seasoning by adding a little more vinegar and lime juice if needed. Add the mint leaves and toss until well coated in the dressing, then transfer to a bowl. When the spatchcocks are cooked, place them on a platter, cover with foil and rest for 5 minutes. Serve with the mint salad and lime halves, and with fresh chilli paste, if desired.

Soy sauce chicken

Serves 6 as part of a shared meal

This is a cinch to make and it's one of those classic dishes that's good to have in your repertoire. All the lovely aromatics in the soy sauce 'stock' (also called 'master stock') permeate the chicken as it cooks. And, whatever you do, don't throw out that cooking liquid. Boil it hard to kill any bugs, then cool and freeze it between uses. It gets better over time, and in China some cooks are using master stocks that have been on the go for decades.

....

125 ml (4 fl oz/½ cup) dark soy sauce

375 ml (12½ fl oz/1½ cups) light soy sauce

80 ml (2½ fl oz/⅓ cup) shaoxing rice wine

250 g (9 oz) rock sugar, chopped

2½ star anise

2 teaspoons fennel seeds

3 pieces dried liquorice root

2 pieces dried tangerine peel

2 cinnamon sticks

6 slices unpeeled ginger

1 x 1.5 kg (3 lb 5 oz) chicken

....

Combine the soy sauces, rice wine, sugar and 1.5 litres (51 fl oz/6 cups) water in a saucepan large enough to snugly hold the chicken and liquid. Bring to a simmer.

Put the star anise, fennel seeds, liquorice root and tangerine peel in a piece of muslin (cheesecloth) and tie securely. Add to the simmering mixture along with the cinnamon sticks and ginger, then add the chicken, breast side down, pushing it down to submerge it. If necessary, add a little extra water to just cover the chicken. Bring the liquid back to a low simmer, then cover the pan and cook over a very low heat for 1 hour. Don't allow the liquid to simmer hard (bubbles should only just be breaking the surface) or the chicken will be tough. Resist the temptation to lift the lid. Remove the pan from the heat, then leave at room temperature for 2–3 hours, or until cooled — the chicken will continue to cook as the liquid cools.

Remove the chicken from the liquid, taking care not to break the skin. Strain the liquid, discarding the solids. Using a sharp cleaver, cut the chicken through the bone into bite-sized pieces. Serve drizzled with a little of the cooking liquid.

Soy sauce chicken: Enoki mushrooms with egg tofu (page 114)

Claypot chicken rice

Serves 4

This is another dish that's easy to make — once all the ingredients are prepared, they are simply thrown in the claypot and cooked together. This home-style dish, common in the south, is traditionally cooked over a charcoal fire, which imparts a special flavour, but it works just as well on the stovetop or in a 180°C (350°F/Gas 4) oven. If you don't have a claypot (although they are easy enough to find in Asian grocers), use a regular saucepan.

....

200 g (7 oz/1 cup) glutinous rice

100 g (3½ oz/½ cup) long-grain rice

40 g (1½ oz/¼ cup) small dried scallops

25 g (1 oz/¼ cup) dried shrimp

5 dried shiitake mushrooms

3 spring onions (scallions), finely chopped

2 Chinese pork sausages (lap cheong), finely sliced

2 tablespoons light soy sauce

2 tablespoons vegetable oil

800 g (1 lb 12 oz) french-cut chicken drumsticks

....

Combine the glutinous and long-grain rice in a bowl, cover with warm water and soak for 1 hour. Put the dried scallops, shrimp and shiitake mushrooms in separate heatproof bowls, cover each with boiling water and soak for 30 minutes. Drain the rice well. Drain the scallops and mushrooms, reserving the soaking water, and drain the shrimp, discarding the soaking water.

Finely chop the mushrooms and shrimp and combine with the spring onions and sausages in a bowl. Using your fingers, pull the scallops into thin shreds, then add them to the bowl.

Measure and combine the reserved soaking liquids in a bowl to make 435 ml (15 fl oz/1¾ cups), adding water as necessary if you don't have enough. Add the soy sauce to the liquid.

Heat the oil in a large claypot over a medium heat, then add the sausage mixture and cook, stirring, for 4–5 minutes. Add the chicken and stir to combine. Cover the pot and cook the chicken for 5 minutes, then add the soy sauce stock and drained rice and bring to a simmer. Cover the pot tightly, reduce the heat to very low and cook for 30 minutes, or until the liquid has been absorbed (try not to remove the lid too much during cooking). Remove the pot from the heat and set aside for 5–10 minutes, covered, or until the rice is tender and the chicken is cooked through. Serve immediately.

Steamed duck with fragrant rice

Serves 4 to 6 as part of a shared meal

Steaming makes duck wonderfully tender. The duck is first steamed whole, then the meat is combined with other ingredients and steamed again. The key here is to use the specified size of bowl for steaming, so the ingredients in the bowl sit level to the rim; this way there's no empty space for it to fall and break when you turn it out. Make sure you let the dish sit for the required amount of time before turning it out, so it can settle and firm up a little.

1 x 2.2 kg (5 lb) duck

2 tablespoons dried shrimp

400 g (14 oz/2 cups) glutinous rice, soaked overnight

50 g (1¾ oz/⅓ cup) dried lotus seeds, soaked overnight

60 ml (2 fl oz/¼ cup) vegetable oil

50 g (1¾ oz) Chinese cured ham (or cured pork), chopped into 5 mm (¼ inch) pieces

1 tablespoon shaoxing rice wine

1 tablespoon light soy sauce

½ teaspoon salt

1 small bunch coriander (cilantro)

Marinade

2 teaspoons caster (superfine) sugar

1 teaspoon salt

2 tablespoons shaoxing rice wine

2 tablespoons light soy sauce

1 teaspoon freshly ground black pepper

Fill a large saucepan one-third full of water and bring to the boil. Place the duck in a heatproof bowl that will fit snugly into the saucepan, then put the bowl into the pan (you may need to adjust the water level in the pan; the water needs to come halfway up the side of the bowl). Cover the pan and steam the duck over a medium–low heat for 1½ hours, adding more water to the pan as necessary. Remove the duck and cool, then place on a chopping board and carefully, using a knife and your fingers, remove all the meat from the bones, discarding the bones. Chop the duck meat into 5 cm (2 inch) pieces. Arrange the duck meat in the base of a 1.5 litre (51 fl oz/6 cup) heatproof bowl. Combine all the ingredients for the marinade, stirring to dissolve the sugar, then slowly pour it over the duck.

While the duck is cooking, put the dried shrimp in a heatproof bowl, cover with boiling water and soak for 30 minutes. Drain, then chop. Drain the rice and wash thoroughly, then place it in a saucepan and cover with 750 ml (25½ fl oz/3 cups) water. Bring to a simmer over a medium heat and cook for 12–15 minutes, or until tender, then drain and set aside to cool.

Drain the lotus seeds and remove any small bitter green shoots. Heat the oil in a large saucepan, then add the lotus seeds, ham and shrimp and cook for 1–2 minutes, then stir in the rice wine, soy sauce and salt. Remove the pan from the heat, add the rice and mix well. Carefully place the rice mixture over the duck and smooth the surface, cover the bowl with foil and put the bowl in a large saucepan (as above), cover and steam over a medium heat for 1 hour. Remove the bowl from the pan, cover and rest for 20 minutes, then invert onto a plate and serve.

Steamed chicken with red dates in lotus leaf

Serves 4 to 6 as part of a shared meal

The French are famous for cooking en papillote — *wrapping their food for cooking — and the Chinese have a similar method too. Bamboo, banana and lotus leaves are often used to wrap food, which seals in all the juices and flavourings. And serving a little wrapped parcel of food to your guests always adds to the air of anticipation, as they unwrap the leaves and breathe in the aromas for the first time.*

8 dried shiitake mushrooms

16 dried large red dates (jujubes)

4 dried lotus leaves

8 chicken thighs, skin on and bone in (or use boneless, skinless fillets if you prefer)

4 spring onions (scallions), green part only, finely sliced (white part reserved for marinade)

Marinade

1 tablespoon oyster sauce

1 tablespoon light soy sauce

2 tablespoons shaoxing rice wine

1 tablespoon sesame oil

4 spring onions (scallions), white part only, cut into 1 cm (½ inch) pieces

2 cm (¾ inch) piece ginger, peeled and finely shredded

2 tablespoons vegetable oil

Put the shiitake mushrooms and red dates (remove the stones if they aren't already pitted) in separate heatproof bowls, cover each with boiling water and soak for 30 minutes, then drain. Slice the mushrooms. Soak the dried lotus leaves in boiling water to soften, then pat dry.

To make the marinade, combine all the ingredients in a large bowl. Add the chicken, mushrooms and dates and turn to coat in the marinade. Cover the bowl with plastic wrap and place in the fridge to marinate for 1 hour. Bring back to room temperature before cooking.

Place two plates into two steamer baskets (or steam in batches), then line each plate with two lotus leaves, slightly overlapping each other. Put half of the chicken mixture on the top of each plate of leaves and wrap the leaves around the chicken to form a parcel. Put the steamer baskets on top of each other, place over a wok or saucepan of simmering water, then cover and steam the chicken for 35–40 minutes, or until cooked through (unwrap a parcel to check if the chicken is cooked). Place the lotus parcels on a platter and unfold the leaves, then sprinkle over the green spring onions. Serve with steamed rice (page 412).

Red-cooked chicken wings with chestnuts

Serves 4 to 6 as part of a shared meal

Anyone who has been to Beijing in autumn or winter (bbbrrr!) will know the enticing smell of roasting chestnuts that fills the streets. But chestnuts, which have a long history in Chinese cuisine, are used for much more than this. From soups and stews to desserts (or ground into a flour that is sometimes used in dumpling skins), they are a much loved ingredient. Around Shanghai they particularly like chestnuts cooked in poultry dishes, such as this one.

20 mid-section chicken wings (about 1.2 kg/ 2 lb 10 oz) or drumettes

125 ml (4 fl oz/½ cup) shaoxing rice wine

1 tablespoon very finely chopped ginger

3 teaspoons cornflour (cornstarch)

½ teaspoon ground white pepper

600 g (1 lb 5 oz) fresh chestnuts

625 ml (21 fl oz/2½ cups) vegetable oil

250 ml (8½ fl oz/1 cup) chicken stock (page 405)

2 tablespoons light soy sauce

2 tablespoons dark soy sauce

1 star anise

2 pieces dried tangerine peel

2 tablespoons sugar

2 spring onions (scallions), green part only, finely sliced on the diagonal

Put the chicken wings in a large bowl. Combine 1 tablespoon of the rice wine, the ginger, cornflour and white pepper, then add to the chicken and toss to combine. Cover the bowl with plastic wrap and refrigerate for 2 hours or overnight. Drain well, reserving the marinade. Pat the chicken wings dry using paper towel.

Preheat the oven to 180°C (350°F/Gas 4). Using a small, sharp knife, cut a cross in the base of each chestnut, then place them in a single layer on a baking tray. Roast for 25 minutes, then cool slightly. When cool enough to handle, peel the chestnuts and remove the papery skin. Set aside.

Heat the oil in a large wok over a high heat, then add the chicken wings in batches and cook for 6–7 minutes, or until golden. Remove with kitchen tongs and drain on paper towel.

Pour off all the oil in the wok. Return the wok to a medium heat, add the remaining rice wine, stock, soy sauces, star anise, tangerine peel and sugar, then add the reserved marinade and chicken wings, and scatter the chestnuts over the top. Bring the mixture to a simmer, cover the wok and cook for 20 minutes, or until the chicken wings and chestnuts are tender and the sauce has reduced and thickened. If the sauce hasn't reduced, remove the lid and boil for 3–4 minutes, or until thick and sticky. Transfer to a platter, scatter over the spring onions and serve.

Tea-smoked duck

Serves 4 to 6 as part of a shared meal

They say China rears over 80 per cent of the world's duck population, and it's not hard to believe that claim; travelling by land around the country, duck farms are evident everywhere. The world-famous Peking duck is beautiful but a little technical to make at home, so here's a recipe that's a little easier but equally rewarding. Try serving this for a crowd — they'll think you're a Chinese master chef.

....

1 x 2 kg (4 lb 6 oz) duck

1 tablespoon sichuan peppercorns

2½ teaspoons sea salt

30 g (1 oz/¼ cup) lapsang souchong tea leaves

2 tablespoons firmly packed soft brown sugar

sesame oil, for brushing

....

Wash the duck thoroughly under cold running water and pat dry with paper towel.

Dry-roast the peppercorns in a small, heavy-based frying pan over a medium–low heat, shaking the pan often, for 3–4 minutes, or until fragrant. Cool, then transfer to a mortar (or an electric spice grinder) and pound with the pestle to form a coarse powder. In a small bowl, combine the ground peppercorns and sea salt, and rub the mixture all over the duck, including the cavity.

Put the duck on a plate, then place the duck in a steamer over a wok or saucepan of boiling water. Cover and steam for 1¼ hours, or until just cooked through. Test to see if the duck is ready by piercing through the thigh — if the juices run clear it is cooked; if the juices are still pink, cook for another 5–10 minutes, then check again.

While the duck is steaming, line the base of a wok (large enough to hold a round cake rack) with a double layer of foil. Combine the tea leaves and sugar and spread over the foil. When the duck is ready, place the cake rack on the foil and then heat the wok over a medium heat until it starts to smoke. Place the duck, breast side up, on the rack, cover with a tight-fitting lid and smoke for 5 minutes, then turn the duck over, cover and smoke for another 5 minutes. Remove from the heat and let the duck rest, covered, for 10 minutes.

Remove the duck to a chopping board and brush all over with sesame oil. Using a cleaver, cut the duck through the bone into bite-sized pieces and serve warm or at room temperature.

Tea-smoked duck; Sweet vinegared lotus (page 77)

Chicken with potatoes and sesame

Serves 4 to 6

This recipe is based on one from the fabulous book, Chinese Home-Style Cooking, *one of the few published in English on the subject, and it indicates the recipe originates in Suzhou. We are drawn to the rustic combo of potato and chicken cooked with all our favourite Chinese flavours: sesame, soy sauce and rice wine.*

4 chicken leg quarters (marylands)

60 ml (2 fl oz/¼ cup) light soy sauce

60 ml (2 fl oz/¼ cup) shaoxing rice wine

340 ml (12 fl oz/1⅓ cups) chicken stock (page 405)

1 litre (34 fl oz/4 cups) vegetable oil

cornflour (cornstarch), for dusting

450 g (1 lb) small desiree or other all-purpose potatoes, peeled

1 tablespoon sesame seeds, toasted (page 413)

4 spring onions (scallions), cut into 4 cm (1½ inch) lengths

2 teaspoons sesame oil

Using a cleaver, chop each chicken leg into four or five pieces widthwise, trimming the bone off at the thin end of the leg. Combine the soy sauce, rice wine and stock in a bowl and set aside.

Pour the vegetable oil into a wok and heat to 180°C (350°F), or until a cube of bread dropped into the oil turns deep golden in 15 seconds. Meanwhile, put the cornflour in a bowl, add the chicken pieces in batches, and turn to coat, shaking off the excess. Fry the chicken in batches for 4–5 minutes, or until light golden. Remove and drain on paper towel. Reserve the oil in the wok.

Cut the potatoes in half or, if slightly large, into three pieces. Add the potatoes to the hot oil in the wok and cook for 5 minutes, or until golden. Remove and drain on paper towel. Pour the oil into a heatproof bowl to cool, then later discard it.

Add the soy sauce mixture to the wok and bring to a simmer over a medium heat, then add the chicken and potatoes, cover the wok and cook for 8–10 minutes, or until the chicken and potatoes are tender and the sauce has thickened. Sprinkle the sesame seeds and spring onions over the top, drizzle with the sesame oil, then cover and cook for another minute. Transfer to a platter and serve.

Hainanese chicken rice

Serves 4

Hainanese chicken rice most likely evolved from a simmered chicken recipe known as Wenchang chicken, from Hainan Island. This is the simplest of dishes — a whole chicken is poached and then cut into bite-sized pieces and served with dipping sauces. Like anything simple, the devil lurks in the details; the proteins in the chicken harden with hard simmering, so to achieve the legendary melting, soft texture of the cooked Hainanese chicken, the cooking liquid should be kept over the lowest possible heat.

4 pandan leaves, bruised and tied in a knot (optional)
2½ teaspoons salt
1 x 1.6 kg (3½ lb) chicken
3 spring onions (scallions), trimmed
8 slices unpeeled ginger
sesame oil, for brushing
1 telegraph (long) cucumber
coriander (cilantro) sprigs, to serve

Rice
1 tablespoon vegetable oil
1 garlic clove, crushed
2 slices unpeeled ginger
400 g (14 oz/2 cups) long-grain rice

Spring onion and ginger dipping sauce
3 large spring onions (scallions), very finely chopped
1 tablespoon finely grated ginger, or to taste
80 ml (2½ fl oz/⅓ cup) vegetable oil

Chilli dipping sauce
5 large red chillies, chopped
1 garlic clove, chopped
2 teaspoons finely chopped ginger
2 teaspoons sugar
1 tablespoon lime juice, or to taste
about 1 tablespoon reserved chicken cooking liquid

Bring 2 litres (68 fl oz/8 cups) water to the boil in a saucepan large enough to snugly fit the chicken. Add the pandan, if using, and 1 teaspoon of the salt. Rub the chicken all over with the remaining salt.

Stuff the whole spring onions and ginger slices into the chicken cavity. Make sure the water is boiling hard, then carefully plunge the chicken, breast side down, into the water to completely submerge it. Cover the pan with a tight-fitting lid, then immediately reduce the heat to very low, using a simmer pad or pulling the pan halfway off the low heat, if necessary — the surface of the water should be just trembling. Cook the chicken for 20 minutes, then remove the pan from the heat and set aside for 1 hour to cool to room temperature, without removing the lid. Carefully remove the chicken from the liquid, reserving the liquid, then transfer the bird to a large bowl of iced water. Leave to cool for 5 minutes, remove and drain well. Pat the chicken dry, brush the skin lightly all over with sesame oil, then cover and set aside. Strain the cooking liquid, discarding the solids.

To prepare the rice, heat the oil in a saucepan over a medium heat, then add the garlic, ginger and rice and cook, stirring, for 2 minutes, or until the rice is glossy. Add 750 ml (25½ fl oz/3 cups) of the reserved chicken cooking liquid and bring to a simmer. Cover the pan with a tight-fitting lid, reduce the heat to low and cook for about 15 minutes, or until the liquid has been absorbed. Remove the pan from the heat and set aside, covered, for another 10 minutes, or until the rice is completely tender.

To make the spring onion and ginger dipping sauce, combine the spring onions and ginger in a heatproof bowl. Heat the oil in a small saucepan over a medium heat for 1–2 minutes, or until it starts to sizzle, then pour the oil over the mixture in the bowl. Stir to combine well, then cool. Add a little more grated ginger, if desired.

To make the chilli dipping sauce, combine all the ingredients in a small food processor or a mortar, then process or pound with the pestle to form a smooth paste. Add a little extra chicken cooking liquid to thin the sauce, if necessary.

Skim any fat from the surface of the remaining chicken cooking liquid, pour it into a clean saucepan, then bring to a simmer over a low heat.

To serve, peel the cucumber, cut it in half lengthwise, then cut into thin slices on the diagonal. Using a cleaver, cut the chicken through the bone into neat, bite-sized pieces. Place on a platter with the cucumber slices and coriander sprigs. Serve the chicken with small bowls of rice, the two dipping sauces and small bowls of the hot chicken stock.

Red tofu chicken

Serves 4 to 6

Fermented tofu smells funky, there's no two ways about it, but it gives food a rich, full flavour in the same way a good sharp cheese does. In fact, the fermentation process gives the tofu an almost creamy, dairy-like texture. Here it's mashed into a marinade to impart a smooth, mellow flavour to the meat that's only made more delicious by deep-frying.

700 g (1 lb 9 oz) boneless, skinless chicken thighs

3 pieces red fermented tofu, plus 1 tablespoon of the tofu liquid

2 garlic cloves, crushed

1½ tablespoons clear rice wine

½ teaspoon five-spice

vegetable oil, for deep-frying

rice flour, for coating

Cucumber and lychee salad

16 fresh lychees

2 Lebanese (short) cucumbers, cut into matchsticks

1½ tablespoons peanut oil

1½ tablespoons sesame oil

1½ tablespoons clear rice vinegar, or to taste

1 teaspoon sugar

Trim the excess fat off the thighs and cut the chicken into 1.5 cm (½ inch) pieces. Combine the tofu, tofu liquid, garlic, rice wine and five-spice in a large bowl. Use a fork to mash the tofu as finely as you can, and mix to form a smooth paste. Add the chicken and toss to coat well. Cover the bowl with plastic wrap and refrigerate for 3 hours or overnight.

Meanwhile, to make the salad, peel the lychees, then cut them in half and remove the seeds. Place the lychees and cucumbers in a bowl. Heat the oils, vinegar and sugar in a small saucepan, swirling the pan to combine well, then pour over the cucumber and lychees. Toss to combine well, then spread the salad out on a serving platter.

Bring the chicken to room temperature. Fill a wok one-third full of oil and heat to 180°C (350°F), or until a cube of bread dropped into the oil turns deep golden in 15 seconds. Toss the chicken pieces in the rice flour, shaking off the excess. Deep-fry the chicken in two batches for 3–4 minutes, or until golden and crisp and cooked through. Using a slotted spoon, remove and drain on paper towel. Transfer the chicken to the platter with the salad and serve immediately.

Xinjiang 'big bowl' chicken

Serves 8

Big, bold flavours and rustic cooking methods are the hallmarks of China's far northwest, where the people are Turkic, not ethnically Chinese. They have more in common culturally and religiously (they're mainly Muslim) with Central Asia, which Xinjiang borders. Cumin, chillies and sichuan peppercorns are common flavourings and vegetables such as tomatoes, eggplant (aubergines) and potatoes are widely eaten. In those parts, a dish like this would be accompanied by copious amounts of thick, chewy, wheat noodles. This recipe can easily be halved if you aren't feeding a crowd.

2 x 1.25 kg (2 lb 12 oz) chickens
60 ml (2 fl oz/¼ cup) vegetable oil
1 onion, chopped
4 garlic cloves, finely chopped
1½ tablespoons finely chopped ginger
2½ teaspoons cumin seeds
1 star anise
1 tablespoon sichuan peppercorns

400 g (14 oz) small desiree or other all-purpose potatoes, peeled
1 large red capsicum (pepper), seeded and cut into 2 cm (¾ inch) pieces
60 ml (2 fl oz/¼ cup) sichuan chilli bean paste
2 teaspoons sugar
1 tablespoon dark soy sauce
500 ml (17 fl oz/2 cups) chicken stock (page 405)
500 g (1 lb 2 oz) roma (plum) tomatoes (about 5)

Ask your butcher to cut each chicken into eight pieces, or alternatively, you can cut the chickens yourself. To do this, place each chicken, breast side up, on a chopping board and remove both leg quarters (marylands) by cutting through the thigh joint nearest the body. Cut each leg quarter in half by cutting through the joint between the drumstick and thigh. Cut down either side of the backbone and discard the backbone (or save it for stock). Place the chicken breast side down, then cut lengthwise through the centre of the breastbone. Cut each breast in half on a slight diagonal just under the wing.

Heat the oil in a large, deep frying pan. Add the chicken in batches and cook, turning often, for 5 minutes, or until browned. Remove the chicken to a plate.

Add the onion, garlic, ginger, cumin seeds, star anise and peppercorns to the pan and cook, stirring, for 2 minutes, or until fragrant. Return the chicken to the pan, then add the remaining ingredients, except the tomatoes. Bring to a simmer, partially cover the pan, and cook over a low heat for about 1 hour, or until the chicken and potatoes are tender. Cut the tomatoes into wedges and remove the seeds, then add to the chicken mixture and cook for 2–3 minutes to heat through. Transfer to a large bowl or platter and serve.

Aromatic fried chilli chicken

Serves 4

The streets of Sichuanese towns are infused with the fragrance of smoky, wok-fried dried chillies and freshly toasted sichuan peppercorns, known as hua jiao, *or 'flower pepper'. The peppercorns are an intriguing mix of fragrant heat and mouth-numbing spice and are used to great effect in this classic dish. This recipe is based on the well-known dish,* lazi jiding, *which traditionally comes to the table slathered in a sea of crisp-fried dried chillies. You're not expected to eat these, they merely impart an earthy flavour to the proceedings.*

5 boneless, skinless chicken thighs (about 650 g/ 1 lb 7 oz)

potato flour, for dusting

vegetable oil, for deep-frying

3 garlic cloves, finely chopped

2 teaspoons finely chopped ginger

50 g (1¾ oz) dried red chillies, cut into thirds, seeds discarded

1½ tablespoons sichuan peppercorns, coarsely ground

1½ tablespoons light soy sauce

1½ tablespoons shaoxing rice wine

1 teaspoon sugar

4 spring onions (scallions), cut into 4 cm (1½ inch) lengths

Marinade

3 teaspoons light soy sauce

2 teaspoons shaoxing rice wine

2 teaspoons sesame oil

1 garlic clove, finely chopped

Trim the excess fat off the thighs and cut the chicken into 1.5 cm (½ inch) pieces. To make the marinade, combine all the ingredients in a large bowl and stir well. Add the chicken, toss to coat in the marinade, then cover and refrigerate for 3–4 hours. Drain the chicken pieces, then dust well in potato flour, shaking off the excess.

Fill a wok one-third full of oil and heat to 180°C (350°F), or until a cube of bread dropped into the oil turns deep golden in 15 seconds. Add the chicken in batches and cook for 4–5 minutes, or until light golden and cooked through. Remove with a slotted spoon and drain on paper towel.

Pour off all but about 60 ml (2 fl oz/¼ cup) of oil from the wok, and reduce the heat to medium. Add the garlic, ginger, chillies and ground peppercorns and stir-fry for about 1 minute, or until fragrant. Return the chicken to the wok, increase the heat slightly, then add the soy sauce, rice wine, sugar and spring onions. Toss for about 2 minutes, or until almost all of the liquid has evaporated and the chicken is heated through, then serve immediately.

Photograph page 202

From left to right: Sichuan flavours of Aromatic fried chilli chicken (page 201); Fish-flavoured pork (page 236); Water-boiled beef (page 280)

Chicken and dried longan soup

Serves 4 to 6 as part of a shared meal

Bright, clear Chinese soups such as this one call for great chicken stock, which is not hard to make from scratch. We've made this a bit more substantially meaty than they would in China, where such soups are consumed as much for their tonic values as their food ones. Dried longan and goji berries are part of a group of tonic seeds that are considered yang, or warming for the body, and are believed to increase sexual potency and fertility. You've been warned ...

2 litres (68 fl oz/8 cups) chicken stock (page 405)
4 chicken leg quarters (marylands)
85 g (3 oz/½ cup) dried longans
25 g (1 oz/⅓ cup) dried yu zhu

2½ tablespoons dried goji berries
2 tablespoons sweet southern apricot kernels (page 425)

Combine all the ingredients in a large saucepan. Very slowly bring to a gentle simmer, skimming the surface as necessary to remove any impurities, then cook over a low heat for 45 minutes, or until the chicken is cooked through.

Remove the chicken from the soup and cool slightly. When it is cool enough to handle, remove the skin and bones from the chicken and tear the meat into large pieces. Skim any fat from the surface of the soup, return the chicken to the pan and reheat the soup. Serve immediately.

Chicken and dried longan soup: Spring onion and ginger noodles (page 307)

Salt-baked chicken

Serves 4

We were inspired to try Hakka Dung Gong Yim Guk Gai *after talking to the local Hakka people in Fujian Province about the traditional salt merchants, who would cook their salt chicken in the ground. If there was ever a centrepiece dish for your table, then this is it — and the chicken is incredibly tasty. You can relax because no salt touches the chicken; it merely acts as a seal to trap the heat and steam ... and you don't need to dig holes in your backyard to cook it either.*

3 kg (6 lb 10 oz) coarse salt or rock salt

1 x 1.6 kg (3½ lb) corn-fed chicken

2 tablespoons shaoxing rice wine

2 teaspoons sea salt

5 cm (2 inch) piece ginger, peeled and finely chopped

4 spring onions (scallions), white part only, cut into 1 cm (½ inch) pieces

Put the coarse salt in a large wok over a medium heat and heat for about 10 minutes, stirring occasionally, or until the salt is hot to the touch.

Remove any fat from the cavity opening of the chicken and around the neck. Rinse the chicken well, then drain and pat dry with paper towel. Combine the rice wine, sea salt and ginger, then rub the mixture into the chicken. Put the spring onions in the cavity, then wrap up the chicken in a piece of muslin (cheesecloth), tucking the ends underneath the chicken. Secure one end with kitchen string and loop it around the muslin, securing the other end, to create an enclosed package.

Using a metal spoon, create a depression in the salt in the wok, large enough to fit the chicken (you need to leave about 2.5 cm/1 inch of salt in the bottom of the wok). Place the chicken in the wok, breast side down, then cover with the salt — the chicken should be completely encased in salt. Cover with the lid.

Place the wok over a medium–low heat and cook for 1½ hours, or until the chicken is cooked through — the juices will run clear when the thigh is pierced with a knife or skewer (you will need to unwrap the chicken to check this). Remove the wok from the heat and use kitchen tongs to remove the chicken, shaking off the salt. Discard the salt. Cut the string and remove the muslin. Carve the chicken into portions and serve on a warm platter.

Chickens' feet braised with soy and black bean

Serves 4 to 6 as part of a shared meal

Chickens' feet are now so popular in China that they import them from all over the world to satisfy demand. Also called 'phoenix claws', they're cooked in a variety of ways. For this classic Cantonese dish (simplified here) they are deep-fried, steamed and then braised; this achieves the classic, soft puffiness so prized by diners.

....

1 kg (2 lb 3 oz) chickens' feet (about 16)

vegetable oil, for deep-frying

1 litre (34 fl oz/4 cups) chicken stock (page 405)

60 ml (2 fl oz/¼ cup) dark soy sauce

60 ml (2 fl oz/¼ cup) shaoxing rice wine

2½ tablespoons black rice vinegar

1½ tablespoons sugar

1 tablespoon oyster sauce

4 cm (1½ inch) piece ginger, peeled and finely shredded

1 tablespoon fermented black beans, rinsed

2 star anise

....

Using a sharp knife, trim the nail ends off each claw, then trim about 1.5 cm (½ inch) from the bone end of each foot. Using paper towel, dry the feet well.

Fill a wok one-third full of oil and heat to 180°C (350°F), or until a cube of bread dropped into the oil turns deep golden in 15 seconds. Fill a large bowl with iced water. Working in two batches, fry the chickens' feet for 6–7 minutes, or until light golden, taking care as you cook them as the feet will spit. Remove the feet with a slotted spoon and place in the bowl of iced water.

Drain the feet well and place in a saucepan with the remaining ingredients. Bring to a simmer, using an inverted plate to keep them submerged if necessary, and cook over a low heat for 40–50 minutes, or until tender. Serve hot with some of the cooking liquid spooned over.

Pickled chickens' feet

Serves 4 to 6 as part of a shared meal

We are always fascinated by packaged Chinese travel snacks whenever we catch a long-distance bus or train. Where we might yearn for a bag of potato crisps or a handful of liquorice allsorts, the Chinese munch on an assortment of vac-packed, salted, smoked, cured and pickled animal parts, including chickens' feet. We saw big drums of cold pickled chickens' feet for sale in markets in Chengdu and other cities; the ultimate convenience food for housewives too busy to make their own. Not that they take that long.

1 kg (2 lb 3 oz) chickens' feet (about 16)

2 carrots, peeled

375 ml (12½ fl oz/1½ cups) clear rice vinegar

115 g (4 oz/½ cup) caster (superfine) sugar

1 tablespoon sesame oil

1 small red onion, halved and finely sliced

6 pickled chillies (page 410)

coriander (cilantro) leaves, to serve

Using a sharp knife, trim the nail ends off each claw, then trim about 1.5 cm (½ inch) from the bone end of each foot. Place in a saucepan, cover with water and bring to a simmer, using an inverted plate to keep them submerged if necessary, and cook over a medium–low heat for 20 minutes, or until tender. Drain well and refresh under cold water. Transfer to a non-reactive bowl.

Meanwhile, cut the carrots in half lengthwise, then thinly slice each half on the diagonal. Combine the vinegar, sugar, 250 ml (8½ fl oz/1 cup) water and the carrots in a saucepan and bring to a simmer. Cover and cook for 5 minutes, or until the sugar has dissolved, then remove the pan from the heat. Cool slightly, then add the sesame oil.

Pour the carrot mixture over the chickens' feet in the bowl, add the onion and chillies and toss to combine well. Cover the bowl with plastic wrap and set aside at room temperature, tossing the feet occasionally, for 2–3 hours to allow the flavours to develop. Transfer to a platter, scatter with coriander leaves and serve.

Deep-fried ginger and five-spice chicken

Serves 4 as part of a shared meal

We were taken by friends to a Sichuan countryside wedding outside of Chengdu and the food, all cooked outside in scorching heat over big fires, was incredible. The guests tucked into chunky pieces of fried chicken like there was no tomorrow — they told us it was a relatively new addition to the local menu. Deep-frying need not mean greasy food either; the trick is in keeping your oil at a constant temperature and not crowding the wok.

1 x 1.8 kg (4 lb) chicken
2 spring onions (scallions), sliced
2 tablespoons dark soy sauce
60 ml (2 fl oz/¼ cup) light soy sauce
80 ml (2½ fl oz/⅓ cup) shaoxing rice wine
1 teaspoon five-spice

3 teaspoons sugar
2.5 cm (1 inch) piece ginger, peeled and finely chopped
vegetable oil, for deep-frying
potato flour, for dusting

Cut the chicken into eight pieces. To do this, place the chicken, breast side up, on a chopping board and remove both leg quarters (marylands) by cutting through the thigh joint nearest the body. Cut each leg quarter in half by cutting through the joint between the drumstick and thigh. Cut down either side of the backbone and discard the backbone (or save it for stock). Place the chicken breast side down, then cut lengthwise through the centre of the breastbone. Cut each breast in half on a slight diagonal just under the wing.

In a large bowl, combine the spring onions, soy sauces, rice wine, five-spice, sugar and ginger and mix well. Add the chicken and turn to evenly coat in the marinade. Cover the bowl with plastic wrap and refrigerate for 3 hours or overnight.

Fill a wok one-third full of oil and heat to 170°C (340°F), or until a cube of bread dropped into the oil turns deep golden in 20 seconds. While the oil is heating, remove the chicken from the marinade and drain well. Discard the marinade. Dust the chicken pieces in the potato flour, shaking off the excess. Add the chicken to the wok in two batches and deep-fry for 12–15 minutes, or until the chicken is deep golden and cooked through. Remove and drain on paper towel, then serve hot.

Roast quail in honey and maltose

Serves 6

Live quails are a common sight in Chinese produce markets and they're brilliantly suited to roasting in the southern Chinese manner. There, a combination of ingredients such as five-spice, honey, hoisin sauce, maltose, and even fermented red tofu are used to burnish (mostly) pork with a deliciously sticky glaze — you've no doubt seen roast meat hanging in Cantonese restaurant windows. We like our quails a little pink in the middle — a very un-Chinese approach to meat cookery.

2 tablespoons maltose

2 tablespoons honey

125 ml (4 fl oz/½ cup) dark soy sauce

2 teaspoons very finely chopped ginger

1 teaspoon five-spice

3 teaspoons sesame oil

6 jumbo quails

Combine all the ingredients, except the quails, in a saucepan. Place over a low heat and cook, stirring occasionally, for 5 minutes, or until well combined. Cool to room temperature.

Meanwhile, using poultry shears or a large, sharp knife, cut down either side of the backbone of each quail, discarding the backbones. Place each quail, skin side down, on a chopping board, then cut each bird in half along the breastbone. Combine the soy sauce mixture and quail halves in a dish, turning to coat well. Cover the dish with plastic wrap and refrigerate for 6–8 hours to allow the flavours to develop, turning the quails occasionally.

Preheat the oven to 220°C (430°F/Gas 7). Place a large piece of foil over an oven rack to catch the drips, tucking the foil around the rack to secure it, then put a cake rack, or similar, on the foil. Remove the quails from the marinade, reserving the marinade, and place them, skin side up, on the cake rack in the hot oven. Cook for 8–10 minutes, brushing the quails occasionally with a little of the marinade, or until just cooked through (but still a little pink in the middle). Serve hot or at room temperature.

Roast quail in honey and maltose; Carrots stir-fried with ginger and gingko nuts (page 93); English spinach with glass noodles (page 74)

Steamed chicken in wine

Serves 4

1 x 1.6 kg (3½ lb) chicken

4 spring onions (scallions), finely sliced

5 cm (2 inch) piece ginger, peeled and finely chopped

1 teaspoon fennel seeds

6 cloves

2 teaspoons sea salt

1 teaspoon sichuan peppercorns

½ teaspoon dahurian angelica root, finely chopped (optional)

60 ml (2 fl oz/¼ cup) clear rice wine

Remove any fat from the cavity opening of the chicken and around the neck. Rinse the chicken well, then drain and pat dry with paper towel.

In a large bowl, combine the spring onions, ginger, fennel seeds, cloves, sea salt, peppercorns, angelica root, if using, and rice wine. Rub the mixture over the chicken, including the cavity.

Fill a large saucepan one-third full of water and bring to the boil. Place the chicken in a heatproof bowl that will fit snugly into the saucepan, then put the bowl into the pan (you may need to adjust the water level in the pan; the water needs to come halfway up the side of the bowl). Cover the pan and steam the chicken over a medium–low heat for 1¼ hours, adding more water to the pan as necessary. Remove the chicken from the bowl and leave to cool a little. Discard the aromatics, skim the stock juices in the bowl, then strain the juices and reserve. Using a cleaver, cut the chicken through the bone into bite-sized pieces, arrange on a platter and pour over the reserved juices. Serve with steamed rice (page 412).

Twice-cooked chicken

Serves 4

1 quantity Steamed chicken in wine (recipe above)

1 litre (34 fl oz/4 cups) vegetable oil

2 eggs, lightly beaten

30 g (1 oz/¼ cup) cornflour (cornstarch)

fresh chilli dip, to serve (page 406)

Carve the cooled chicken into 10–12 pieces. Pour the oil into a wok and heat to 180°C (350°F), or until a cube of bread dropped into the oil turns deep golden in 15 seconds. Meanwhile, mix the eggs and cornflour in a large bowl until combined, then add the chicken pieces and thoroughly coat each piece in the egg mixture. Add the chicken to the wok in two batches and cook for 5–7 minutes, or until evenly browned and crisp. Remove and drain on paper towel. Serve with the fresh chilli dip.

Duck hotpot

Serves 4

Langzhong is a city in northeastern Sichuan Province and it's worth a visit for its grid of intact, centuries-old streets and lovely old architecture, sadly a rarity in China these days. It was here we ate duck hotpot. Served without fanfare in an enormous enamel basin, it came complete with every duck part known to mankind, floating among a slew of dried chillies and peppercorns. This was Chinese food at its most rustic and honest — and at its most spicy.

1 x 2.2 kg (5 lb) duck

170 ml (5½ fl oz/⅔ cup) peanut oil

35 g (1¼ oz/1 cup) dried red chillies

5 cm (2 inch) piece ginger, peeled and finely shredded

5 garlic cloves, finely sliced

2 tablespoons sichuan peppercorns

80 ml (2½ fl oz/⅓ cup) sichuan chilli bean paste, or to taste

2½ tablespoons fermented black beans, rinsed and mashed with a fork

2 tablespoons sugar

60 ml (2 fl oz/¼ cup) light soy sauce

125 ml (4 fl oz/½ cup) shaoxing rice wine

1 bunch coriander (cilantro), chopped

Using a cleaver or large, sharp knife, remove the neck from the duck and reserve. Cut between the legs and body to remove the leg quarters (marylands), then cut each in half at the middle thigh joint. Cut down each side of the backbone and set aside, then cut the duck in half down the breastbone. Cut each breast in half on a slight diagonal. Set aside.

Heat the oil in a large saucepan or stockpot over a medium–high heat, then add the chillies and cook, stirring, for 3 minutes, or until lightly browned, taking care that they don't burn. Remove to a bowl using a slotted spoon, reserving the oil in the pan. Add the ginger and garlic to the pan and cook, stirring, for 1 minute, then add the peppercorns and cook for another minute, or until the mixture is fragrant. Add the chilli bean paste and stir-fry for 30 seconds or so, then add the black beans, sugar, soy sauce, rice wine and 2.5 litres (85 fl oz/10 cups) water.

Add the duck, including the reserved neck and backbone for extra flavour, if desired (you may need to cut the backbone in half), and bring the mixture slowly to a simmer; cook over a low heat for 2 hours, or until the duck is very tender. Add the coriander, stir to combine and serve.

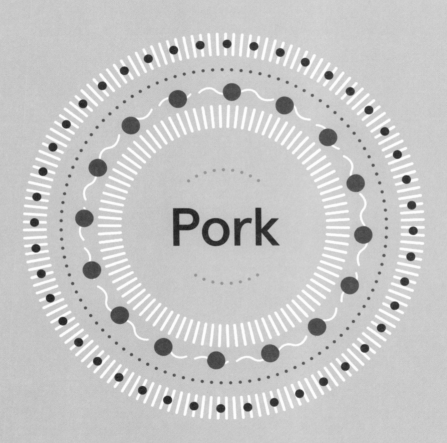

Pork

The Chinese consume more pork than any other nation and they have been eating it since around 5000 BC ... so it's fair to say they're rather good at cooking it. Their written word for 'home' involves fashioning a character that puts a 'roof' over a 'pig', and even today when you use a rural bathroom, chances are you'll be sharing it with an oinking swine.

Crisp roast pork belly

Serves 6 to 8 as part of a shared meal

Roasted pork, or siu yuk, is one of the most recognisable Asian foods the world over. We've all passed a Chinese restaurant and drooled at the glistening, burnished roasted cuts hanging from meat hooks in the window, ready to be weighed and consumed. Making your own roast pork at home isn't that hard — the trick is to make sure the pork skin is well and truly dry, which helps it to crisp and blister in the oven.

1.2 kg (2 lb 10 oz) piece boneless pork belly, skin on

1 tablespoon shaoxing rice wine

35 g (1¼ oz/¼ cup) sea salt

½ teaspoon five-spice

2 tablespoons vegetable oil

hoisin sauce, to serve

Place the pork belly on a chopping board, skin side down. Make two long, deep cuts (about 2 cm/¾ inch deep) into the meat across the width (this will help the flavours to absorb). Rub the rice wine all over the pork meat, but not the skin. Combine 1 teaspoon of the sea salt and the five-spice, then sprinkle it evenly over the pork, again making sure not to get any on the skin. Put the pork, skin side up, on a plate and rub the remaining sea salt over the skin. Place the pork in the fridge, uncovered, overnight. This helps the skin to dry out and crisp up when cooked.

Preheat the oven to 200°C (400°F/Gas 6). Wipe off the excess salt, then place the pork on a baking tray, skin side up, and bring back to room temperature. Rub the oil all over the pork. Using a skewer, pierce the skin all over. Place the pork in the oven and roast for 45 minutes.

Turn the oven grill (broiler) on, then place the pork under the hot grill and cook for 5–6 minutes, or until the skin is crisp (cooking time will depend on how close to the grill the pork is sitting), keeping a close eye on it, as it burns quickly. Remove to a chopping board, rest for 10 minutes, then slice and serve with hoisin sauce and steamed Asian greens.

Sticky pork in bean sauce with pancakes

Serves 4

Deep-fried pork, coated in sticky sauce then rolled in soft pancakes with thin strips of raw leek — nothing could be better. Baby leeks are best here as their flavour is mild, but spring onions (scallions) will also work at a pinch. This is a fabulous dish to make and set in the middle of the table for everyone to help themselves. And it goes perfectly with cold beer.

500 g (1 lb 2 oz) boneless pork loin, excess fat trimmed

1 baby leek, washed well, white part only, cut into matchsticks

750 ml (25½ fl oz/3 cups) vegetable oil

20 Mandarin pancakes (page 354)

Marinade

2 tablespoons light soy sauce

2 tablespoons water

1 tablespoon cornflour (cornstarch)

Sweet bean sauce

2 tablespoons sweet bean sauce

2 tablespoons light soy sauce

2 teaspoons sugar

1 tablespoon water

Cut the pork into 5 mm (¼ inch) slices. Stack three or four slices on top of each other and cut them into thin strips. Combine the marinade ingredients in a bowl, add the pork and toss to coat well, then set aside to marinate for 30 minutes. Combine the ingredients for the sweet bean sauce in another bowl and set aside. Place the leeks in a serving bowl.

Heat the oil in a large wok over a medium–high heat. Working in two batches, carefully lower the pork into the hot oil with a slotted spoon. Deep-fry for about 2 minutes, or until the pork is cooked through. Remove and drain on paper towel.

Pour off all but 2 tablespoons of oil from the wok, then return the wok to a medium heat. Add the sweet bean sauce, stir to heat through, then add the pork and toss for 2–3 minutes, or until evenly coated and well glazed. Place the pork in a serving bowl (or arrange both the leeks and pork on a large platter) and serve with the pancakes on the side. To eat, add some pork and leeks to the middle of a pancake, turn up the bottom edge to enclose the filling and roll up.

Pork with preserved mustard leaf and wine

Serves 6

This was a dish we ate in unhealthy quantities in Shaoxing, a city famous for its fermented and preserved foods and fragrant rice wine. They have a word there, mei, for an entire course of foods that involves preserved ingredients and tofu, and this is one such dish. Go to Shaoxing and you'll see preserved mustard leaf (sold in packets as 'potherb mustard') in aromatic, brown piles — it smells incredibly sweet and not unlike tobacco.

180 g (6½ oz) preserved mustard leaves

115 g (4 oz/½ cup) caster (superfine) sugar

100 ml (3½ fl oz) dark soy sauce

60 ml (2 fl oz/¼ cup) shaoxing rice wine

1.5 kg (3 lb 5 oz) piece boneless pork belly, skin on

Put the mustard leaves in a bowl, cover with water and soak for 5 minutes, then drain well and gently squeeze out as much liquid as possible.

Put the mustard leaves in a large claypot with the sugar, soy sauce, rice wine and 250 ml (8½ fl oz/1 cup) water. Using a large, sharp knife, cut the pork belly in half widthwise and place, skin side down, on top of the mixture in the pot. Place the claypot over a medium heat and bring the liquid to a simmer, then reduce the heat to very low, using a simmer pad if necessary, cover the pot and cook for 1 hour. Carefully turn the pork over, then cook for another 4 hours, turning the meat every hour. After 4 hours the pork should be very tender and positioned skin side up. Remove the pot from the heat and set aside to cool to room temperature, then refrigerate overnight.

The next day, remove the pork from the claypot and, using a sharp knife, cut it into neat 3 cm (1¼ inch) square pieces. Return the pork pieces to the claypot, cover and gently reheat the mixture over a low heat for 30–40 minutes. Serve immediately.

Taro and pork soup

Serves 4

Variations of this combination of ingredients are seen throughout China and Southeast Asia. The use of fermented tofu, available in jars from Asian grocers, gives the soup a deep, earthy taste that really shines through. Hearty and filling, it's perfect for the colder seasons.

400 g (14 oz) piece boneless pork belly, skin on, cut into 1.5 cm (½ inch) pieces

2 tablespoons light soy sauce

500 g (1 lb 2 oz) taro

2 tablespoons vegetable oil

1 tablespoon sugar

3 pieces red fermented tofu, plus 1 tablespoon of the tofu liquid

1.5 litres (51 fl oz/6 cups) chicken stock (page 405)

2 star anise

2 garlic cloves, finely sliced

2 spring onions (scallions), white and green parts finely sliced, kept separate

2 teaspoons cornflour (cornstarch)

1 large red chilli, finely sliced

Fill a saucepan with 2 litres (68 fl oz/8 cups) water and bring to the boil. Add the pork, then reduce the heat to medium–low and simmer for 10 minutes. Drain well. Combine the pork and soy sauce in a bowl and toss to coat, set aside for 20 minutes, then drain.

Peel the taro and cut into 1.5 cm (½ inch) pieces. Put the taro in a steamer over a wok or saucepan of boiling water, then cover and steam for about 20 minutes, or until tender.

Heat the oil in a large wok over a medium–high heat, add the pork and stir-fry for 5 minutes, or until evenly browned, then add the sugar and stir well. Transfer the pork to a bowl.

Put the tofu and liquid in a small bowl and mash together with a fork. Bring the stock to the boil in a large saucepan over a medium–high heat, then add the pork, mashed tofu, star anise, garlic, white spring onion and taro. Reduce the heat to medium–low and simmer for 30 minutes. Combine the cornflour with 60 ml (2 fl oz/¼ cup) water, add this to the soup and stir to combine; cook for another 2–3 minutes, or until thickened. Remove from the heat and serve in a soup tureen or individual bowls, with the green spring onion and chilli scattered over the top.

Photograph page 349

Pork hocks, ginger and eggs in sweet vinegar

Serves 6 to 8

Also called 'confinement pork', this dish is as much about the ginger as it is about the lip-smacking elasticity of the pork hocks and the sweet tang of black vinegar. It's a dish fed to new mothers for 'building blood' and 'warming'. Indeed, nutritionists have noted that ginger boosts blood circulation, and collagen (the pork cuts here are oozing it) supports tissue repair. Ultimately, though, it's just delicious.

500 g (1 lb 2 oz) young ginger, peeled

2 litres (68 fl oz/8 cups) sweet black rice vinegar (Pun Chun brand)

400 ml (13½ fl oz) black rice vinegar

2.5 kg (5½ lb) whole pork hocks with feet, cut through the bone into 5 cm (2 inch) pieces (ask your butcher to do this)

8 hard-boiled eggs, peeled

Cut the ginger into large pieces, then use the blade of a heavy cleaver to smash the ginger on a board to flatten the pieces as much as possible. Heat a large wok over a medium heat, then add the ginger and dry-fry, stirring often, for about 20 minutes, or until the ginger has dried out somewhat and is starting to turn a little brown around the edges.

Place the ginger in a saucepan, add half the sweet vinegar and all the black vinegar and bring to a simmer. Cook over a medium–low heat for 1½ hours, then remove the pan from the heat and cool the mixture to room temperature. Cover and leave overnight.

Transfer the mixture to a large saucepan and add the remaining sweet vinegar and the pork hocks, adding enough water to just cover the meat, if necessary. Bring the mixture to a gentle simmer, then cook over a low heat for 2 hours. Add the eggs, pushing them into the liquid, and cook for another 30 minutes. Serve with steamed rice and stir-fried green vegetables.

Steamed sweet red bean pork on sticky rice

Serves 6

Here's our attempt at a crazy dish we loved at a Sichuan country wedding and one that was entirely new to us — pork slices stuffed with red bean paste, steamed over sticky rice, then served sprinkled liberally with sugar. Yes ... sugar. In the mix with loads of spicy dishes and foods, its sweet succulence made for a great change of pace and taste. It's even better, arguably, made using pork belly. But, really, what isn't?

400 g (14 oz/2 cups) glutinous rice

1 kg (2 lb 3 oz) pork neck or boneless pork belly, in one piece, skin on

1.25 litres (42 fl oz/5 cups) chicken stock (page 405)

about 200 g (7 oz) red bean paste (page 412)

sugar, to serve

Wash the rice thoroughly in a sieve under cold running water, then tip into a bowl, cover with water and soak overnight. Drain well.

Place the pork in a saucepan large enough to hold it snugly. Add the stock and a little water to just cover the pork, if necessary. Bring the pork to a gentle simmer, then cook over a low heat for about 1 hour, or until cooked through. Leave to cool in the liquid, then drain well, reserving the cooking liquid for another use. Refrigerate the pork for 2 hours or overnight to firm it.

Meanwhile, place the rice in a steamer lined with a tea towel (dish towel). Place the steamer over a wok or saucepan of boiling water, then cover and steam for 20 minutes, or until the rice is just tender. Transfer the rice to a large heatproof bowl (one that will fit in your steamer).

Using a large, sharp knife, and cutting through the fat first, slice the pork as thinly as you can — the first slice should stop just short of cutting all the way through the pork and the second should cut all the way through, and so on, so you can create 'sandwiches' of the meat and bean paste. Working with one piece of sliced pork at a time, carefully spread a few teaspoons of bean paste over the inside of each double slice, then gently press the two slices of pork together to seal.

Arrange the stuffed pork slices, neatly overlapping, over the rice. Put the bowl in the steamer and place over a wok or saucepan of boiling water, then cover and steam for 40 minutes, or until the pork is tender. Sprinkle with sugar to taste, and serve.

Steamed minced pork with salted fish

Serves 4 as a light meal

*Cantonese food is, for the Chinese, considered the epitome. Of their eight recognised major culinary styles —
Guangdong (Cantonese), Shandong, Anhui, Hunan, Jiangsu, Fujian, Zhejiang and Sichuan — Cantonese cooking
is revered for its sophisticated, polished techniques, dainty presentation and refined flavours. But the cooking
does have a rustic, simple side too, as seen in this tasty home-style recipe that features pork and salted mackerel.
The salted fish may be a tad odoriferous uncooked but don't, whatever you do, skimp on it — it's absolutely vital
for depth of flavour in the final dish.*

6 dried shiitake mushrooms

100 g (3½ oz) salted mackerel cutlet

700 g (1 lb 9 oz) minced (ground) pork,
   not too lean

8 tinned water chestnuts, drained and finely
   chopped

2 spring onions (scallions), finely sliced

1 tablespoon soy paste

1 garlic clove, finely chopped

1 tablespoon shaoxing rice wine

2½ tablespoons cornflour (cornstarch)

sea salt and freshly ground black pepper

4 cm (1½ inch) piece ginger, peeled and finely
   shredded

Put the shiitake mushrooms in a small heatproof bowl, cover with boiling water and soak for 30 minutes,
or until softened. Drain well, squeeze dry, then very finely chop.

Rinse the mackerel cutlet, then cut it in half lengthwise along the bone. Very finely chop one half and slice
the other lengthwise into thin strips. In a large bowl, combine the mushrooms and finely chopped mackerel
with the pork, water chestnuts, spring onions, soy paste, garlic, rice wine and cornflour. Using your hands,
mix to combine well, then season with sea salt and pepper.

Divide the mixture among four lightly greased 300 ml (10 fl oz) heatproof bowls, smoothing the tops. Place
some fish strips and ginger on the top of each bowl, then cover tightly with foil. Put the bowls in a steamer
over a wok or saucepan of boiling water, then cover and steam for about 30 minutes, or until the juices run
clear when the pork is pierced in the middle with a skewer. Serve with steamed rice (page 412).

Red rice pork belly

Serves 6 to 8 as part of a shared meal

Red yeast rice is made by fermenting rice with a type of yeast called Monascus purpureus, *which gives the grains a ruby-red colour. This rice has long been used in China as a preservative, flavouring agent and a natural food colouring, and here it gives the pork its gorgeous ruddy hue. Sold as 'spareribs' in supermarkets, this cut of pork here is actually strips of belly.*

4 pieces red fermented tofu, plus 1 tablespoon of the tofu liquid

80 ml (2½ fl oz/⅓ cup) shaoxing rice wine

¾ teaspoon five-spice

2 tablespoons red yeast rice

80 ml (2½ fl oz/⅓ cup) vegetable oil

3 cm (1¼ inch) piece ginger, peeled and finely shredded

1.5 kg (3 lb 5 oz) pork belly on the bone, cut into 2.5 cm (1 inch) wide strips

500 ml (17 fl oz/2 cups) chicken and pork stock (page 405)

1½ tablespoons sugar

1 star anise

Put the tofu and liquid in a small bowl and mash together with a fork, then stir in the rice wine and five-spice. Using an electric spice grinder, grind the red yeast rice until a powder forms, then stir it into the tofu mixture. Set aside.

Heat half of the oil in a large claypot over a medium–low heat, then add the ginger and cook, stirring, for 2 minutes, or until fragrant. Remove the claypot from the heat. Heat the remaining oil in a large, non-stick frying pan over a medium–high heat, then add the pork and cook for 3 minutes on each side, or until golden. Put the pork in the claypot with the tofu mixture, add the stock, sugar and star anise, then return the pot to a medium heat and bring to a simmer. Reduce the heat to low, cover the pot and cook for 1½ hours, or until the pork is very tender.

Red rice pork belly; Oil-braised bamboo (page 127)

Cress and pork ball soup

Serves 4 as part of a shared meal

Soups play a big part in Chinese cuisine, from comforting, thick broths to light and flavoursome soups such as this one. This healthy soup is packed with watercress; it's meant to aid the respiratory system and is an excellent source of vitamin C and iron. If you like, you could swap the watercress for any green leafy vegetable — try Chinese broccoli (gai larn) or bok choy (pak choy) — or make the meatballs with beef instead of pork.

....

200 g (7 oz) bean thread (glass) vermicelli
   noodles

500 g (1 lb 2 oz) minced (ground) pork or beef

2 cm (¾ inch) piece ginger, peeled and finely
   chopped

½ teaspoon sugar

1½ tablespoons cornflour (cornstarch)

1 tablespoon shaoxing rice wine

1 egg, lightly beaten

sea salt and freshly ground black pepper

1.5 litres (51 fl oz/6 cups) chicken stock
   (page 405)

1 bunch watercress (about 400 g/14 oz),
   picked over, large stems discarded

....

Put the vermicelli noodles in a small heatproof bowl, cover with boiling water and soak for 5 minutes, or until softened, then drain. Using scissors, cut the noodles into smaller pieces.

Put the pork in a bowl with the ginger, sugar, cornflour, rice wine and egg, then season with sea salt and pepper and mix well. Wet your hands a little, then take small handfuls of the pork mixture and roll it into small balls, about the size of a walnut. As you complete each ball, place it on a tray lined with baking paper.

Bring the stock to a simmer in a saucepan over a medium heat, add the meatballs and cook for 5–7 minutes. In a separate saucepan, bring 2 litres (68 fl oz/8 cups) water to the boil, then add the watercress and cook for 1–2 minutes, or until wilted. Drain and cool under cold running water, then drain again. Divide the watercress and noodles among four soup bowls. Add some meatballs to each bowl, then ladle over the hot stock and serve.

Cress and pork ball soup: Wood ear fungus salad (page 75)

Rock sugar pork hock

Serves 4 as part of a shared meal

Red cooking is a method of slow braising that is famous in and around the region of Shanghai. The 'red' in the title comes from the pork hock being cooked in soy sauce and sugar (in this case, rock sugar). The slow cooking renders the pork so meltingly soft that you should be able to eat it with a pair of chopsticks. Whatever you do, make sure you eat the skin and fat — it's all part of the textural adventure.

1 x 1.8 kg (4 lb) pork hock
120 g (4½ oz) rock sugar
5 cm (2 inch) piece ginger, peeled and finely
    sliced

6 spring onions (scallions), roughly chopped
250 ml (8½ fl oz/1 cup) shaoxing rice wine
200 ml (7 fl oz) light soy sauce
200 ml (7 fl oz) black rice vinegar

Put the pork hock into a large, heavy-based saucepan and cover with cold water. Bring to the boil over a high heat, then reduce the heat to medium and simmer for 10 minutes. Drain the pork, rinse under cold water and drain again.

Pound the rock sugar in a mortar using the pestle, or wrap it in a tea towel (dish towel) and pound it with a rolling pin until roughly crushed. Return the hock to the cleaned saucepan, then add the sugar and the remaining ingredients. Top up with 750 ml (25½ fl oz/3 cups) water, or enough to just cover the pork. Bring to the boil over a high heat, then reduce the heat to medium–low and simmer for 2½–3 hours, skimming the fat off the surface every 30 minutes or as required, until the hock is fork tender (turn the pork over every 30 minutes to ensure it cooks evenly). Keep an eye on the liquid and top it up with water if it gets too low. Transfer the pork to a platter, strain over some of the braising liquid and serve with rice and a bowl of wok-fried greens.

Fish-flavoured pork

Serves 4

Just to make life confusing, there is actually no fish in the fish-flavoured pork; the origin of the name derives from the flavourings that were traditionally used in the preparation and cooking of fish. This dish may not have any fish, but what it does have are the hallmarks of Sichuanese food: pungent heat and satisfyingly savoury flavours.

500 g (1 lb 2 oz) pork tenderloin, cut into thin strips

50 g (1¾ oz) dried wood ear fungus

80 ml (2½ fl oz/⅓ cup) vegetable oil

3 garlic cloves, finely chopped

3–4 spring onions (scallions), finely sliced

3 cm (1¼ inch) piece ginger, peeled and finely chopped

2 red chillies, seeded and finely chopped

2–3 teaspoons sichuan chilli bean paste

80 g (2¾ oz/½ cup) tinned water chestnuts, roughly chopped

1 small bunch coriander (cilantro), leaves roughly chopped

Marinade

1 tablespoon clear rice wine

1 tablespoon water

2 tablespoons light soy sauce

1½ tablespoons cornflour (cornstarch)

Sauce

60 ml (2 fl oz/¼ cup) clear rice wine

1 tablespoon clear rice vinegar

80 ml (2½ fl oz/⅓ cup) light soy sauce

2 tablespoons sugar

1 tablespoon sesame oil

250 ml (8½ fl oz/1 cup) water

To make the marinade, combine the ingredients in a large bowl. Add the pork and mix well, then cover and marinate for 30 minutes. Put the wood ear fungus in a small heatproof bowl, cover with boiling water and soak for 30 minutes, or until softened, then drain. Remove any hard bits from the wood ears and tear into large pieces. To make the sauce, combine the ingredients in a bowl and set aside.

Heat 2 tablespoons of the oil in a large wok over a medium–high heat until just smoking. Add the pork in two batches and cook for 2–3 minutes, or until just cooked. Remove to a plate and set aside.

Wipe the wok clean with paper towel, then return the wok to a medium–high heat. Add the remaining oil, then add the garlic, spring onions, ginger and chillies and fry for 30 seconds, or until fragrant. Add the chilli bean paste, water chestnuts and wood ears and toss to combine. Add the pork and the sauce, thoroughly combine and bring to a simmer. Divide among four bowls, garnish with the coriander and serve.

Photograph page 203

White-cut pork with garlic sauce

Serves 4 to 6

Another punchy Sichuan dish but this time potent with garlic, not spice. It's easy to make (you just need to cook the meat the day before, then chill and slice it finely) but depends, for optimum success, on the best pork money can buy. Choose a cut with a good ratio of fat to lean: belly, shoulder or neck all work well. It rightly needs some skin in the equation too, as the contrasting textures of melting fat, soft meat and slightly chewy skin, all cut through with a hot jolt of garlic sauce, are nothing short of sublime.

1 kg (2 lb 3 oz) piece boneless pork belly, skin on

coriander (cilantro) sprigs, to serve (optional)

Sugared peanuts

80 g (2¾ oz/½ cup) small, raw red-skinned peanuts

1 tablespoon sugar

Garlic sauce

1 large head garlic, cloves peeled and coarsely chopped

2½ tablespoons light soy sauce

1½ tablespoons caster (superfine) sugar

2 tablespoons clear rice vinegar

To make the sugared peanuts, preheat the oven to 180°C (350°F/Gas 4). Put the peanuts on a baking tray and roast for 15 minutes, or until golden, then cool. Rub off some of the skins — you don't need to be too fastidious, but get rid of the skins from about half of the peanuts. Combine the peanuts with the sugar in a food processor and, using the pulse button, coarsely chop. Set aside.

To make the garlic sauce, combine the garlic, soy sauce, sugar and vinegar in a food processor and process until a smooth purée forms. Thin with 2–3 teaspoons water if necessary — the sauce should have a thick, flowing consistency.

Put the pork belly in a saucepan large enough so the pork can lie completely flat, then add enough water to just cover. Place over a medium heat and bring to a gentle simmer. Reduce the heat to low and cook the pork at a bare simmer for 2–2½ hours, or until very tender — do not let it simmer hard or the meat will be tough. Remove the pan from the heat and leave the pork to cool in the liquid. Drain the pork well, reserving the liquid for another use if you like, then wrap the pork in plastic wrap and refrigerate. The pork can be cooked up to 2 days in advance.

When ready to serve, use a large, sharp knife to cut the pork as evenly and thinly as you can, slicing the pork against the grain. Arrange the cut pieces neatly on a platter (reserve any less than perfect pieces or scraps for a salad or some other use). Drizzle some of the garlic sauce over the pork and scatter over some of the sugared peanuts and coriander sprigs, if using. Serve immediately, with the remaining garlic sauce and peanuts on the side.

Photograph page 238

From left to right: Chilli-peanut cucumbers (page 59); White-cut pork with garlic sauce (page 237); Cold noodles with sesame sauce and chicken (page 312); Sichuan radish salad (page 75)

Steamed black bean pork ribs

Serves 4 to 6 as part of a shared meal

No doubt you'll recognise this tasty steamed dish from yum cha restaurants. Guangzhou is the home of this leisurely breakfast/brunch tradition and we've eaten our way around the city according to its best dim sum venues. Hands down our favourite is Liu Hua Zhou Cheng, a 24-hour place inside a park off Renmin North Road. Full of locals, who position themselves outdoors among the trees and around the fish pond, it's the best place we know on earth to sit and scoff steamed dumplings, buns, chickens' feet, egg tarts and black bean pork ribs until we simply can't move.

750 g (1 lb 11 oz) short pork spareribs

2 tablespoons fermented black beans, rinsed

3 garlic cloves, crushed

2½ tablespoons light soy sauce

2½ teaspoons caster (superfine) sugar

1½ tablespoons clear rice wine

2 teaspoons sesame oil

2 tablespoons cornflour (cornstarch)

2 tablespoons chicken and pork stock (page 405)

Cut the pork ribs between the bones into 3 cm (1¼ inch) pieces. Put the pork pieces in a heatproof bowl, then add the remaining ingredients and use your hands to mix everything together. Cover the bowl with plastic wrap and refrigerate for 2–3 hours.

Remove the plastic wrap and cover the bowl tightly with foil. Place the bowl in a steamer over a wok or saucepan of boiling water, then cover and steam for 1–1½ hours, or until the meat is tender. Transfer the ribs to a platter and serve.

Hunan red-braised spareribs

Serves 4 as part of a shared meal

This dish is a nod to the red-braised pork belly made famous by Hunan's own Chairman Mao. They say he loved it so much he had his Hunanese chefs regularly cook it for him in Beijing. Although traditionally it's cooked with pork belly, we think a good-sized rack of ribs works equally as well.

2 kg (4 lb 6 oz) piece American-style pork
    spareribs

Glaze
60 ml (2 fl oz/¼ cup) vegetable oil
110 g (4 oz/½ cup) sugar
125 ml (4 fl oz/½ cup) shaoxing rice wine
125 ml (4 fl oz/½ cup) light soy sauce

5 cm (2 inch) piece ginger, unpeeled and
    finely sliced
2 star anise
12 dried red chillies
2 pieces cassia bark

Preheat the oven to 180°C (350°F/Gas 4). To make the glaze, heat the oil and sugar in a large ovenproof saucepan (large enough to fit the ribs) over a medium heat until the sugar melts, then increase the heat to high and swirl the pan until the sugar caramelises and turns a deep brown colour — be careful once it starts to caramelise, as it burns easily. Reduce the heat to medium, then add 750 ml (25½ fl oz/3 cups) water, the rice wine, soy sauce (be careful as the liquid may bubble up), ginger, star anise, chillies and cassia and bring to the boil. Remove the pan from the heat and add the ribs, cutting them in half if necessary to fit in the pan.

Place the pan in the oven and cook for 2 hours, turning the ribs over every 30 minutes or so and basting them with the glaze, until tender. When cooked, the meat should pull away from the bone easily; if not, continue cooking for another 15–20 minutes. Remove from the oven, slice between the bones into individual ribs, and serve.

Black vinegar and sweet bean glazed spareribs (variation)

Make the recipe as above, but replace the star anise, dried chillies and cassia with 100 ml (3½ fl oz) black rice vinegar and 100 ml (3½ fl oz) sweet bean sauce.

Soy-braised pork belly

Serves 4 to 6 as part of a shared meal

This dish represents a bit of creative licence on our part, as it's loosely based on any number of braised pork belly dishes we ate around China. Long, slow cooking renders belly fat chopstick-tender (don't even think about trimming the fat off) and the skin turns wonderfully lip-smacking and soft.

2½ tablespoons peanut oil

1 kg (2 lb 3 oz) boneless pork belly, skin on, cut into 4 cm (1½ inch) pieces

1 litre (34 fl oz/4 cups) chicken and pork stock (page 405)

5 cm (2 inch) piece ginger, unpeeled and finely sliced

8 spring onions (scallions), cut into 5 cm (2 inch) lengths

2½ tablespoons dark soy sauce

2½ tablespoons shaoxing rice wine

75 g (2¾ oz/⅓ cup) sugar

1 star anise

sea salt and freshly ground black pepper

Heat the oil in a large saucepan over a medium–high heat until just starting to smoke. Add the pork and stir-fry for 2–3 minutes, or until lightly browned, then add the stock, ginger, spring onions, soy sauce, rice wine, sugar and star anise. Bring to the boil, then reduce the heat to medium–low and simmer, uncovered, for 1½–2 hours, or until the pork is very tender (you should be able to cut the meat with a fork), skimming the fat off the surface every 30 minutes or so.

Remove the pan from the heat and strain the mixture into a bowl, reserving the liquid. Cover the pork with foil and set aside. Return the liquid to the pan and bring to a steady boil over a high heat for 10–12 minutes, or until the liquid has reduced to about 250 ml (8½ fl oz/1 cup) and is thick and syrupy. Return the pork to the pan, stir to coat with the sauce and warm through. Season to taste with sea salt and pepper and serve with steamed rice (page 412).

Pork stir-fried with king oyster mushrooms

Serves 4 to 6 as part of a shared meal

We are convinced that king oyster mushrooms were purely created with stir-frying in mind. Their meaty texture and full-on fungi flavour means they don't get lost in the vigorous cooking process. We ate a dish similar to this in Shanghai, and there it was intensely heavy and sweet from bean sauce and probably lots of sugar too, but even then the mushrooms didn't get swamped. You really must use king oysters for this recipe.

550 g (1 lb 3 oz) piece pork scotch fillet
400 g (14 oz) king oyster mushrooms
80 ml (2½ fl oz/⅓ cup) vegetable oil
1 tablespoon finely shredded ginger
2½ tablespoons chicken stock (page 405)

1 tablespoon hoisin sauce
1 tablespoon shaoxing rice wine
1 teaspoon sugar
2 teaspoons light soy sauce
2 teaspoons dark soy sauce

Cut the pork into slices about 1 cm (½ inch) thick, then cut the slices into strips about 1 cm (½ inch) wide. Cut the oyster mushrooms into 1 cm (½ inch) slices and set aside.

Heat 1½ tablespoons of the oil in a wok over a high heat, then add the pork and stir-fry for 3 minutes, or until nearly cooked through. Remove the pork and any juices to a bowl.

Return the wok to a medium–high heat, add the remaining oil, then add the mushrooms and ginger and stir-fry for about 4 minutes, or until the mushrooms are nearly cooked. Add the remaining ingredients and bring the liquid to a simmer, then cook for 3–4 minutes, or until the liquid has reduced and thickened and the mushrooms look glossy. Return the pork and juices to the wok and cook, tossing the wok often, for about 2 minutes, or until the pork is cooked through. Serve immediately.

Stir-fried pork, peanuts and tofu

Serves 4 to 6 as part of a shared meal

This little combo is our simple ode to some of our favourite ingredients, flavours and textures. Firstly, there's pork — no, wait … that should read PORK!! — then there's tofu, which, in any of its multitudinous guises (many of which are sadly unavailable outside of China) we consider to be one of the most versatile substances around. Then there are peanuts — crunchy, savoury and nutty. Fresh wood ears are wonderful too, but substitute soaked dried ones if fresh are not available.

1 tablespoon light soy sauce

2 teaspoons dark soy sauce

2 teaspoons caster (superfine) sugar

1½ tablespoons shaoxing rice wine

1 tablespoon oyster sauce

1 large pork fillet (about 465 g/1 lb), trimmed

2½ tablespoons peanut oil

2 garlic cloves, finely chopped

100 g (3½ oz) wood ear fungus, torn in half if large

150 g (5½ oz) firm tofu, cut into batons

1½ teaspoons cornflour (cornstarch)

2 tablespoons chicken stock (page 405) or water

50 g (1¾ oz/⅓ cup) raw, skinned peanuts, roasted (page 413)

Put the soy sauces, sugar, rice wine and oyster sauce in a bowl and stir to combine well. Set aside.

Slice the pork across the grain into pieces about 5 mm (¼ inch) thick. Heat half of the oil in a wok over a medium–high heat, then add the pork and stir-fry for 2 minutes, or until the pork is light golden but not quite cooked through. Remove to a bowl.

Heat the remaining oil in the wok, add the garlic and wood ears and stir-fry for 2 minutes, then add the tofu and cook for 1–2 minutes, or until the tofu is heated through. Add the soy sauce mixture and the pork (with any juices) and toss to combine.

Combine the cornflour and stock in a small bowl and mix to form a smooth paste. Add the cornflour mixture and peanuts to the wok and gently toss to combine. Cook, stirring occasionally, for 1 minute, or until the liquid thickens and the pork is cooked through. Transfer to a warmed platter or large bowl and serve.

Lion's head meatballs

Serves 4

So called because the bok choy (pak choy) looks like a lion's mane and the meat looks like ... well, you can work that out. Don't be fooled into thinking these are just another meatball; the texture of these is incredible. They're a specialty in and around Shanghai where they are variously cooked in stock, as here, or in a more rugged red-cooked mixture (soy, sugar, shaoxing wine). By rights you should make your own mince by hand-chopping the best quality, fatty pork you can find — after 30 minutes of chopping with two cleavers the meat will be fluffy, creamy and soft — but using good quality, not-too-lean minced pork gives delicious results too (and you can then work that with cleavers if you want, to lighten your meatballs the cheat's way).

500 g (1 lb 2 oz) minced (ground) pork

60 g (2 oz/⅓ cup) chopped, tinned water chestnuts

1 egg, beaten

1½ teaspoons shaoxing rice wine

2 teaspoons oyster sauce

2 teaspoons light soy sauce

2 teaspoons finely chopped ginger

1 garlic clove, finely chopped

2½ tablespoons cornflour (cornstarch)

8 heads baby bok choy (pak choy), trimmed and halved lengthwise

Cooking liquid

1 litre (34 fl oz/4 cups) chicken and pork stock (page 405)

60 ml (2 fl oz/¼ cup) light soy sauce

2 teaspoons sugar

Combine the pork, water chestnuts, egg, rice wine, oyster sauce, soy sauce, ginger, garlic and cornflour in a bowl and stir to combine. Use your hands to knead the mixture for 5 minutes, or until slightly elastic. Divide the pork mixture into four even portions and form each portion into a large ball.

To make the cooking liquid, combine all the ingredients in a saucepan large enough to hold all the meatballs in a single layer, and bring to a gentle simmer. Add the meatballs and bring the liquid back to a gentle simmer, then cover and cook over a medium heat for 10 minutes, turning the balls over once.

Add the halved bok choy to the pan, then cover and cook for another 15 minutes, or until the meatballs are cooked through and the bok choy is tender. Divide the liquid, meatballs and bok choy among four large bowls and serve immediately.

Pork in bamboo leaves

Serves 4 as part of a shared meal

The historical beauty of China is breathtaking and nowhere is this more evident than in Anchang, an old village just west of Shaoxing, in Zhejiang Province. To our delight this area is also a food gem. It's famous for its dried fermented sausages and sausage makers fill casings in the street and hang the sausages from their ceilings to cure and dry. Canal-side eating houses are where you can sit and eat the wonderful hairy crab, when in season, and your body weight of pork wrapped in bamboo leaves.

8 dried bamboo leaves

1 kg (2 lb 3 oz) boneless, skinless pork belly (ask your butcher to remove the skin, or see the step below)

125 ml (4 fl oz/½ cup) dark soy sauce, plus a little extra for drizzling

2 tablespoons shaoxing rice wine

2 garlic cloves, finely chopped

5 cm (2 inch) piece ginger, peeled and finely chopped

Bring a large saucepan of water to the boil, then reduce the heat to low, add the dried bamboo leaves and simmer for 10–15 minutes, or until softened. Drain, refresh under cold water, and pat dry with paper towels.

If your pork has skin on it, place the pork on a chopping board, skin side down. Slide a sharp knife between the skin and fat and slowly (while holding one corner of the skin) cut your way along the skin, trying not to cut into the fat. Discard the skin. Cut the pork belly across the grain into eight equal pieces.

Put the soy sauce, rice wine, garlic and ginger in a bowl (large enough to fit the pork) and stir to combine. Add the pork and massage the marinade into each piece, then cover with plastic wrap and refrigerate for 2–3 hours.

Fold each bamboo leaf in half lengthwise. Wrap each piece of pork in a bamboo leaf, then tie up firmly with kitchen string. Place the pork parcels on a rimmed, heatproof plate. Put the pork in a large steamer over a wok or saucepan of boiling water, then cover and steam for 20–25 minutes, or until the pork is cooked through. Remove, reserving any juices on the plate, and let the pork rest for 5 minutes, then unwrap the bamboo and place the opened parcels on a serving plate. Pour over the juices, drizzle with a little extra soy sauce and serve.

Pearly meatballs

Serves 4 as part of a shared meal

A stone's throw away from our hotel in Changsha in Hunan is the rather popular restaurant, Huogongdian, apparently frequented by a young Mao Zedong. The waitresses there wheel around trolleys with the most amazing assortment of steamed, fried, braised and smoked local foods, but what really caught our eye were these beautifully crafted meatballs coated in glutinous rice.

200 g (7 oz/1 cup) glutinous rice

6 dried shiitake mushrooms

2 spring onions (scallions), green part only, finely chopped

2 tablespoons potato starch

100 g (3½ oz) raw prawn (shrimp) meat, finely chopped

6 tinned water chestnuts, finely chopped

250 g (9 oz) minced (ground) pork

1 tablespoon finely chopped ginger

1 tablespoon shaoxing rice wine

1 egg, lightly beaten

2 teaspoons sesame oil

sea salt and freshly ground black pepper

Wash the rice thoroughly in a sieve under cold running water, then tip into a bowl, cover with water and soak overnight. Drain well.

Put the shiitake mushrooms in a small heatproof bowl, cover with boiling water and soak for 30 minutes, or until softened. Drain well, then finely chop the mushrooms and combine with the spring onions and soaked rice in a bowl. Set aside.

Combine the potato starch in a small bowl with 1 tablespoon water and stir until smooth. Put the prawn meat in a bowl with the water chestnuts, pork, ginger, rice wine, egg, sesame oil and potato starch mixture. Season with sea salt and pepper, then mix well to combine.

Wet your hands a little, then take small handfuls of the pork mixture and roll it into small balls, about the size of a walnut. Roll each ball in the rice mixture to coat evenly and place on an oiled plate. Working in batches if necessary, put the plate in a steamer over a wok or saucepan of boiling water, then cover and steam for 10–12 minutes, or until the meat is cooked through and the rice is tender. Serve immediately.

Salt and pepper spareribs

Serves 4 as part of a shared meal

The dry-roasting of the peppercorns and salt is a key process in the flavouring of these spareribs, but to lift them even higher in the flavour stakes, the ribs are also marinated and then twice-fried. You can buy the small, meaty ribs from your Asian butcher. The recipe for the spiced salt and pepper makes more than you'll need here; store the leftover mixture in an airtight container for next time.

1 tablespoon shaoxing rice wine

1 tablespoon light soy sauce

2 tablespoons cornflour (cornstarch)

600 g (1 lb 5 oz) short pork spareribs, cut into individual ribs

1 litre (34 fl oz/4 cups) vegetable oil

Spiced salt and pepper

1 tablespoon black peppercorns

40 g (1½ oz/⅓ cup) sea salt

To make the spiced salt and pepper, dry-roast the peppercorns in a small, heavy-based frying pan over a medium–low heat, shaking the pan often, for 3–4 minutes, or until fragrant. Cool, then transfer to a mortar (or an electric spice grinder) and pound with a pestle to form a powder. Return the pan to a medium heat and add the salt. Stir constantly for about 5 minutes, or until the salt starts to turn golden. Remove from the heat and cool, then add to the ground peppercorns.

In a large bowl, combine the rice wine, soy sauce and cornflour with 2–3 tablespoons water to form a paste. Add the spareribs and evenly coat them in the mixture.

Heat the oil in a large, heavy-based saucepan to 180°C (350°F), or until a cube of bread dropped into the oil turns deep golden in 15 seconds. Add the spareribs in two batches and deep-fry for 1–2 minutes, or until lightly browned. Remove and drain on paper towel.

Reheat the oil to 200°C (400°F), or until a cube of bread dropped into the oil turns deep golden in 5 seconds (be careful as the oil is very hot). Add the spareribs in two batches and deep-fry until evenly browned and cooked through — remove a rib from the wok and slice the meat to see if it is cooked through. Remove, drain on paper towel, and serve with the spiced pepper and salt on the side.

Twice-cooked pork

Serves 6 as part of a shared meal

This is Sichuanese in style, and represents simple Chinese cookery at its best. The pork is first simmered whole until tender, then sliced and seared in a hot wok to give it a charred, smoky flavour. The key to getting even slices is to make sure the pork is cold after the first stage of cooking, as it will have firmed up.

800 g (1 lb 12 oz) piece boneless pork belly, skin on

1½ tablespoons shaoxing rice wine

1 tablespoon sichuan chilli bean paste

2 tablespoons sweet bean sauce

2 teaspoons sugar

1 tablespoon fermented black beans, rinsed

80 ml (2½ fl oz/⅓ cup) chicken stock (page 405)

about 2½ tablespoons vegetable oil

5 spring onions (scallions), cut into 3 cm (1¼ inch) lengths

3 garlic cloves, finely sliced

2 teaspoons finely chopped ginger

Place the pork in a saucepan large enough to hold it snugly, then cover with cold water. Slowly bring to a simmer over a medium–low heat, then cook for 40–50 minutes, depending on the thickness of the pork, or until just cooked through. Leave the pork to cool in the liquid, then drain well. Wrap the pork in plastic wrap and refrigerate for 2 hours, or overnight. Cut the pork lengthwise into 3 cm (1¼ inch) pieces, then cut across the grain into 5 mm (¼ inch) thick slices.

Combine the rice wine, chilli bean paste, sweet bean sauce, sugar, black beans and stock in a bowl and stir to combine well, then set aside.

Heat 1 tablespoon of the oil in a wok over a medium–high heat, add half the pork and stir-fry for about 5 minutes, or until golden, then remove to a plate using a slotted spoon. Add another tablespoon of oil to the wok and cook the remaining pork; remove to the plate using a slotted spoon.

If necessary, add the remaining oil to the wok (there should be enough oil remaining from the pork) and cook the spring onions, garlic and ginger for 2 minutes, or until the spring onions are lightly browned. Add the rice wine mixture and pork and toss to combine well, then cook for another 2–3 minutes, or until everything is heated through and the pork is evenly coated in the syrup.

Lamb & Beef

'If you like good food, cook it yourself,' penned the famous seventeenth-century playwright Li Liweng, and we like his thinking. Some of the simplest Chinese dishes to cook at home are the rugged, hearty ones from far-flung regions, where the meat is flavoursome, the spices are strong and the cooking methods (simmering, braising and steaming) are most forgiving.

Sesame seed beef

Serves 4

The Chinese affection for sesame seeds knows no bounds. You find them on and in all sorts of cakes, biscuits and desserts, and it's not just in sweet dishes where they shine. Here their nutty crunch is a perfect match for the beef — just watch the cooking heat and times, as overcooked sesame seeds will, naturally, ruin your dish.

500 g (1 lb 2 oz) beef eye fillet, trimmed of any fat

2 teaspoons sea salt

90 g (3 oz/½ cup) rice flour

155 g (5½ oz/1 cup) sesame seeds

2 eggs, beaten

1 litre (34 fl oz/4 cups) vegetable oil

chilli oil (page 407), or ready-made, to serve

Cut the beef across the grain into 1 cm (½ inch) thick slices, then season with the sea salt. Put the rice flour and sesame seeds on separate plates, and put the eggs into a bowl. Working with one slice at a time, dip the beef into the flour, shaking off the excess, then dip it into the beaten egg, allowing the excess to drain off. Finally, dip it into the sesame seeds, turning to coat well and pressing the sesame seeds onto the beef. Repeat for all the beef, placing each slice on a tray lined with baking paper as you complete it. Refrigerate for 3 hours or overnight to help the sesame coating stick to the beef.

Heat the oil in a large wok over a medium–high heat until just beginning to smoke (if the oil is too hot the sesame seeds will burn). Add the beef in small batches and deep-fry for about 2 minutes, then turn the slices over and fry for another minute, or until evenly browned and just cooked through. Remove and drain on paper towel, then cover and keep warm near the stovetop while you cook the next batch. Serve with a small bowl of chilli oil for dipping.

Sesame seed beef; Vinegared potato shreds (page 92)

Xi'an lamb soup with pickled garlic

Serves 6 to 8

Stock

1.8 kg (4 lb) lamb bones

2 kg (4 lb 6 oz) lamb shoulder on the bone

8 slices unpeeled ginger

1 onion, chopped

1 carrot, chopped

3 star anise

2 teaspoons cumin seeds

3 teaspoons sichuan peppercorns

2½ teaspoons fennel seeds

1 piece cassia bark

2 black cardamom

125 ml (4 fl oz/½ cup) clear rice wine

Soup

12 dried wood ear fungus

20 g (¾ oz/½ cup) dried lily buds

100 g (3½ oz) bean thread (glass) vermicelli

6 buns (page 340), 2 days old

60 ml (2 fl oz/¼ cup) vegetable oil

2 tablespoons light soy sauce

1 tablespoon clear rice wine

1½ tablespoons black rice vinegar

2 teaspoons sesame oil

3 spring onions (scallions), finely sliced

fresh chilli paste (page 406), to serve

pickled garlic, to serve (page 409)

To make the stock, put the lamb bones in a large stockpot, then add the shoulder and the remaining stock ingredients. Add 5 litres (169 fl oz/20 cups) water or enough to just cover the shoulder. Bring to a simmer, skimming off any fat, and weighting the shoulder down with an inverted plate and a heavy pan. Cook for 3 hours over a low heat, or until the meat is nearly falling off the bone. Remove the shoulder from the pot and cool slightly, then remove the meat in large pieces. Return the bones to the pot and cook the stock for another 3–4 hours. Skim the stock, then strain it through a colander lined with muslin (cheesecloth), discarding the solids. Let the stock settle, then skim off any fat. The stock can be made up to 2 days in advance. If making it in advance, cool to room temperature, then transfer to a container and refrigerate.

Cut the lamb into thin slices. Place in a large frying pan with 500 ml (17 fl oz/2 cups) of the stock, bring to a simmer, then cover and keep hot over a low heat.

To make the soup, put the wood ear fungus and lily buds in separate heatproof bowls, cover each with boiling water and soak for 30 minutes, then drain. Tear each wood ear into three or four pieces. Cut any hard tips off the lily buds and discard. Place the vermicelli noodles in a large heatproof bowl, cover with boiling water and soak for 5 minutes, or until softened, then drain. Tear or cut the buns into small pieces.

Heat the vegetable oil in a stockpot over a medium heat, then add the wood ears, lily buds and noodles and stir to combine well. Add the remaining stock, the soy sauce, rice wine, vinegar and sesame oil and bring to a simmer. Stir in the bread pieces and strain the stock from the lamb slices into the soup. Divide the soup among large bowls, then arrange the lamb slices neatly on top. Scatter over the spring onions and spoon over some chilli paste. Serve with the pickled garlic on the side.

Crisp lamb ribs with cumin, spring onions and chillies

Serves 4 to 6 as part of a shared meal

Lamb ribs are considered a secondary cut; they are relatively cheap and easy to find at Asian butchers or in some supermarkets. The ribs have a high fat ratio, but that's exactly why they are so delicious. Crisp and charred, and packed with heat and spice, these ribs are perfect with steamed rice and a bowl of fresh chilli paste for slathering. And, as for the fat, just do as the Chinese do and embrace it! Repeat after us: 'Embrace the fat. Embrace the fat.'

2 egg whites

60 ml (2 fl oz/¼ cup) clear rice wine

30 g (1 oz/¼ cup) cornflour (cornstarch)

2 teaspoons sea salt

1 tablespoon freshly ground black pepper

2 kg (4 lb 6 oz) lamb ribs, cut into individual ribs

30 g (1 oz/¼ cup) cumin seeds

125 ml (4 fl oz/½ cup) vegetable oil

20 dried red chillies, or to taste

4 spring onions (scallions), finely sliced

1 tablespoon sesame oil

fresh chilli paste (page 406), to serve

Put the egg whites in a large bowl with the rice wine, cornflour, sea salt and pepper and whisk until well combined. Add the lamb ribs and turn to coat, then cover and refrigerate for 1 hour. Bring back to room temperature before cooking. Lightly pound the cumin seeds using a mortar and pestle, then set aside.

Heat 2 tablespoons of the oil in a large wok over a medium–high heat, add half the lamb ribs and cook for 10 minutes, turning frequently, or until browned all over, then reduce the heat to medium and cook for another 12–15 minutes. Transfer to a plate, cover and keep warm. Repeat with another 2 tablespoons of oil and the remaining lamb ribs.

Wipe out the wok and return it to a medium–high heat. Add the remaining oil, then the cumin seeds and chillies and cook for about 1 minute, or until the spices are fragrant and the chillies are slightly charred. Add the spring onions and stir-fry for 1 minute, then add the lamb ribs and stir-fry for another 2–3 minutes, or until everything is well combined and the lamb is hot. Remove the wok from the heat, season the ribs with sea salt and drizzle over the sesame oil. Serve with chilli paste and steamed rice (page 412).

Crisp lamb ribs with cumin, spring onion and chillies; Spicy Xi'an carrot and daikon (page 123)

Taiwanese beef rice

Serves 4

We know, we know ... Taiwan isn't strictly 'China' in any geopolitical sense, but we love this simple, tasty dish so much we couldn't leave it out. This easy recipe can be simplified even more by using ready minced (ground) beef — and pork mince works well too. To make your own pork mince, for this or other recipes, use neck or boneless shoulder meat for the best flavour and texture.

700 g (1 lb 9 oz) beef scotch fillet or sirloin, trimmed
60 ml (2 fl oz/¼ cup) vegetable oil
1 tablespoon finely chopped ginger
2 garlic cloves, finely chopped
1 onion, sliced
1 large carrot, sliced
80 ml (2½ fl oz/⅓ cup) soy paste

2 tablespoons oyster sauce
2 tablespoons clear rice wine
1½ tablespoons caster (superfine) sugar
2 tablespoons black rice vinegar
1 star anise
½ teaspoon five-spice
500 ml (17 fl oz/2 cups) beef stock (page 404)
2 teaspoons cornflour (cornstarch)

Finely slice the beef, then, using two cleavers or a large knife, chop the beef on a heavy chopping board until it has the texture of coarse mince.

Heat half of the oil in a saucepan over a medium heat, then add the ginger, garlic, onion and carrot and cook, stirring often, for 7–8 minutes, or until the onion is soft.

Meanwhile, heat the remaining oil in a wok or large frying pan over a high heat. Add the beef and cook, stirring with a wooden spoon to break up the meat, for 4–5 minutes, or until it changes colour. Add the beef and any juices to the vegetables in the pan, then add all the remaining ingredients, except the cornflour. Bring to a simmer over a low heat and cook for 30 minutes.

Combine the cornflour with 1 tablespoon water in a small bowl and stir to form a paste, then add to the beef mixture, stirring constantly until the mixture starts to simmer and thicken. Remove from the heat and serve with steamed rice (page 412).

Chargrilled spicy lamb

Serves 4

One of our abiding memories of Xi'an is the shambolic charm of the Muslim Quarter, where you can poke your nose into bakeries, watch butchers hack into freshly slaughtered carcasses and observe young chefs stretch slippery lengths of dough into impossibly long biang biang mian, *or 'belt noodles', so unique to this city. But one memory remains the strongest and that is of the intoxicating aromas of chargrilled lamb, chilli and cumin wafting through the air, tempting us with some of the most sensationally tasty meat we've ever eaten.*

2.2 kg (5 lb) lamb shoulder on the bone
6 garlic cloves, finely chopped
30 g (1 oz/¼ cup) cumin seeds, freshly ground

2½ tablespoons chilli flakes, or to taste
about 125 ml (4 fl oz/½ cup) peanut oil
sea salt

Place the lamb on a rimmed plate large enough to fit snugly in a large steamer. Put the plate in the steamer over a wok or saucepan of boiling water, then cover and steam the lamb for 2–2½ hours, or until well cooked (you may need to top up the water in the wok from time to time). Remove the lamb from the steamer and set aside to cool to room temperature.

In a large bowl, combine the garlic, cumin, chilli flakes and enough oil to make a thin paste. Alternatively, put the whole garlic cloves, cumin, chilli flakes and oil in a small food processor and process until combined. Tear the cooked lamb shoulder into large chunks, about 6 cm (2½ inches), discarding any large pieces of fat. Add the lamb to the paste and toss to coat well.

Heat a chargrill pan or barbecue grill over a medium–high heat, add the lamb, season with sea salt and cook for 8–10 minutes, turning occasionally, or until the lamb is browned and crisp all over. Arrange the lamb on a platter and serve.

Photograph page 267

From left to right: Spring onion pancakes (page 345); Coriander salad (page 104); Garlic cucumbers (page 59); Chargrilled spicy lamb (page 265); sliced tomatoes sprinkled with sugar

Hunan orange beef

Serves 6 as part of a shared meal

Subtropical Hunan Province sits on the southern side of the mighty Yangtze River and has spawned one of China's most famous cuisines, Xiang cuisine. Little wonder, as the area is exceedingly fertile, producing more rice than any other province and comes second in producing the most pork, beef and lamb. Although often lumped in with the food of nearby Sichuan, its cooking is rather distinct, with over 4000 unique dishes. Orange beef epitomises the region's cuisine beautifully, incorporating chillies, ginger and citrus. Traditional recipes use dried orange or tangerine peel, but we've added a modern twist by using fresh orange.

....

1 kg (2 lb 3 oz) flank steak, trimmed

1 teaspoon sea salt

2 egg whites

1½ tablespoons cornflour (cornstarch)

2½ tablespoons dark soy sauce

2 tablespoons clear rice wine

2 tablespoons sweet bean sauce

2 teaspoons sesame oil

finely grated zest and juice of 1 orange

1 tablespoon sugar

1 litre (34 fl oz/4 cups) vegetable oil

12 dried red chillies

3 cm (1¼ inch) piece ginger, peeled and finely chopped

3 garlic cloves, finely chopped

2 spring onions (scallions), finely sliced

3 celery stalks, finely sliced on the diagonal

....

Slice the beef across the grain into 5 mm (¼ inch) thin slices. Place in a large bowl with the sea salt, egg whites and cornflour and mix thoroughly. Cover the bowl with plastic wrap and place in the fridge to marinate for 1–2 hours. Bring back to room temperature before cooking.

To make the sauce, combine 60 ml (2 fl oz/¼ cup) water in a bowl with the soy sauce, rice wine, sweet bean sauce, sesame oil, orange juice and sugar. Mix well and set aside.

Heat the oil in a wok over a medium–high heat. When the oil starts to smoke, reduce the heat to medium, add the beef in batches and fry for 2–3 minutes. Remove and drain on paper towel. Increase the heat to high, return the beef to the wok in batches and cook for another 2–3 minutes, or until crisp. Remove and drain on paper towel.

Pour off all but 2 tablespoons of oil from the wok. Return the wok to a medium–high heat, add the chillies and fry for 1 minute, or until they darken, then add the orange zest, ginger, garlic, spring onions and celery; fry for another 1–2 minutes, or until aromatic. Pour the sauce into the wok, bring to the boil, then reduce the heat to medium, add the beef and heat through. Serve with steamed rice (page 412).

Hunan orange beef; Garlic stems with speck (page 115)

Stir-fried lamb with leeks and coriander

Serves 4 to 6

We love the old-world, gruff charm of Kao Rou Ji restaurant in Beijing's Houhai precinct. This gorgeous area is right on the lake and although it has been hijacked somewhat by souvenir shops and pizza joints, it still speaks of a time when life was a little less polished and a lot less Westernised. The dining room is filled with the smells of cumin and lamb and barbecued meat and this dish reminds us of being there.

700 g (1 lb 9 oz) boneless lamb leg, trimmed of excess fat

2 tablespoons cornflour (cornstarch)

1 teaspoon cumin seeds

1½ tablespoons dark soy sauce

60 ml (2 fl oz/¼ cup) clear rice wine

2 leeks, white part only

80 ml (2½ fl oz/⅓ cup) vegetable oil

3 garlic cloves, crushed

2 cm (¾ inch) piece ginger, peeled and finely shredded

2 teaspoons sugar

1 tablespoon light soy sauce

1½ tablespoons black rice vinegar

1 bunch coriander (cilantro), leaves and stems coarsely chopped

Using a sharp knife, cut the lamb across the grain into very thin slices. Place in a large bowl with the cornflour, cumin seeds, dark soy sauce and 2 tablespoons of the rice wine. Use your hands to gently toss everything together, then cover the bowl with plastic wrap and refrigerate for 2 hours. Bring back to room temperature before cooking.

Cut the leeks in half lengthwise and wash well, then cut the halves on the diagonal into thin strips. Heat half of the oil in a large wok over a medium–high heat, then add the leeks and garlic and cook, stirring constantly so the leeks don't turn brown, for 2–3 minutes, or until softened slightly. Remove to a bowl.

Add the remaining oil to the wok and increase the heat to high, then add the lamb, using kitchen tongs to open the slices out so they cook evenly (as best as you can). Cook the lamb, stirring often, for 2–3 minutes, or until all the slices have changed colour. Add the remaining ingredients (reserving a handful of coriander leaves), the leeks and the remaining rice wine and cook, stirring, for about 2 minutes, or until well combined and heated through. Divide among bowls, scatter over the reserved coriander and serve immediately.

Stir-fried lamb with leeks and coriander; Sesame buns (page 344)

Braised beef with daikon and chu hou sauce

Serves 6 as part of a shared meal

This classic southern stew of beef braised with chu hou *and daikon is home-style cooking at its best. The luscious, sticky bits of meat and sweet nubs of daikon taste even better reheated in the sauce the next day, once the flavours have had a chance to develop. Chu hou sauce is a 200-year-old invention from Foshan, near Guangzhou. Named after the chef who first concocted it, it's a sweet, hoisin-based braising sauce with an aromatic, spiced edge. The Cantonese might use brisket — you can too.*

1 kg (2 lb 3 oz) oyster blade steak

125 ml (4 fl oz/½ cup) vegetable oil

4 garlic cloves, smashed

6 slices unpeeled ginger

125 ml (4 fl oz/½ cup) shaoxing rice wine

100 ml (3½ fl oz) chu hou sauce

2 tablespoons dark soy sauce

2 tablespoons light soy sauce

1½ star anise

1 black cardamom

1 cinnamon stick

2 pieces red fermented tofu, mashed with 1 tablespoon of the tofu liquid

2 tablespoons chopped rock sugar

800 ml (27 fl oz) beef stock (page 404)

1 daikon (white radish) (about 600 g/1 lb 5 oz), cut into 3 cm (1¼ inch) pieces

1 tablespoon cornflour (cornstarch)

Cut the beef into 5 cm (2 inch) pieces. Heat the oil in a wok over a high heat, then add half of the beef and cook, turning occasionally, for 4–5 minutes, or until browned. Using a slotted spoon, remove to a large saucepan. Repeat with the remaining beef, then discard the oil from the wok.

Add all the remaining ingredients to the pan, except the daikon and cornflour, adding a little extra stock or water if needed, to just cover the beef. Bring the mixture slowly to a simmer over a low heat, skimming any fat off the surface as needed. Partially cover the pan with a lid and cook over a low heat for 2 hours, skimming occasionally, or until the beef is tender. Add the daikon, pushing it under the surface of the liquid, then cover the pan and cook for another 20–30 minutes, or until the daikon is tender.

Combine the cornflour with 60 ml (2 fl oz/¼ cup) water in a small bowl and stir to form a smooth paste. Add to the beef mixture and cook, stirring, for 2–3 minutes, or until the sauce boils and thickens slightly. Serve immediately with steamed rice (page 412).

Oxtail soup

Serves 4

You couldn't get more rustic, rural and hearty than this soup, a simple broth with incredible depth of flavour. After long, slow cooking the oxtail is deliciously beefy and sticky — you have to suck the meat off the bones, but by all means pull the meat off the bones, shred it, then add it to the soup. Eat this with bowls of steamed rice and pickled vegetables, and perhaps some chunks of pumpkin (winter squash) cooked down to an intensely flavoursome purée in nothing but some oil and its own juices.

800 g (1 lb 12 oz) oxtails, cut into 4 or 5 pieces (ask your butcher to do this)

5 cm (2 inch) piece ginger, peeled and finely chopped

500 g (1 lb 2 oz) desiree or other all-purpose potatoes, skins scrubbed and cut into 2 cm (¾ inch) pieces

4 tomatoes, roughly chopped

2 large carrots, cut into 2 cm (¾ inch) pieces

sea salt and freshly ground black pepper

Rinse the oxtail pieces in cold water. Put the oxtail in a large saucepan, add 2.5 litres (85 fl oz/10 cups) water (or enough to cover) and bring to the boil over a high heat. Reduce the heat to medium–low and simmer for 30 minutes, skimming the fat off the surface every 10 minutes, or as required. Remove the saucepan from the heat and transfer the oxtail to a plate. Skim the stock again, then strain it through a colander lined with muslin (cheesecloth).

Clean the saucepan and return the oxtail and stock to the pan over a low heat. Add the ginger, then cover and simmer for 3½ hours, or until the oxtail is tender. You may need to add a little more water during the simmering process.

Add the potatoes, tomatoes and carrots to the pan. Cover and simmer for a further 40 minutes, or until the vegetables are tender. Season to taste with sea salt and pepper. Remove the oxtail and cool slightly (if you like, pull the meat off the bones). Divide the meat and vegetables among four large bowls, ladle over the stock and serve.

Simmered lamb shanks

Serves 6

Here we head north to Dongbei, to the Manchuria of old. This vast region, northeast of Beijing, has a distinctive cuisine, thanks to an incredibly harsh climate, some interesting neighbours (Russia and Korea) and some great local produce. Stews and braises, often involving hefty pieces of meat, are common, with game and lamb popular. Typically the shanks are served with accompaniments such as pickled cabbage and steamed breads, but we like them with roast potatoes, even though this is slightly cross-regional.

6 frenched lamb shanks

2 tablespoons vegetable oil

4 garlic cloves, finely sliced

10 cm (4 inch) piece ginger, unpeeled and finely sliced

2 star anise

2 pieces cassia bark

2 tablespoons light soy sauce

2½ tablespoons dark soy sauce

60 ml (2 fl oz/¼ cup) clear rice wine

2½ tablespoons black rice vinegar

sea salt and freshly ground black pepper

2 teaspoons sesame oil

2 spring onions (scallions), green part only, finely sliced

First blanch the lamb. Bring a large saucepan of water to the boil, add the lamb shanks and bring back to the boil, then immediately drain the lamb into a colander and set aside.

Heat a large, heavy-based saucepan or stockpot over a medium–high heat. Add the oil, garlic and ginger and stir-fry for about 30 seconds, or until fragrant. Add the star anise, cassia, soy sauces, rice wine and vinegar, season with sea salt and pepper, then stir to combine. Add the lamb shanks, then pour in 1.5 litres (51 fl oz/6 cups) water, or enough to cover the lamb. Bring to the boil, then reduce the heat to medium–low and simmer gently for 1½ hours, or until tender. Test by inserting a skewer or fork into the lamb; if the meat pulls away easily, it is ready.

Transfer the lamb to a platter, reserving the cooking stock in the pan. Cover the lamb with foil and keep warm. Bring the cooking stock to the boil and reduce by half, to intensify the flavour. Pour a little stock over the lamb (the remaining stock can be frozen and used for other purposes), drizzle with the sesame oil and scatter the spring onions over the top.

Simmered lamb shanks; Roasted cumin and chilli potatoes (page 118); Dongbei cabbage salad (page 119)

Fragrant braised beef tendons

Serves 4 as part of a shared meal

OK squeamish types, close your eyes and think 'texture'. Tendons, which are essentially pure cartilage, have the ability to suck in the flavours of the aromatic ingredients they're cooked with, as well as impart their own distinctive beefy savour to a dish. We personally love their unctuous qualities; when cooked, they're jelly-like, soft and rich. Rather like fat, really, but without the fat — in fact, we think they're the 'new pork belly'. You heard it here first, folks.

1 kg (2 lb 3 oz) beef tendons (from an Asian butcher)

1 teaspoon sichuan peppercorns

60 ml (2 fl oz/¼ cup) vegetable oil

3 garlic cloves, finely chopped

2 cm (¾ inch) piece ginger, peeled and finely chopped

2 red chillies, finely sliced

1 tablespoon sichuan chilli bean paste

1½ tablespoons shaoxing rice wine

1½ tablespoons light soy sauce

2 spring onions (scallions), finely sliced

sea salt and freshly ground black pepper

1 small handful coriander (cilantro) leaves, to serve

1 small handful watercress sprigs, to serve

Put the beef tendons in a large saucepan, add 2 litres (68 fl oz/8 cups) water (or enough water to cover) and bring to a simmer. Reduce the heat to low and simmer for 3–3½ hours, or until the beef is tender, topping up the water as required. Drain the tendons, leave to cool, then cut into slices about 4 cm (1½ inches) long.

Dry-roast the peppercorns in a small, heavy-based frying pan over a medium–low heat, shaking the pan often, for 3–4 minutes, or until fragrant. Cool, then transfer to a mortar (or an electric spice grinder) and pound with the pestle to form a coarse powder. Set aside.

Heat the oil in a large wok over a high heat, add the garlic, ginger and chillies and stir-fry for 1–2 minutes, or until fragrant. Add the beef tendons, ground peppercorns and chilli bean paste and stir to combine, then add the rice wine, soy sauce and spring onions and stir-fry for 2–3 minutes, or until well combined and heated through. Season with sea salt and pepper. Transfer to a platter, scatter over the coriander leaves and watercress and serve.

Beef ribs with vinegar and honey dates

Serves 6

Around thirty years ago, beef was so scarce and expensive in China that any dish cooked with it was known as a 'millionaire's meal'. For better or worse, with steadily increasing wealth, the demand for meat of all types is rising. Here's our contribution to the Chinese beef lexicon, a synthesis of all the long-simmered, lip-smacking flavours we love. Use vinegar labelled as 'aged' from Shanxi if you can find it, otherwise just use regular Chinese black vinegar.

1 litre (34 fl oz/4 cups) vegetable oil

1.25 kg (2 lb 12 oz) beef ribs, cut into 4 cm (1½ inch) pieces (ask your butcher to do this)

250 ml (8½ fl oz/1 cup) aged black rice vinegar (such as shanxi vinegar)

185 ml (6 fl oz/¾ cup) light soy sauce

125 ml (4 fl oz/½ cup) shaoxing rice wine

750 ml (25½ fl oz/3 cups) beef stock (page 404)

1½ star anise

1 black cardamom

8 slices unpeeled ginger

1 piece cassia bark

100 g (3½ oz/½ cup lightly packed) soft brown sugar

12 dried honey dates

Heat the oil in a large wok over a medium–high heat. Add the ribs in three batches and cook for 5–6 minutes, turning as necessary, or until browned all over. Remove and drain on paper towel.

Place the ribs in a large saucepan, then add all the remaining ingredients, pushing the pieces of meat down to submerge them. Bring slowly to a simmer, skimming any fat off the surface as necessary, then cook over a low heat for about 2 hours, or until the meat is just starting to fall off the bones. Serve the beef ribs with steamed rice (page 412).

Photograph pages 278–9

From left to right: Chinese cabbage with mustard (page 109); Beef ribs with vinegar and honey dates (page 277); Spicy buckwheat noodles (page 297)

Water-boiled beef

Serves 4 to 6

In Chinese this dish is called shui zhu niu rou. Shui zhu *refers to a technique called 'water cooking' where thin, tender pieces of meat are cooked in a stock enlivened with lots of sichuan chilli bean paste (rabbit, fish, sliced pork or tripe are also cooked this way). Even by Sichuanese standards, this dish is spicy — in restaurants there it's served with dozens and dozens of dried chillies bobbing on the surface. This recipe has been tempered a little for Western palates ... but it's still hot.*

3 teaspoons sichuan peppercorns
800 g (1 lb 12 oz) beef scotch fillet, in one piece
½ teaspoon sea salt
1½ tablespoons shaoxing rice wine
2½ tablespoons vegetable oil
12–15 dried red chillies

80 ml (2½ fl oz/⅓ cup) sichuan chilli bean paste, or to taste
800 ml (27 fl oz) chicken stock (page 405)
1 tablespoon dark soy sauce
1 tablespoon cornflour (cornstarch)

Dry-roast the peppercorns in a small, heavy-based frying pan over a medium–low heat, shaking the pan often, for 3–4 minutes, or until fragrant. Cool, then transfer to a mortar (or an electric spice grinder) and pound with the pestle to form a coarse powder. Set aside.

Trim the beef of all fat and sinew, then use a sharp knife to cut it across the grain into thin slices. Combine in a bowl with the sea salt and rice wine, using your hands to mix well, then set aside.

Heat the oil in a wok over a medium–high heat until just beginning to smoke, then add the dried chillies and cook, tossing the wok, for 2–3 minutes, or until the chillies are blistered all over. Remove using a slotted spoon, leaving the oil in the wok. When the chillies have cooled a little, coarsely chop them.

Reheat the oil in the wok over a medium–high heat, add the chilli bean paste and cook, stirring, for 1 minute, or until fragrant. Add the stock and soy sauce and bring to the boil.

Combine the cornflour with 2 tablespoons water in a small bowl and mix well. Add to the beef mixture, using your hands to mix well. Add the beef to the boiling liquid in the wok and, using chopsticks, move the beef around in the liquid to separate the slices. Cook for 3 minutes, or until the liquid returns to the boil and the beef is just cooked. Transfer to a large serving bowl and scatter over the ground peppercorns and chopped chillies.

Photograph page 203

Beef, red onion and black bean stir-fry

Serves 4 to 6 as part of a shared meal

Stir-frying is a real art and requires a very grunty gas supply, plus knowing how to harness and moderate it — if you've ever seen wok cooks at work in Asia or in a local restaurant, you'll know what we mean. Achieving good results at home is possible; the trick is to have everything prepped and ready to go. Here's one of our favourite stir-fries, made with beef and red onion, but feel free to add or swap other vegetables — broccoli florets, chopped and seeded tomatoes or capsicum (pepper) — for the onion.

....

500 g (1 lb 2 oz) beef scotch fillet or skirt steak, trimmed

1 tablespoon light soy sauce

2 tablespoons shaoxing rice wine

3 teaspoons cornflour (cornstarch)

3 cm (1¼ inch) piece ginger, peeled and very finely chopped

2 garlic cloves, crushed

2½ teaspoons sesame oil

2½ tablespoons oyster sauce

1 tablespoon dark soy sauce

2 tablespoons fermented black beans, rinsed

80 ml (2½ fl oz/⅓ cup) peanut oil

2 large red onions, cut into 2 cm (¾ inch) pieces

....

Cut the steak across the grain into strips about 3 mm (⅛ inch) thick. Combine the light soy sauce, half the rice wine, the cornflour, ginger and garlic in a large bowl and whisk well. Add the beef to the bowl and use your hands to toss the meat in the marinade. Set aside.

Combine the sesame oil, oyster sauce, dark soy sauce, black beans and 60 ml (2 fl oz/¼ cup) water in a bowl and stir to combine well. Set aside. Heat half of the peanut oil in a wok over a medium–high heat, then add the onions and stir-fry for 4–5 minutes, or until the onions are softened and a little charred. Remove to a bowl. Heat the remaining oil in the wok over a high heat until just beginning to smoke, then add the beef mixture and stir-fry for 2 minutes, or until the beef is browned all over. Return the onion to the wok and add the oyster sauce mixture. Cook, tossing the wok, for 1 minute, or until heated through, then serve.

Beef shin steamed in fragrant rice powder

Serves 4 to 6

We've provided an easy recipe for the rice powder needed for this dish, but you can buy it ready-to-go if you prefer — just make sure you get the one called zhen *(steam)* rou *(meat)* fen *(rice) and not the cosmetic version that goes on your face! We've used beef shins here, but it's arguably even better made with slices of pork, especially our fatty favourite — pork belly. For a spicier version, you can marinate the meat in a few tablespoons each of chilli bean paste, light soy and shaoxing wine, with a couple of teaspoons of sugar.*

2 boneless beef shins (about 1 kg/2 lb 3 oz), trimmed

2 tablespoons dark soy sauce

2 teaspoons sugar

3 teaspoons sesame oil

ready-made pickled mustard greens, to serve

ready-made chilli paste, to serve

Rice powder

100 g (3½ oz/½ cup) long-grain rice

100 g (3½ oz/½ cup) glutinous rice

1 teaspoon five-spice

Cut the beef shins across the grain into 5 mm (¼ inch) thick slices. Combine the soy sauce, sugar and sesame oil in a large bowl, add the meat and use your hands to coat the meat in the mixture. Cover the bowl with plastic wrap and refrigerate for 3–4 hours or overnight.

To make the rice powder, combine the long-grain and glutinous rice in a heavy-based frying pan over a medium–low heat and cook, shaking the pan often, for about 20 minutes, or until the rice is a light golden colour and smells nutty. Remove the rice from the pan and cool. Transfer the cooled rice to an electric spice grinder and grind to a coarse powder. Alternatively, you can do this using a large mortar and pestle. Place in a bowl and stir in the five-spice.

Drain the beef well, reserving the marinade. Working with one piece of beef at a time, coat each piece well in the rice powder, reserving the left-over powder. Drizzle half of the reserved marinade over the base of a large rimmed plate (that will fit snugly into a large steamer or will sit on a rack in a large wok). Arrange the beef on the plate, then combine the remaining marinade with 80 ml (2½ fl oz/⅓ cup) water and drizzle over the meat. Sprinkle 3–4 tablespoons of the reserved rice powder over the meat. Place the plate in the steamer over a wok or saucepan of boiling water, then cover and steam for 1 hour, or until the beef is tender and the rice coating is cooked through (you may need to top up the water in the wok from time to time). Serve with steamed rice (page 412), pickled mustard greens and chilli paste.

Braised beef cheeks with ginger and rock sugar

Serves 6 as part of a shared meal

Here we've applied Chinese flavours to what has become a fashionable cut of meat in the West. Being a secondary cut, the cheeks — which are indeed the facial muscles of a cow — need long, slow cooking to render them deliciously tender. Technically classed as offal, beef cheeks are highly perishable, so need to be cooked when very fresh. You may need to order them in advance from the butcher.

1.2 kg (2 lb 10 oz) beef cheeks (4 cheeks)

rice flour, for dusting

60 ml (2 fl oz/¼ cup) vegetable oil

2 red chillies, seeded and finely sliced

5 cm (2 inch) piece ginger, unpeeled and sliced

70 g (2½ oz) light brown rock sugar or soft brown sugar

2 pieces cassia bark

1½ star anise

6 garlic cloves, peeled

125 ml (4 fl oz/½ cup) light soy sauce

125 ml (4 fl oz/½ cup) shaoxing rice wine

about 1 litre (34 fl oz/4 cups) beef stock (page 404)

40 g (1½ oz/¼ cup) sesame seeds, toasted (page 413)

Coat the beef cheeks well in the rice flour, shaking off the excess. Heat the oil in a large, heavy-based frying pan over a medium–high heat, then add the beef in two batches and cook for 3–4 minutes on each side, or until well browned. Transfer to a large saucepan.

Add all the remaining ingredients, except the sesame seeds, to the pan, adding a little extra stock or water if needed, to just cover the beef cheeks. Bring to a simmer, skimming the surface to remove any impurities, then reduce the heat to low and simmer for 2½ hours, skimming occasionally, or until the beef cheeks are tender. Remove from the pan and cut into slices. Serve with rice noodles or steamed rice (page 412) and sprinkle with the sesame seeds.

Twice-fried cumin beef

Serves 6 as part of a shared meal

Skirt steak, not to be confused with flank, is cut from the front belly region of the cow, near the brisket. It is probably not the world's most tender cut, but what it does have is flavour in spades, which is needed here for this spicy treatment. Use sirloin, scotch or fillet if you prefer.

1 kg (2 lb 3 oz) skirt steak, finely sliced

60 ml (2 fl oz/¼ cup) shaoxing rice wine, plus extra to taste

2 tablespoons dark soy sauce, plus extra to taste

30 g (1 oz/¼ cup) cornflour (cornstarch)

1 litre (34 fl oz/4 cups) peanut oil

2 tablespoons finely chopped ginger

2 tablespoons finely chopped garlic

3 small red chillies, seeded and finely chopped

1 tablespoon chilli flakes

1 tablespoon ground cumin

1 tablespoon sesame oil

4 spring onions (scallions), green part only, finely sliced

Put the beef in a large bowl, then add the rice wine, soy sauce and cornflour and stir until well combined. Set aside.

Heat the peanut oil in a large wok over a high heat until just beginning to smoke, then add half the beef and cook for 2–3 minutes, stirring to separate the pieces, until evenly browned. Remove the beef with a slotted spoon and drain on paper towel. Repeat with the remaining beef.

Pour off all but 2 tablespoons of oil from the wok. Return the wok to a medium heat, then add the ginger, garlic, chillies, chilli flakes and cumin and stir for about 1 minute, or until fragrant. Return the beef to the wok (at this stage you can add more rice wine and soy sauce, to taste) and stir until the beef is hot and everything is well combined. Stir in the sesame oil and remove from the heat. Transfer the beef to a large bowl, scatter the spring onions over the top and serve.

Simmered oxtail

Serves 4 as part of a shared meal

The Chinese regularly champion what many other food cultures regard as 'lesser' cuts of meat. Oxtail may not top everyone's list, but personally we adore it. Served with a plate of steamed greens and plenty of rice, this is a perfect dish for casual feasting. You can easily double this recipe, refrigerate what you don't eat and the next day extract the meat from the bones and you've got a fantastic filling for Mandarin pancakes (page 354).

1 kg (2 lb 3 oz) oxtail, cut into 4 cm (1½ inch) pieces (ask your butcher to do this)

60 ml (2 fl oz/¼ cup) vegetable oil

3 spring onions (scallions), white part only, finely sliced

2 cm (¾ inch) piece ginger, finely chopped

3 garlic cloves, finely chopped

2 star anise

1 tablespoon sweet bean sauce

60 ml (2 fl oz/¼ cup) light soy sauce

1 litre (34 fl oz/4 cups) beef stock (page 404)

1 teaspoon sesame oil, or to taste

Put the oxtail in a heavy-based saucepan and cover with cold water. Bring to the boil, then reduce the heat to low and simmer for 2½ hours, or until tender, skimming off the fat as required. Remove from the heat and drain in a colander.

Heat the vegetable oil in a large wok over a medium–high heat, then add the spring onions, ginger and garlic and stir-fry for 2–3 minutes, or until fragrant. Add the star anise, sweet bean sauce, soy sauce, stock and oxtail. Bring to the boil, then reduce the heat to medium and simmer for 20–30 minutes, or until the liquid has reduced and glazes the oxtail. Sprinkle with sesame oil, to taste, and serve.

Noodles
&
Rice

The mighty Yangtze River, which roughly bisects China in half, delineates the country into two distinct culinary regions. These are the wheat-eating north (home to noodles that are legendarily diverse in shape, raw materials and methods of construction) and the south, where rice (glutinous and non, steamed and fried, as rice flour and grain) is king.

Wonton noodle soup

Serves 4

Many is the market we've walked around and watched, in complete awe, as the fresh dumpling makers ply their craft. What takes mere mortals an hour of painstaking folding takes them the seeming blink-of-an-eye, as they smear a small dab of filling over a corner of a wrapper, then deftly fold (or, in some cases, artfully scrunch) the dumplings into life. This recipe makes more wontons than you will need for four serves, so add more wontons if you like or increase the quantities of the soup to serve six — or simply freeze any leftover for next time.

Pork and prawn wontons

3 dried shiitake mushrooms

250 g (9 oz) raw prawn (shrimp) meat, chopped

200 g (7 oz) minced (ground) pork, not too lean

1 garlic clove, very finely chopped

6 tinned, drained water chestnuts, finely chopped

2 spring onions (scallions), very finely chopped

1 tablespoon light soy sauce

1 tablespoon shaoxing rice wine

sea salt and ground white pepper

60 square wonton wrappers (not frozen)

Noodle soup

250 g (9 oz) fresh, thin wheat noodles

1.5 litres (51 fl oz/6 cups) chicken stock (page 405)

4 heads baby bok choy (pak choy), trimmed and halved lengthwise

To make the pork and prawn wontons, put the shiitake mushrooms in a small heatproof bowl, cover with boiling water and soak for 30 minutes, or until softened. Drain well, squeeze very dry, then finely chop. Put the mushrooms, prawn meat, pork, garlic, water chestnuts, spring onions, soy sauce and rice wine in a food processor and process until a sticky paste forms. Season with sea salt and white pepper.

Place a teaspoon of filling in the centre of a wonton wrapper, then use your finger to dampen around the edge with a little water. Fold the wrapper in half to form a rectangle (make sure the edges are neat and aligned) and press to seal. Bring the two folded corners together and press firmly to seal. Place the completed wontons on a lightly floured tray. Bring a large saucepan of salted water to the boil. Add the wontons in batches and cook for 4–5 minutes, or until they rise to the surface and are cooked through. Drain well and set aside.

To make the noodle soup, cook the noodles in a saucepan of boiling water for 2–3 minutes (or according to the packet instructions), or until softened, then drain well.

Bring the stock to the boil in a large saucepan, add the bok choy, then cover and simmer for 2–3 minutes, or until cooked through. Add the cooked wontons to the stock to heat through. Divide the noodles, bok choy and wontons among four large bowls, pour over the hot stock and serve immediately.

Mung bean jelly noodles

Serves 4 to 6

These aren't so much 'noodles' as 'noodle-like'. They're made by cooking mung bean starch until it becomes a translucent goop, which is then left to set until it's firm enough to be cut, grated or sliced into pieces. Called liang fen (literally 'cold powder') in Chinese, these are usually served cold (although sometimes stir-fried in chunks) and usually teamed with sharp, pungent flavours such as vinegar, chilli and sichuan peppercorns. They are, we promise, WAY more delicious than we've probably made them sound.

85 g (3 oz/⅔ cup) mung bean starch

2 teaspoons sichuan peppercorns, or to taste

2 tablespoons peanut oil

1½ tablespoons fermented black beans, rinsed

3 teaspoons finely chopped ginger

3 garlic cloves, finely chopped

2 tablespoons sichuan chilli bean paste

1 tablespoon sugar

2 tablespoons light soy sauce

2½ tablespoons black rice vinegar

1 tablespoon sesame oil

2 spring onions (scallions), green part only, finely shredded

crisp, fried soybeans or roasted, salted peanuts, to serve

Bring 875 ml (29½ fl oz/3½ cups) water to a simmer in a saucepan over a low heat. Meanwhile, combine the mung bean starch with 125 ml (4 fl oz/½ cup) water in a bowl and stir until smooth. Whisking constantly to avoid lumps forming, add the starch paste to the simmering water and whisk vigorously for 2–3 minutes, or until the mixture is well combined and very thick. Cook, stirring often, for another 3–4 minutes. Rinse a 26 x 14 cm (10¼ x 5½ inch) dish with cold water, shaking out the excess water, then quickly pour the hot starch mixture into the dish. Cool to room temperature, cover the dish with plastic wrap and refrigerate for 2–3 hours, or until well chilled and very firm.

Dry-roast the peppercorns in a small, heavy-based frying pan over a medium–low heat, shaking the pan often, for 3–4 minutes, or until fragrant. Cool, then transfer to a mortar (or an electric spice grinder) and pound with the pestle to form a coarse powder. Set aside.

Heat the peanut oil in a wok over a medium heat, then add the black beans, ginger and garlic and stir-fry for about 2 minutes, or until fragrant. Add the chilli bean paste, sugar, soy sauce, vinegar and sesame oil and stir for 1–2 minutes, or until the sugar has dissolved. Remove from the heat and cool to room temperature.

Turn the mung bean jelly out of the dish onto a chopping board and cut into quarters. Working with one piece at a time and slicing along a long side, cut the jelly as thinly as you can to form flat, noodle-like ribbons. Pile the jelly noodles on a platter, spoon the black bean dressing over the top, then scatter with the spring onions, fried soybeans and ground peppercorns. Serve immediately.

Sa cha noodles

Serves 4

Here's a surprise from Fujian: a noodle dish with a sauce not too far removed from Malaysian satay! Stroll down Xiamen's Zhongshan Road, with its myriad dining options, and you'll see locals eating these 'sand tea' noodles from paper takeaway cartons, slurping up the distinctive spicy, peanutty sauce. You can choose from a number of meaty inclusions — chicken, liver, seafood and the like. We like seafood the best in ours. For optimal results, make the sa cha *sauce from scratch, rather than buying the ready-made version.*

500 g (1 lb 2 oz) small squid

2 tablespoons vegetable oil

310 ml (10½ fl oz/1¼ cups) sa cha sauce (page 408)

1 litre (34 fl oz/4 cups) chicken stock (page 405)

800 g (1 lb 12 oz) fresh, wide rice noodles

500 g (1 lb 2 oz) raw king prawns (shrimp), peeled, leaving tails intact, and cleaned

250 g (9 oz) fried tofu puffs, sliced

180 g (6½ oz/2 cups) mung bean sprouts

3 spring onions (scallions), finely sliced on the diagonal

1 small handful coriander (cilantro) leaves

To clean the squid, gently pull the tentacles away from the tube (the intestines should come away at the same time). Remove the intestines from the tentacles by cutting under the eyes, then remove the beak if it remains in the centre of the tentacles by using your fingers to push up the centre. Reserve the tentacles. Pull the transparent cartilage from inside the body and remove. Clean out the inside of the tube. Hold the tube under running water and peel the skin off; the wings can also be used. Place the cleaned squid tubes on a chopping board and cut the tube into thin rings.

Heat the oil in a large saucepan over a medium heat. Add the sa cha sauce and cook, stirring, for 1–2 minutes, or until fragrant. Add the stock and bring to a simmer, stirring constantly to combine the sauce and stock. Cover the pan and simmer for 5 minutes. Meanwhile, place the rice noodles in a large heatproof bowl and cover with boiling water.

While the noodles are soaking, add the prawns, tofu, squid rings and tentacles to the simmering stock in the pan and cook for 3 minutes, or until the seafood is just cooked through. Add the bean sprouts.

Drain the noodles and divide among four large bowls. Divide the seafood mixture among the bowls, scatter over the spring onions and coriander and serve immediately.

Prawn and fish congee

Serves 6

Mmmmm ... congee. This is our go-to dish when we feel under the weather; there's just something about its soothing texture, that kick of ginger and stomach-lining goodness that cures whatever ails us. Some find this 'bland' and if that's you, then try adding some chopped preserved Chinese vegetables or some pungent century egg. The great thing about congee is it can be a blank canvas for whatever ingredients you have on hand — use chicken or vegetables here instead of the seafood or just eat this plain, with your toppings of choice.

200 g (7 oz/1 cup) medium-grain rice, washed

1 kg (2 lb 3 oz) raw large king prawns (shrimp), peeled, cleaned and cut into 2 cm (¾ inch) pieces

400 g (14 oz) skinless snapper fillets, cut into 2 cm (¾ inch) pieces

peanut oil, for deep-frying

60 g (2 oz) egg wonton wrappers, cut into 5 mm (¼ inch) wide strips

2 tablespoons finely shredded ginger

2 spring onions (scallions), finely sliced

1 large handful coriander (cilantro) leaves, chopped

Marinade

1 tablespoon shaoxing rice wine

1 teaspoon very finely chopped ginger

2½ teaspoons light soy sauce

1½ teaspoons caster (superfine) sugar

2½ teaspoons peanut oil

2½ teaspoons clear rice vinegar

½ teaspoon salt

large pinch of ground white pepper

Combine the rice and 3.75 litres (126½ fl oz) water in a large saucepan and bring to the boil. Reduce the heat, partially cover with the lid, then gently simmer over a low heat for 1½–2 hours, or until the rice is very soft and the mixture has the consistency of thin porridge — you may need to add a little more water.

To make the marinade, combine all the ingredients in a large bowl, stirring to dissolve the sugar. Add the prawns and snapper and toss gently to combine well. Cover the bowl with plastic wrap and refrigerate until ready to use.

Fill a wok one-third full of oil and heat to 180°C (350°F), or until a cube of bread dropped into the oil turns deep golden in 15 seconds. Working in batches, add the strips of wonton wrappers to the hot oil and fry for 20 seconds, or until golden, then remove with a slotted spoon and drain well on paper towel.

Add the ginger, half the spring onions and most of the coriander (reserving some for garnish) to the rice mixture and stir to combine. Bring to a simmer, then add the seafood mixture and cook, stirring, over a medium heat for 2 minutes, or until the seafood is just cooked. Check the seasoning, then add extra salt and white pepper if needed. Divide the congee among six bowls, sprinkle with the remaining spring onion and coriander, scatter the fried wrappers over the top and serve immediately.

Spicy buckwheat noodles

Serves 4 as an accompaniment

400 g (14 oz) dried soba (buckwheat) noodles

2 tablespoons vegetable oil

80 ml (2½ fl oz/⅓ cup) soy sauce

80 ml (2½ fl oz/⅓ cup) black rice vinegar

1–2 tablespoons chilli oil (page 407), or ready-made, to taste

2 teaspoons sugar

2 teaspoons finely chopped garlic

3 spring onions (scallions), finely sliced on the diagonal

1 large chilli, finely sliced

50 g (1¾ oz/⅓ cup) sesame seeds, toasted (page 413)

Bring 2 litres (68 fl oz/8 cups) water to the boil in a saucepan, add the noodles and cook for 3–5 minutes, or until softened. Drain and rinse under cold running water, then drain again and place in a bowl. Add the oil, soy sauce, vinegar, chilli oil, sugar, garlic and spring onions. Mix well, then turn out onto a platter and scatter with the chilli and sesame seeds.

Photograph page 279

Fried noodle cake

Serves 6 as an accompaniment

300 g (10½ oz) dried, thin egg noodles

80 ml (2½ fl oz/⅓ cup) vegetable oil

3 spring onions (scallions), sliced

black rice vinegar and sugar, to serve

Cook the noodles in a saucepan of boiling water for 4 minutes (or according to the packet instructions), or until softened, then drain.

Heat the oil in a 22 cm (8¾ inch) heavy-based frying pan over a medium–low heat. Place half the cooked noodles in an even layer in the pan to cover the base. Scatter the spring onions over the top, then place the remaining noodles on top. Cook for 15 minutes, or until the underside is golden, then slip the noodle cake carefully onto a large plate, uncooked side up. Invert the noodle cake back into the pan. Place a lightly greased saucepan lid, or similar, directly onto the cake, then place a board on top to weight it down. Cook for another 10–15 minutes, or until deep golden, then transfer to a chopping board and cut into wedges. Serve the noodle cake with small bowls of vinegar and sugar, for dipping.

Photograph page 157

Hand-cut noodles with mustard greens, vinegar and chilli

Serves 4

Oh, how we wish we had the skill and dexterity to make the famous pulled wheat flour noodles of China's west and north. Called la mian *(*la *here means 'stretch'), it's mesmerising watching guys (it's invariably men — you need powerful arms) make these. They start by stretching the dough and folding it to line up the gluten strands, then what ensues is a miraculous succession of looping, pulling, doubling the dough back onto itself, then pulling again, until a pile of perfectly even-sized noodles lies waiting to be cooked. It's beyond us, so we satisfy ourselves with knife-cut ones instead.*

750 g (1 lb 11 oz/5 cups) strong plain (all-purpose) flour, plus extra

125 ml (4 fl oz/½ cup) peanut oil

2 bunches (about 600 g/1 lb 5 oz) baby mustard greens, trimmed

4 spring onions (scallions), finely sliced

4 garlic cloves, finely chopped

pinch of five-spice

chilli flakes, to taste

50 g (1¾ oz/⅓ cup) sesame seeds, toasted (page 413)

chilli oil with sediment (page 407), finely chopped garlic, black rice vinegar and light soy sauce, to serve

To make the noodles, combine the flour and 435 ml (15 fl oz/1¾ cups) water in a bowl and stir with a wooden spoon to just bring the dough together. Using your hands, mix the dough, adding a little extra water, a tablespoon at a time, until a soft, smooth dough forms. Turn the dough out onto a floured surface and knead for 10 minutes, or until very smooth and elastic. Cover the dough loosely with a damp tea towel (dish towel) and rest for 40 minutes.

Cut the dough into four even pieces. Working with one piece at a time, roll the dough out on a well-floured surface to form a 48 x 28 cm (19 x 11 inch) rectangle. Scatter some flour generously over the surface of the dough, then fold the dough over onto itself several times until it measures about 10 cm (4 inches) in width. Cut the roll into 1.5 cm (½ inch) wide strips — don't cut the noodles too thin, or they will be hard to unroll. Using your fingers, lightly toss the noodles to unravel them, then place them on a tray and dust again with flour to stop them sticking to each other. Repeat with the remaining dough pieces. Bring a large saucepan of water to the boil. Add the noodles in batches and cook for 2–3 minutes, or until tender, then drain.

Heat 1½ tablespoons of the oil in a large wok over a medium–high heat, then add the mustard greens and stir-fry for 2 minutes, or until the leaves have wilted and the stems have softened. Add the noodles and toss to combine well. Divide the noodles and mustard greens among four large bowls, then top each with some spring onions and garlic. Add a pinch of five-spice and chilli flakes, to taste, to the middle of each bowl of noodles. Heat the remaining oil in a small saucepan until it is sizzling hot, then pour the hot oil over the spices in the bowls. Sprinkle with sesame seeds and serve with chilli oil with sediment, chopped garlic, vinegar and soy sauce, to add to the noodles as desired.

Sticky rice in lotus leaves

Serves 4 to 6 as part of a shared meal

The lotus is an incredible plant. In sweltering August, ladies harvest the heads from plants in beautiful lotus fields in Jiangxi — these are sold for their fresh seeds as a snack. The flower is legendarily gorgeous and the lotus root, with its refreshing, crunchy texture, is often used in salads, soups, stir-fries and desserts. The dried leaves are used as a food wrapping, imparting a special fragrance, as here in this classic southern dish.

650 g (1 lb 7 oz/3¼ cups) glutinous rice

2 tablespoons light soy sauce

2 tablespoons dried shrimp

4 dried shiitake mushrooms

1½ tablespoons peanut oil, plus extra for brushing

1 boneless, skinless chicken thigh, trimmed and cut into 1 cm (½ inch) pieces

2 Chinese pork sausages (lap cheong), chopped

1 tablespoon oyster sauce

3 teaspoons caster (superfine) sugar

1 teaspoon sesame oil

1½ teaspoons cornflour (cornstarch)

3 dried lotus leaves

2 cooked, salted duck egg yolks, coarsely chopped

Put the rice in a large bowl with 1 tablespoon of the soy sauce, cover with water and soak for 4 hours. Drain well. Put the rice in a steamer lined with a tea towel (dish towel), place the steamer over a wok or saucepan of boiling water, then cover and steam for 30 minutes. Meanwhile, put the dried shrimp and mushrooms in separate heatproof bowls, cover each with boiling water and soak for 30 minutes, or until softened. Drain well, reserving 60 ml (2 fl oz/¼ cup) of the mushroom liquid. Chop the shrimp and mushrooms.

Heat the peanut oil in a wok over a medium heat, then add the chicken, sausages, mushrooms and shrimp and cook, stirring, for 3 minutes, or until the chicken is cooked through. Add the remaining soy sauce, the oyster sauce, sugar and sesame oil and toss to combine. Combine the cornflour and reserved mushroom liquid in a small bowl, then add to the mixture in the wok and cook, stirring, until the liquid boils and thickens. Transfer the chicken mixture to a bowl and leave to cool slightly.

Place the dried lotus leaves in a large saucepan and cover with water. Cover the pan with the lid and simmer for 10–15 minutes, or until softened. Drain well and cool. Cut the lotus leaves in half crosswise. Divide the rice into six even portions. Place a half lotus leaf on the work surface, dark green side up, and brush the middle of the leaf with some peanut oil. Take a portion of the rice and press it over the middle of the leaf to form a 13 cm (5 inch) square. Place about a sixth of the chicken mixture along the middle of the rice, then put a few pieces of the egg yolk on top; use your hands to roll the rice around the filling to form a cylinder. Wrap the rice cylinder tightly in the leaf, bringing the sides of the leaf over the filling, then roll up firmly to enclose. Using kitchen string or the ties that sometimes come with the leaves, tie the lotus leaf packages at both ends and around the length to secure. Repeat the process with the remaining leaves, rice, chicken mixture and egg yolk. Place the packages in a steamer, cover and steam for 20 minutes. Serve hot.

Thunder tea rice

Serves 6

Here's an interesting dish and a great one for feeding a crowd. It is believed to have originated in the mountainous, tea-producing area of Fujian during the turbulent Three Kingdoms period of Chinese history. A general and his men fighting there became ill and a local herbal practitioner taught them to forage the hills for herbs, then pound them with ginger, nuts and tea to make a restorative elixir. The dish today involves pouring the hot 'tea' over bowls of rice and an assembled collection of blanched vegetables, fried anchovies, chopped tofu and the like.

600 g (1 lb 5 oz/3 cups) long-grain rice

Rice toppings

125 g (4½ oz) salted radish, finely chopped

50 g (1¾ oz/½ cup) dried shrimp

4 heads baby bok choy (pak choy), chopped into 1 cm (½ inch) pieces

250 g (9 oz) snake (long) beans, cut into 5 mm (¼ inch) pieces

250 g (9 oz) Chinese broccoli (gai larn), cut into 5 mm (¼ inch) pieces

250 g (9 oz) Chinese cabbage (wombok), trimmed and cut into 1 cm (½ inch) pieces

750 ml (25½ fl oz/3 cups) vegetable oil

90 g (3 oz/1½ cups) dried anchovies

10 spring onions (scallions), finely sliced

250 g (9 oz) fried tofu puffs, cut into 1 cm (½ inch) pieces

240 g (8½ oz/1½ cups) roasted, salted peanuts, coarsely chopped

Herb and peanut 'tea'

30 g (1 oz/¼ cup) oolong tea leaves

2½ tablespoons sesame seeds, toasted (page 413)

120 g (4½ oz/¾ cup) roasted, salted peanuts

2½ tablespoons finely chopped ginger

1 very firmly packed cup each of mint, Thai basil and coriander (cilantro) leaves

To prepare the toppings, put the salted radish in a bowl, cover with cold water and set aside for 40 minutes. Drain, then squeeze the radish to get rid of as much liquid as possible. Put the dried shrimp in a heatproof bowl, cover with boiling water and soak for 30 minutes, or until soft, then drain.

Cook the bok choy for 1–2 minutes in a large saucepan of boiling salted water. Using a slotted spoon, transfer to a colander. Using the back of a large spoon, press down on the bok choy to get rid of as much water as possible, then transfer to a bowl. Repeat the process with the snake beans, Chinese broccoli and cabbage, cooking them separately and draining well.

Heat the oil in a wok over a medium–high heat. Add the anchovies and cook for 2–3 minutes, or until crisp, then remove using a slotted spoon and drain on paper towel. Reserve one-third of the fried anchovies for the tea and place the remaining anchovies in a small serving bowl. Place the cooked toppings and the remaining toppings in individual bowls and set aside.

Put the rice in a saucepan, add 1.125 litres (38 fl oz/4½ cups) water, then cover the pan tightly and cook over a medium heat for 12–15 minutes, or until the water has been absorbed. Remove from the heat and set aside for 5–10 minutes.

Meanwhile, to make the 'tea', put the oolong leaves in an electric spice grinder and grind to a powder. Remove to a bowl. Put the sesame seeds in the spice grinder and grind to a fine powder, then add to the tea in the bowl. Put the peanuts and ginger in a food processor and process until as finely ground as possible. Add the mint, Thai basil and coriander leaves and process until the leaves are very finely chopped. Add the ground sesame seeds and tea leaves and the reserved fried anchovies and process briefly to combine well.

Just before you are ready to serve, transfer the mixture in the food processor to a large heatproof bowl. Using a whisk, add 1 litre (34 fl oz/4 cups) boiling water, whisking to combine well. To serve, divide the rice and hot 'tea' separately among individual serving bowls (or serve the hot tea from a communal bowl to pour over the rice). Serve with the toppings, to add as desired.

Photograph pages 304–5

Thunder tea rice (pages 302–3)

Rice with lamb, carrot, cumin and raisins

Serves 6

If this sounds suspiciously Central Asian, it's because it comes from Xinjiang, where food is heavily influenced by the surrounding 'Stans'. This part of China is on the old Silk Route, with ingredients and influences historically coming from places like Persia, which is most likely the ultimate origin of this dish. Raisins are a common ingredient in these parts — Xinjiang is a huge grape-growing area. You find dishes like this all over China in Uyghur and Hui (ethnic Chinese) Muslim areas.

600 g (1 lb 5 oz) boneless lamb shoulder or leg pieces, trimmed

650 g (1 lb 5 oz) carrots (about 7)

60 ml (2 fl oz/¼ cup) vegetable oil

1 onion, chopped

4 garlic cloves, chopped

2 teaspoons cumin seeds

400 g (14 oz/2 cups) long-grain rice

60 g (2 oz/½ cup) raisins

580 ml (19½ fl oz/2⅓ cups) chicken stock (page 405)

sea salt and freshly ground black pepper

Preheat the oven to 180°C (350°F/Gas 4). Cut the lamb into 1 cm (½ inch) pieces and set aside. Peel the carrots, then cut into thick matchsticks (alternatively, coarsely grate the carrots).

Heat half of the oil in a large ovenproof saucepan or flameproof casserole dish over a medium–high heat, then add the lamb and cook, stirring, for 4–5 minutes, or until browned all over. Remove to a bowl.

Add the remaining oil to the pan, reduce the heat to medium, then add the onion and garlic and cook, stirring, for 4–5 minutes, or until the onion has softened slightly. Add the cumin seeds, rice and raisins and stir to combine well. Add the carrots and stock, bring to the boil, then cover the pan tightly and transfer to the oven. Cook for 25 minutes, or until the rice is nearly tender, then remove the pan from the oven and set aside, covered, for 10–15 minutes for the rice to cook through. Season to taste with sea salt and pepper before serving.

Spring onion and ginger noodles

Serves 4 as an accompaniment or light meal

This is a quick, no-fuss dish when you want something noodley to accompany a meat dish or soup. Throw in some prawns (shrimp) or finely sliced chicken, and you have an easy main course on your hands. Young ginger, called for here, has thin, translucent skin and a brighter, clearer flavour than 'old' ginger. It's also less fibrous and feels much heavier due to the fact it hasn't dried out like its mature counterpart.

---

80 ml (2½ fl oz/⅓ cup) peanut oil

8 cm (3¼ inch) piece young ginger, peeled and finely shredded

2 garlic cloves, finely chopped

80 ml (2½ fl oz/⅓ cup) oyster sauce

80 ml (2½ fl oz/⅓ cup) chicken stock (page 405) or water

1 leek, cut into shreds about 6 cm (2½ inches) long

10 spring onions (scallions), cut into shreds about 6 cm (2½ inches) long

500 g (1 lb 2 oz) fresh, flat egg noodles

40 g (1½ oz/¼ cup) sesame seeds, toasted (page 413)

Heat half of the oil in a saucepan over a medium heat, then add the ginger and garlic and cook, stirring often, for 2 minutes, or until fragrant. Add the oyster sauce and stock and bring to a simmer. Remove the pan from the heat and set aside. Heat the remaining oil in a wok over a medium–high heat, then add the leek and half of the spring onions and stir-fry for 2 minutes, or until softened.

Meanwhile, cook the noodles in a saucepan of boiling water for 2–3 minutes (or according to the packet instructions), or until softened, then drain well. Add the noodles and oyster sauce mixture to the wok and toss to combine well and heat through. Divide among four bowls, sprinkle with the sesame seeds and serve.

Photograph page 205

Chongqing noodle hotpot

Serves 4

This dish is inspired by the legendary food of Chongqing, which, even by Sichuan standards of spicy is off-the-dial hot. Locals caution the visitor to go into chilli-training mode before they visit, so they'll be able to tolerate the food. One of us, unhappily, came ... er ... unstuck after consuming a Chongqing fish hotpot in Chengdu. But don't fear, this noodle hotpot is hot, but it's not truly Chongqing hot.

2½ tablespoons peanut or vegetable oil

250 g (9 oz) minced (ground) pork

3 garlic cloves, crushed

2½ tablespoons sichuan chilli bean paste

80 g (2¾ oz/⅓ cup) ready-made sichuan preserved vegetables, chopped

1½ tablespoons light soy sauce

1 tablespoon sugar

250 g (9 oz) Chinese cabbage (wombok), sliced

300 g (10½ oz) sweet potato starch noodles

4 spring onions (scallions), sliced

1 tablespoon finely chopped ginger

1 handful coriander (cilantro) leaves

1.5 litres (51 fl oz/6 cups) boiling chicken and pork stock (page 405)

roasted broad (fava) beans or raw peanuts, roasted (page 413), to serve

Hot–sour chilli sauce

2 teaspoons sichuan peppercorns

80 ml (2½ fl oz/⅓ cup) chilli oil with sediment (page 407)

1 tablespoon sesame oil

60 ml (2 fl oz/¼ cup) black rice vinegar

1½ tablespoons light soy sauce

1 tablespoon caster (superfine) sugar

To make the hot–sour chilli sauce, dry-roast the peppercorns in a small, heavy-based frying pan over a medium–low heat, shaking the pan often, for 3–4 minutes, or until fragrant. Cool, then transfer to a mortar (or an electric spice grinder) and pound with the pestle to form a coarse powder. Put the ground peppercorns in a bowl, then combine with the remaining ingredients. Cover and set aside.

Heat 2 tablespoons of the oil in a wok over a medium heat, then add the pork and garlic and cook, stirring, for 4–5 minutes, or until the pork is cooked and any liquid has evaporated. Add the chilli bean paste, preserved vegetables, soy sauce and sugar and toss to combine. Remove from the heat and set aside.

Heat the remaining oil in a saucepan over a medium heat, add the cabbage, then cover and cook, stirring occasionally, for 5 minutes, or until softened. Remove from the heat and set aside.

Cook the noodles in a large saucepan of boiling water for 6 minutes (or according to the packet instructions), or until softened, then drain well. Divide the noodles among four warmed large bowls and top with some of the pork mixture and cabbage, then with some spring onions, ginger and coriander. Pour the hot stock over each to cover, place some broad beans on top and then spoon over the hot–sour chilli sauce to taste, serving any remaining sauce separately.

Fried mixed mushroom noodles

Serves 4

Unfortunately, we're never quite in seasonal synch on our trips to Yunnan, so we've missed out on the summer mushroom crop there more than once. The region is famed for having an incredible diversity of fungi (over 600 types), with around thirty edible ones commonly available, including morels, boletus, porcini and the prized matsutake. However, we have dined on a range of wild mountain mushrooms in Sichuan, and although the mushrooms used in this recipe aren't quite as exotic, they still make for a mighty tasty noodle dish.

150 g (5½ oz) each oyster, king oyster, shimeji and shiitake mushrooms

250 g (9 oz) enoki mushrooms

60 ml (2 fl oz/¼ cup) vegetable oil

2 garlic cloves, finely sliced

2 tablespoons finely shredded ginger

150 g (5½ oz/1⅔ cups) mung bean sprouts

60 ml (2 fl oz/¼ cup) shaoxing rice wine

2 tablespoons mushroom soy sauce

1 tablespoon light soy sauce

2 teaspoons sugar

500 g (1 lb 2 oz) fresh, flat wheat noodles

3 teaspoons sesame oil

To prepare the mushrooms, tear the oyster mushrooms lengthwise into 1 cm (½ inch) wide pieces. Finely slice the king oyster mushrooms widthwise. Trim the shimeji mushrooms at the base and separate the mushrooms into clusters. Finely slice the shiitake mushrooms. Trim the enoki and separate the mushrooms from each other. Put each type of mushroom into a separate bowl.

Heat the vegetable oil in a wok over a medium–high heat, then add the king oyster and shiitake mushrooms, garlic and ginger and stir-fry for 2 minutes, or until the mushrooms just start to soften. Add the oyster and shimeji mushrooms and cook for 1 minute, then add the enoki and bean sprouts. Stir-fry for another 2 minutes, or until the mushrooms have softened, then add the rice wine, soy sauces and sugar. Bring to the boil, tossing to combine well.

Meanwhile, cook the noodles in a saucepan of boiling water for 3–4 minutes (or according to the packet instructions), or until softened. Drain well, then add to the simmering mushroom mixture in the wok, along with the sesame oil. Toss to combine well, then divide among four bowls and serve immediately.

Cold noodles with sesame sauce and chicken

Serves 4 to 6

A great way to present this dish is to have all the various ingredients prepared and assembled in bowls on the table; guests can then help themselves to as much or as little of what they want, and mix it all together, to taste. This recipe is inspired by a classic Sichuanese dish and makes a terrific cold summer meal when the weather is sultry. Add blanched shreds of carrot or some finely sliced radish for extra zing and colour if you want. Fans of heat can add a drizzle of chilli oil and a sprinkle of ground toasted sichuan peppercorns for a nice, numbing edge.

500 g (1 lb 2 oz) fresh, thin wheat noodles

Sesame sauce

80 ml (2½ fl oz/⅓ cup) Chinese sesame paste, plus 2 tablespoons oil from the jar

1 tablespoon dark soy sauce

1½ tablespoons light soy sauce

2½ tablespoons red rice vinegar

1 tablespoon caster (superfine) sugar

1 tablespoon sichuan chilli bean paste, or to taste

Accompaniments

2 boneless chicken breasts, skin on

270 g (9½ oz/3 cups) mung bean sprouts

4 spring onions (scallions), finely sliced

1 large handful coriander (cilantro) sprigs

To prepare the accompaniments, place the chicken in a saucepan and add enough water to just cover. Very slowly bring the chicken to a simmer over a medium–low heat, then reduce the heat to very low just as bubbles start to break the surface; simmer for 30 minutes. The water should tremble and not simmer hard or the chicken will be tough — place the pan on a simmer pad if necessary. Remove the pan from the heat and leave the chicken in the liquid for 1 hour, or until cooked through and cooled slightly. Remove the chicken, reserving the stock for another use. Remove and discard the skin, then use your hands to very finely shred the chicken. Place in a serving bowl.

Bring a saucepan of water to the boil, add the bean sprouts, then bring the water back to the boil. Cook the sprouts for 2–3 minutes, or until wilted, then drain and refresh under cold running water. Drain well, then spread the sprouts on paper towel to absorb the remaining water. Place in a serving bowl. Put the spring onions and coriander sprigs in separate serving bowls.

To make the sesame sauce, put all the ingredients in a bowl and whisk until smooth and well combined. Pour into a serving jug.

Cook the noodles in a saucepan of boiling water for 2–3 minutes (or according to the packet instructions), or until softened. Drain, then cool under running water. Drain again, then divide among large bowls. Serve the noodles with the accompaniments and sesame sauce for diners to add and mix their own, to taste.

Photograph page 239

Sweet potato congee and deep-fried eggs

Serves 6

We wandered down a residential alleyway in the character-filled village of Zhuxianzhen in Henan Province, and came upon an elderly lady eating her lunch. She sat us down, fed us a stodgy chunk of wheat dough steamed with vegetables and a massive bowl of sweet potato congee straight from her kitchen, right there in the dusty lane. It was one of those magical gestures of hospitality so often encountered when venturing off beaten Chinese paths.

265 g (9½ oz/1⅓ cups) medium-grain rice

2.5 litres (85 fl oz/10 cups) chicken stock (page 405)

500 g (1 lb 2 oz) white sweet potato

sea salt and ground white pepper

sesame oil, to serve

preserved bamboo shoots or other ready-made preserved vegetables, to serve

Sweet deep-fried eggs

12 eggs

vegetable oil, for deep-frying

6 spring onions (scallions), finely sliced

1½ tablespoons soy paste

1 tablespoon oyster sauce

2 tablespoons clear rice vinegar

2 tablespoons caster (superfine) sugar

Combine the rice and stock in a large saucepan and bring to a simmer. Cook over a low heat for 1½ hours, or until the rice is soft and the mixture has thickened. Peel the sweet potato and cut into 1 cm (½ inch) pieces, then add to the rice mixture. Cover the pan and cook for another 30–40 minutes, or until the sweet potato is soft. Season with a little sea salt and white pepper, but not too much, as congee should not be salty.

Meanwhile, to make the deep-fried eggs, cook the eggs in a saucepan of simmering water for 5 minutes. Drain, then cool under running water. Peel the eggs, then pat dry with paper towel.

Fill a wok one-third full of oil and heat to 190°C (375°F), or until a cube of bread dropped into the oil turns deep golden in 10 seconds. Add the spring onions and cook for 5 minutes, or until golden, then remove using a slotted spoon and drain on paper towel. Working in two batches, add the eggs and cook for 6–7 minutes, or until golden. Remove and drain on paper towel.

Pour off all but 1 tablespoon of oil from the wok. Add the soy paste, oyster sauce, vinegar and sugar to the wok and bring to a simmer over a medium heat, swirling the wok to combine the ingredients well.

Cut each egg in half and place on a serving platter. Drizzle the sweet sauce over the eggs, then scatter the fried spring onions over the top. Divide the congee among six large bowls and drizzle with a little sesame oil. Serve the congee with the sweet eggs and preserved bamboo, to add to the congee as desired.

Photograph pages 314–15

From left to right: Mantou: spring onion 'flower' rolls (page 338);
Sweet potato congee and deep-fried eggs (page 313)

Noodles with fish and home-salted mustard greens

Serves 4

Perhaps the best noodles we ate in China were at the celebrated Kuiyuan Restaurant in the lovely city of Hangzhou. Founded in 1867 by a businessman from Anhui Province, it's gone on to become legendary for its 150 or so noodle recipes. Their stocks are out of this world and they hand-make their noodles according to special 100-year-old techniques. All their ingredients are hand-selected, and oh how we wish we could conjure noodles like their famous prawn (shrimp) and eel ones.

600 g (1 lb 5 oz) skinless monkfish, or other firm white fish fillets

1 quantity home-salted mustard greens (page 409), or ready-made

375 g (13 oz) dried, thin egg noodles

5 cm (2 inch) piece young ginger, peeled and finely shredded (optional)

Stock

2 kg (4 lb 6 oz) fish bones and heads from white fish

2 tablespoons vegetable oil

250 g (9 oz) boneless pork belly, skin on

4 spring onions (scallions), chopped

6 slices unpeeled ginger

35 g (1¼ oz/⅓ cup) dried shrimp

125 ml (4 fl oz/½ cup) clear rice wine

To make the stock, use a cleaver to cut the fish bones and heads into 10 cm (4 inch) pieces. Heat the oil in a stockpot over a medium heat, then add the fish bones and heads, pork belly, spring onions and ginger and cook, stirring occasionally, for 10 minutes, or until the fish bones and pork have changed colour and have released some juices. Add the dried shrimp, rice wine and about 2.5 litres (85 fl oz/10 cups) water, or enough to just cover the pork and fish bones. Bring to a simmer over a low heat, then cook for about 1 hour, skimming off any impurities as they rise to the surface. Strain the stock through a fine sieve, discarding the solids, then return to a clean pan and bring to a simmer.

Cut the fish widthwise into 10–12 cm (4–4¾ inch) pieces. Add the fish to the gently simmering stock and cook over a low heat for 5 minutes, depending on the thickness of the fish, or until cooked through.

Meanwhile, rinse the mustard greens well and roughly slice. Cook the noodles in a saucepan of boiling water for 4 minutes (or according to the packet instructions), or until softened, then drain. Divide the noodles among four bowls and scatter over the mustard greens. Place the fish on the noodles and ladle the hot stock over the top. Scatter over the ginger, if using, and serve immediately.

Dan dan mian

Serves 4

Once upon a time, the streets of Chengdu rang with the cries of snack sellers, including the dan dan *noodle man (the name comes from the shoulder pole used to balance the baskets carrying the sauce and noodles). Alas, those days are long gone and the city has rushed headlong into complete modernity. Luckily, there's still a ton of character in her denizens ... and in the food. Such dishes may not be found on the street anymore, but they're still very much a part of the dining fabric.*

3 teaspoons sichuan peppercorns

2½ tablespoons peanut oil

50 g (1¾ oz/⅓ cup) tianjin preserved vegetables, rinsed and dried

200 g (7 oz) minced (ground) pork

2 teaspoons shaoxing rice wine

80 ml (2½ fl oz/⅓ cup) light soy sauce

80 ml (2½ fl oz/⅓ cup) chilli oil (page 407), or ready-made

1 tablespoon black rice vinegar

4 spring onions (scallions), green part only, finely sliced

600 g (1 lb 5 oz) fresh, thin egg noodles

Dry-roast the peppercorns in a small, heavy-based frying pan over a medium–low heat, shaking the pan often, for 3–4 minutes, or until fragrant. Cool, then transfer to a mortar (or an electric spice grinder) and pound with the pestle to form a coarse powder. Set aside.

Heat 1 tablespoon of the peanut oil in a wok over a medium–high heat, then add the preserved vegetables and cook, stirring constantly, for 30 seconds. Remove with a slotted spoon and place in a large bowl.

Heat the remaining oil in the wok, then add the pork and stir-fry over a high heat for 2 minutes, or until browned. Add the rice wine and 1½ tablespoons of the soy sauce and cook, stirring constantly, for another 5 minutes, or until almost all the liquid has evaporated. Remove the pork from the wok and add to the bowl with the preserved vegetables. Add the remaining soy sauce, the chilli oil, vinegar and spring onions to the bowl and toss to combine well.

Meanwhile, cook the noodles in a saucepan of boiling water for 2–3 minutes (or according to the packet instructions), or until softened, then drain. Divide the noodles among four bowls, spoon the pork mixture over the top and serve immediately, allowing diners to mix their own noodles at the table.

Photograph page 357

Ants climbing trees

Serves 4

Food magazines are full of those recipes that promise a meal on the table in under an hour. Well, this classic Sichuan dish is one Chinese answer to the 'feed me fast' dilemma. Its rather poetic name comes from the way the pieces of meat look as they cling to the vermicelli noodles, just like a whole pile of ants on a twig or branch.

---

5 dried shiitake mushrooms

300 g (10½ oz) minced (ground) beef or pork, not too lean

2 tablespoons light soy sauce

1 tablespoon dark soy sauce

3 teaspoons sugar

2 garlic cloves, finely chopped

½ teaspoon cornflour (cornstarch)

200 g (7 oz) bean thread (glass) vermicelli noodles

4 spring onions (scallions), trimmed

2½ tablespoons peanut oil

1 tablespoon finely chopped ginger

1½ tablespoons sichuan chilli bean paste

375 ml (12½ fl oz/1½ cups) chicken stock (page 405)

Put the shiitake mushrooms in a small heatproof bowl, cover with boiling water and soak for 30 minutes, or until softened. Drain well, squeeze dry, then finely chop.

Combine the mince, soy sauces, sugar, garlic and cornflour in a bowl, then use your hands to combine well. Cover and set aside at cool room temperature for 30 minutes.

Put the vermicelli noodles in a large heatproof bowl, cover with boiling water and soak for 5 minutes, then drain. Using kitchen scissors, cut the noodles in half. Finely slice the white part of the spring onions and set aside. Finely slice the green part and set aside.

Heat half of the oil in a large wok over a medium–high heat, then add the meat mixture and cook, stirring constantly with the back of a metal spoon to break up the meat, for 6–7 minutes, or until brown. Remove to a bowl and wipe the wok dry.

Add the remaining oil to the wok over a medium–high heat, then add the white spring onion, the ginger and chilli bean paste and cook, stirring, for 1–2 minutes, or until fragrant. Add the noodles and stock, then return the meat mixture to the wok and toss to combine well. Bring the liquid to the boil and cook, stirring, for another 3–4 minutes, or until the liquid has evaporated and the noodles are tender. Divide the noodle mixture among four bowls, scatter the green spring onion over the top and serve immediately.

Beef and tomato noodles

Serves 4 to 6

If there's one ingredient that's a revelation to the food tourist in China, it's vinegar. There are a few notable centres of production: in Zhenjiang (previously spelled 'Chinkiang'), in Jiangsu Province, and in the northern city of Taiyuan, in Shanxi. Made from rice, water and salt and according to processes of natural fermentation, the best Chinese vinegars are worthy of any Italian balsamic, with mellow, full and complex flavours and a slightly sweet edge. In Shanxi, people routinely drink a little for medicinal purposes, and it's not unheard of to take a bottle with them when they travel. We love it in cooked dishes too, as in this meaty braise for noodles.

10 dried wood ear fungus

2 boneless beef shins (about 1 kg/2 lb 3 oz), trimmed

100 ml (3½ fl oz) vegetable oil

1 large onion, finely chopped

2 tablespoons finely shredded ginger

3 teaspoons cumin seeds

2 teaspoons sichuan peppercorns

1 black cardamom

1 piece cassia bark

600 g (1 lb 5 oz) tomatoes (about 4), chopped

80 ml (2½ fl oz/⅓ cup) black rice vinegar

2½ tablespoons light soy sauce

1 litre (34 fl oz/4 cups) beef stock (page 404)

large pinch of ground fennel

sea salt and freshly ground black pepper

500 g (1 lb 2 oz) fresh, flat wheat noodles

chilli flakes, to serve

coriander (cilantro) leaves, to serve

Put the wood ear fungus in a small heatproof bowl, cover with boiling water and soak for 30 minutes, or until softened, then drain. Remove any hard bits from the wood ears and tear into large pieces. Set aside.

Trim the beef and cut into 5 mm (¼ inch) thick slices. Heat about one-third of the oil in a wok over a medium–high heat, then add half the beef and stir-fry for 3 minutes, or until browned. Transfer to a large saucepan. Repeat with another one-third of the oil and the remaining beef.

Add the remaining oil to the wok, then add the onion and ginger and stir-fry for 3–4 minutes, or until starting to brown. Add the cumin seeds and sichuan peppercorns and cook for another minute, or until fragrant. Add the mixture to the beef in the pan, along with the cardamom, cassia, tomatoes, vinegar, soy sauce, stock and fennel. Place the pan over a medium heat and bring to a simmer, skimming any fat off the surface as necessary. Reduce the heat to low and cook for 1 hour, then add the wood ears and cook for another 30 minutes, or until the meat is very tender. Remove the cardamom and cassia and season to taste with sea salt and pepper.

Cook the noodles in a saucepan of boiling water for 2–3 minutes (or according to the packet instructions), or until softened, then drain well. Divide the noodles among bowls, ladle the meat mixture over the top, then sprinkle with some chilli flakes, garnish with coriander and serve.

Vermicelli with mushrooms and fermented tofu

Serves 4

It's not hard to mistake rice vermicelli for bean thread noodles so take care when buying them, as it's a common mistake. This variety of noodle is manufactured mainly in Shandong Province, one of our favourite places for food in China. They are one of those fantastic ingredients that, while they don't have much flavour themselves, are wonderful vehicles for other ingredients, such as the punchy fermented tofu and peppery watercress here.

250 g (9 oz) bean thread (glass) vermicelli noodles

60 ml (2 fl oz/¼ cup) peanut oil

3 garlic cloves, very finely sliced

1 tablespoon finely shredded ginger

300 g (10½ oz) shiitake or portobello mushrooms, sliced

200 g (7 oz) enoki mushrooms, trimmed

2 pieces red fermented tofu, plus 1 tablespoon of the tofu liquid

2½ tablespoons mushroom soy sauce

1½ tablespoons shaoxing rice wine

250 ml (8½ fl oz/1 cup) chicken stock (page 405)

120 g (4½ oz/4 cups) watercress sprigs

Put the vermicelli noodles in a large heatproof bowl, cover with boiling water and soak for 15 minutes, or until softened, then drain. Using kitchen scissors, cut the noodles into smaller pieces.

Heat the oil in a wok over a medium–high heat, then add the garlic, ginger and shiitake mushrooms. Cook, tossing the wok often, for 3–4 minutes, or until the mushrooms have softened. Add the enoki and cook for another 2 minutes, or until softened.

Put the tofu and liquid in a small bowl and mash together with a fork. Add the mashed tofu to the wok along with the soy sauce, rice wine, stock and noodles. Stir to combine well, then cook for 5 minutes, stirring occasionally, or until most of the liquid has been absorbed. Add the watercress to the wok and cook for another 2 minutes, or until the cress has wilted. Divide the noodle and mushroom mixture among four warmed bowls and serve immediately.

Chinese fried rice

Serves 4

The key to this home-style classic is to use very dry, cooked rice, which makes it a perfect dish for using up any left-over steamed rice sitting in your fridge. In China, fried rice is closely associated with the city of Yangzhou, near Nanjing, where they've turned the making of it into a serious art. They meticulously cut all the vegetables and other ingredients into perfectly small pieces. In fact, the townsfolk there are so serious about it they've even trademarked Yangzhou fried rice and only certified restaurants are allowed to serve it!

850 g (1 lb 14 oz/4½ cups) cooked, cold long-grain rice, or 300 g (10½ oz/1½ cups) uncooked long-grain rice

2 eggs, lightly beaten

1 tablespoon sesame oil

2 tablespoons peanut oil

150 g (5½ oz) Chinese pork sausages (lap cheong) (about 4), finely sliced on the diagonal

2 spring onions (scallions), finely sliced

400 g (14 oz) peas, podded, or 200 g (7 oz) frozen peas, blanched

400 g (14 oz) raw king prawns (shrimp), peeled, cleaned and halved lengthwise

2 garlic cloves, finely chopped

1 tablespoon light soy sauce

1 tablespoon oyster sauce

If using uncooked rice, wash the rice in a sieve under cold running water until the water runs clear. Place the rice in a saucepan and cover with 500 ml (17 fl oz/2 cups) cold water, or enough so the water level is about 2.5 cm (1 inch) above the rice. Bring to the boil, cover, then reduce the heat to low and cook for 12 minutes, or until the rice is tender and has absorbed the water. Remove from the heat, spread the rice out on a tray and leave to cool to room temperature. Cover and refrigerate for at least 3 hours.

Combine the eggs and half the sesame oil in a bowl. Heat a large wok over a high heat, add 1 tablespoon of the peanut oil, then add the egg mixture and swirl it around the wok to coat. Cook for 1–2 minutes, or until the egg is just set. Remove the omelette to a chopping board, roll it up, then finely slice and reserve.

Return the wok to a high heat, add the remaining peanut oil, then add the sausages, spring onions, blanched peas and prawns and stir-fry for 2 minutes. Add the garlic and stir-fry for 1 minute, or until fragrant. Add the rice, soy sauce, oyster sauce, omelette strips and the remaining sesame oil. Stir-fry for another minute, or until heated through, then serve.

Taro and dried shrimp fried rice (variation)

Peel 500 g (1 lb 2 oz) taro, then chop it into 1 cm (½ inch) dice. Steam or boil until tender. Meanwhile, put 50 g (1¾ oz/½ cup) dried shrimp in a heatproof bowl, cover with boiling water and soak for 30 minutes, or until softened. Following the same method as for the recipe above, replace the prawns with the dried shrimp, and the peas with the taro. Sprinkle 100 g (3½ oz) chopped peanuts over the top and serve.

Cat's ears noodles

Serves 4

The old walled city of Pingyao, about 600 kilometres west of Beijing, holds UNESCO World Heritage status. It's a beautiful place. It's also 'noodle central' with around 200 varieties in the local repertoire. These are formed using a range of techniques, from cutting, pushing, pulling, tucking, folding, dragging and pinching to these cute 'cat's ears', made by rolling small pieces over onto themselves into a tight curl. We can't promise they're easy to make but they are good fun.

600 g (1 lb 5 oz/4 cups) plain (all-purpose) flour

1 teaspoon salt

80 ml (2½ fl oz/⅓ cup) peanut oil

4 garlic cloves, finely chopped

2 teaspoons cumin seeds

250 g (9 oz) garlic stems (1 bunch), cut into 1 cm (½ inch) pieces

2 red capsicums (peppers), seeded and chopped

2 large red chillies, seeded and finely sliced

5 firm ripe tomatoes (about 750 g/1 lb 11 oz), coarsely chopped

60 ml (2 fl oz/¼ cup) black rice vinegar

1 small bunch coriander (cilantro), leaves coarsely chopped (optional)

Put the flour and salt in a large bowl. Add 500 ml (17 fl oz/2 cups) water, stirring with a wooden spoon to bring the dough together, adding a little extra water if needed, 1 tablespoon at a time. Turn the dough out onto a floured board and knead for 5 minutes, or until smooth and elastic. Cover with a damp tea towel (dish towel) and rest for 30 minutes.

Flatten the dough into a disc with your hands, then pinch off small pieces of dough about the size of your fingertip. Working with one piece of dough at a time, use your thumb to press down on each small piece of dough and then gently roll it forward — the dough will curl a little, resembling a cat's ear.

Heat a large wok over a medium–high heat, add the oil, then the garlic and cumin seeds and stir-fry for 1 minute, or until fragrant. Add the garlic stems, capsicums, chillies and tomatoes and stir-fry for another 3–4 minutes. Add the vinegar and 60 ml (2 fl oz/¼ cup) water, toss well and cook for another minute.

Meanwhile, bring a large saucepan of salted water to the boil, add the cat's ear noodles and cook, stirring frequently, to prevent them sticking together, for 2–3 minutes, or until they float to the surface, then cook for another 2 minutes. Drain in a colander, then add to the vegetables and sauce in the wok and toss to combine and heat through. Divide among four bowls and scatter with the coriander, if using.

Beijing meat sauce with noodles

Serves 4

Here's the spaghetti bolognese of China — called za jiang mein, *which literally means 'fried sauce noodles'. The crucial ingredient here is thick, sweet soybean sauce. In Beijing they use yellow soybean sauce (although confusingly it's not actually yellow but dark brown), while in Tianjin, just down the road, they favour hoisin sauce, which you can substitute here. Some versions top the noodles with scrambled eggs, or coriander (cilantro) or mung bean sprouts, so feel free to experiment.*

2 tablespoons vegetable oil

3 garlic cloves, finely chopped

1½ tablespoons finely chopped ginger

4 large spring onions (scallions), white part only, finely chopped

500 g (1 lb 2 oz) minced (ground) pork

150 ml (5 fl oz) sweet bean sauce

60 ml (2 fl oz/¼ cup) shaoxing rice wine

1½ tablespoons dark soy sauce

250 ml (8½ fl oz/1 cup) chicken stock (page 405)

500 g (1 lb 2 oz) fresh, thick wheat noodles

2 Lebanese (short) cucumbers, halved lengthwise, then cut into long pieces

1 small handful coriander (cilantro) sprigs

Heat the oil in a large wok over a medium heat. Add the garlic, ginger and spring onions and cook, stirring, for 2–3 minutes, or until softened. Add the pork and cook, stirring to break up the meat, for 5–6 minutes, or until it changes colour. Add the sweet bean sauce, rice wine, soy sauce and stock, stir to combine well, then bring to a simmer. Reduce the heat to low and cook for about 20 minutes, or until the pork is cooked and the sauce has reduced and thickened.

Cook the noodles in a saucepan of boiling water for 3–4 minutes (or according to the packet instructions), or until softened, then drain well. Divide the noodles among four large bowls, then spoon over the sauce. Top each bowl with some of the cucumber, scatter over the coriander and serve.

Pumpkin, ham and chicken congee

Serves 4 to 6

By mistake we ended up eating at the breakfast table reserved for a group of primary school art students and their parents in the incredibly pretty village of Little Likeng in Jiangxi Province. Kind to the core, they urged us to stay and eat with them and we observed, amazed, as the pint-sized kids put away serious amounts of thin, plain congee, platefuls of steamed mantou, *fried breadstick (youtiao) and boiled eggs. Everything went into the congee bowl together, washed down with copious amounts of tea and hot soy milk. Here's our slightly more elegant interpretation of this beloved staple, well suited for lunch or as a light dinner.*

2 tablespoons vegetable oil

750 g (1 lb 11 oz) jap or kent pumpkin (winter squash), peeled, seeded and chopped

200 g (7 oz) short- or medium-grain rice

75 g (2¾ oz) piece Chinese cured ham, shredded

2½ tablespoons finely shredded ginger

2 litres (68 fl oz/8 cups) chicken stock (page 405)

2 tablespoons clear rice wine

2 boneless, skinless chicken breasts (about 450 g/1 lb)

sea salt and freshly ground black pepper

small raw, red-skinned peanuts, roasted (page 413), to serve

Heat the oil in a large saucepan over a medium–low heat. Add the pumpkin, then cover the pan and cook, stirring occasionally, for 15 minutes, or until the pumpkin is very soft. Remove the pan from the heat and use a potato masher or a hand-held stick blender to purée the pumpkin.

Return the pan of puréed pumpkin to the heat, then add the rice, ham, ginger, stock and rice wine and stir to combine well. Bring the mixture to a simmer, cover the pan and cook over a low heat, stirring occasionally, for 1 hour, or until the rice is very soft.

Meanwhile, cut the chicken across the grain into very thin slices. Add to the congee, stir to combine, then cook for 2–3 minutes, or until the chicken is just cooked through. Season to taste with sea salt and pepper, then divide among warm bowls. Scatter the peanuts over the top and serve.

Stir-fried beef and rice noodles

Serves 4

Built around fresh he fen, or wide rice noodles, this dish is like most simple Cantonese ones in that it relies on the best and freshest possible ingredients. With their bouncy, slippery smoothness, these noodles, which originated in what is now the Tianhe District of Guangzhou, are the perfect textural foil for all those black beans, beef, sprouts and spring onion (scallion).

500 g (1 lb 2 oz) beef eye fillet, trimmed

1 tablespoon dark soy sauce

3 teaspoons cornflour (cornstarch)

2 teaspoons sesame oil

2½ tablespoons oyster sauce

2 tablespoons shaoxing rice wine

80 ml (2½ fl oz/⅓ cup) peanut oil

4 garlic cloves, finely chopped

2 teaspoons finely chopped ginger

800 g (1 lb 12 oz) fresh, wide rice noodles

180 g (6½ oz/2 cups) mung bean sprouts

1 tablespoon fermented black beans, rinsed and crushed with a fork

4 spring onions (scallions), cut into 5 cm (2 inch) lengths

Cut the beef into 5 mm (¼ inch) thick slices, then cut the slices in half lengthwise. Combine the soy sauce, cornflour and sesame oil in a bowl, add the beef and toss to coat well. Combine the oyster sauce and rice wine in a small bowl and set aside.

Heat 1 tablespoon of the peanut oil in a wok over a high heat. Add half of the undrained beef and half of the garlic and ginger and stir-fry for 3 minutes, or until the meat is browned and nearly cooked through. Remove to a plate with any juices. Heat another tablespoon of the peanut oil in the wok and cook the remaining beef, ginger and garlic, then remove to the plate.

Heat the remaining oil in the wok over a high heat, then add the noodles and stir-fry for 4–5 minutes, or until the noodles are heated through and slightly crusty in places. Add the bean sprouts and black beans and stir-fry for 2–3 minutes, or until the sprouts soften. Add the beef and any juices, the oyster sauce mixture and the spring onions and toss well. Cook for 1 minute, or until the beef is cooked through, then divide among four bowls and serve.

Shanghai fried noodles

Serves 4

This dish isn't really Shanghainese at all. It apparently originated with Shanghai immigrants into Hong Kong in the 1950s, many of whom set up Shanghai-style restaurants, adapting dishes to suit local tastes. Whatever its origins, this is a great meal when you need something quick and tasty in an almighty great rush — assuming you have all ingredients to hand, that is.

1 tablespoon light soy sauce

2 tablespoons dark soy sauce

2 teaspoons oyster sauce

2 teaspoons caster (superfine) sugar

80 ml (2½ fl oz/⅓ cup) chicken stock (page 405)

500 g (1 lb 2 oz) fresh, thick, round egg noodles

80 ml (2½ fl oz/⅓ cup) vegetable oil

500 g (1 lb 2 oz) Chinese cabbage (wombok), trimmed and cut into 3 cm (1¼ inch) pieces

2 garlic cloves, finely chopped

Pork

450 g (1 lb) pork loin, trimmed and cut into very thin strips

1 tablespoon light soy sauce

2 teaspoons caster (superfine) sugar

2 teaspoons sesame oil

To prepare the pork, combine all the ingredients in a bowl, toss to coat well, then cover and set aside at cool room temperature for 30 minutes.

Combine the soy sauces, oyster sauce, sugar and stock in a bowl and stir to combine well. Set aside.

Cook the noodles in a saucepan of boiling water for 5 minutes (or according to the packet instructions), or until softened. Drain in a colander, then toss the noodles with a little of the vegetable oil to prevent them from sticking together.

Meanwhile, heat half of the oil in a wok over a medium–high heat, add the cabbage and garlic and stir-fry for 4 minutes, or until the cabbage has softened. Remove to a bowl. Heat the remaining oil in the wok, then add the pork mixture and stir-fry for 3–4 minutes, or until the pork is cooked through. Return the cabbage to the wok, then add the noodles and the soy sauce mixture and cook, tossing the wok, for 2–3 minutes, or until everything is well combined and heated through. Divide among four bowls and serve immediately.

Sweet bean and black rice congee

Serves 6

Hands down the two best sweet red bean congees we have eaten were in Suzhou — at the wonderful Wumen Renjia restaurant down Panru Lane, where the focus is on traditional Suzhou cooking, and at the 130-year-old Pin Von Teahouse, right on the canal on historic Pingjiang Street. These versions were suave, smooth and unctuous; ours is decidedly more rustic, but no less delicious for it.

440 g (15½ oz/2 cups) dried adzuki beans

100 g (3½ oz/½ cup) black glutinous rice

2 pieces dried tangerine peel

230 g (8 oz/1 cup) caster (superfine) sugar, or to taste

steamed mantou (page 336) or sweet sesame buns (page 344, refer to recipe introduction for sweet version), to serve (optional)

Put the adzuki beans and black rice in separate bowls, cover with cold water and leave to soak overnight. Drain well.

Transfer the beans and rice to a large saucepan, then add the tangerine peel and 2.5 litres (85 fl oz/10 cups) water. Bring to a simmer, skimming any impurities from the surface, then continue to simmer over a medium–low heat for 1 hour, or until the beans and rice are very soft.

Remove the pan from the heat and use a hand-held stick blender to briefly process the beans and rice so they are partially puréed but still have some texture. Alternatively, transfer about half of the mixture to a food processor and process until smooth, then return to the pan. Return the pan to the heat, add the sugar and cook over a low heat to warm through, stirring to dissolve the sugar, and adding a little more water if it is too thick. Divide among six bowls and serve immediately with a small bowl of sugar, to add to the congee to taste, and with the mantou or sweet sesame buns, if using.

Breads, Buns
&
Dumplings

Dumplings, fried or steamed; flatbreads, stuffed or plain and
oily from the griddle; hefty, fist-sized *mantou* (steamed breads);
flaky spring onion pancakes; and eggy *jian bing* (breakfast crepes)
slathered in sticky hoisin sauce — these are the rustic foods that
fuel every corner of Chinese life. Here are just a few of the ones
we love the best.

Mantou

Makes 12

These steamed breads are a staple all over northern China, where wheaten foods are analogous to the rice of the south. The basic formula comes in various guises, from small, pillowy mouthfuls to fist-sized buns with a chewy firmness. There are also numerous spin-off variations, such as the couple here: the distinctive flower-shaped roll cooked with a sprinkling of spring onion (scallion) inside, and our all-time favourite, small deep-fried ones you eat dipped in condensed milk, straight from the tin.

2 teaspoons instant dried yeast

500 g (1 lb 2 oz/3⅓ cups) strong plain (all-purpose) flour

1½ tablespoons caster (superfine) sugar

1 teaspoon salt

1 tablespoon vegetable oil

1 teaspoon baking powder

Sprinkle the yeast over 340 ml (12 fl oz/1⅓ cups) lukewarm water in a large bowl, then set aside in a draught-free place for 5–6 minutes, or until foamy. Add the flour, sugar, salt and oil and stir with a wooden spoon to just bring the dough together. Turn the dough out onto a lightly floured surface and knead for 8–10 minutes, or until smooth and elastic (alternatively, knead using an electric mixer with a dough hook attachment).

Form the dough into a ball, then place in a large, lightly oiled bowl, turning the dough to coat. Cover the bowl with plastic wrap and set aside in a draught-free place for 45–60 minutes, or until the dough has doubled in size. Knock back the dough and turn it out onto a lightly floured surface, then sprinkle with the baking powder and knead well to distribute the baking powder through the dough (or return the dough to the mixer to do this). Rest the dough for 20 minutes, loosely covered with a damp tea towel (dish towel).

Using a rolling pin, roll out the dough into a long rectangle, about 70 cm (27½ inches) long and 25 cm (10 inches) wide. Fold one-third of the dough back over onto itself, then fold the remaining third over the top, to form a triple-folded piece of dough that now measures about 23 cm (9 inches) in length. Roll out the dough until it is about 55 cm (22 inches) long, then brush liberally with water. Turn the dough so a long side is facing you. Starting from a long side, roll the dough up into a log. Using a sharp knife, cut the roll into 12 even pieces. Place each roll on a square of baking paper, placing the rolls so a smooth side is facing up (with the cut sides on the side).

Working in two batches, if necessary, put the rolls in a large steamer and place over a wok or saucepan of boiling water, then cover and steam for 12–15 minutes, or until cooked through.

Mantou: spring onion 'flower' rolls

Makes 10

Make the dough following the recipe on page 336. After the dough has rested, divide it evenly into two pieces. Working with one piece at a time, roll out on a floured surface to a 38 x 28 cm (15 x 11 inch) rectangle. Repeat with the second piece of dough.

Brush each piece with 1 tablespoon vegetable oil, or enough to coat it well. Finely chop 3 or 4 spring onions (scallions) and sprinkle half the spring onions over each rectangle. Turn the dough so a short side is facing you, then roll up to form a log. Push the ends in a little to make the log about 25 cm (10 inches) and to bulk up the ends a little so the log has an even thickness along its length. Repeat with the second piece. Cut each log into five 5 cm (2 inch) pieces. Use a chopstick to firmly press across each roll widthwise until the sides open and turn upwards (this will give them their 'flower' appearance when cooked). Place each roll on a small square of baking paper. Put the rolls in a large steamer and place over a wok or saucepan of boiling water, then cover and steam for about 8 minutes, or until cooked through. Serve warm.

Photograph page 314

Mantou: sweet variation

Makes 16

Make the dough following the recipe on page 336. After the dough has rested, divide it evenly into two pieces. Working with one piece at a time, roll out on a floured surface to a 45 x 20 cm (18 x 8 inch) rectangle, then roll up from a long side. Repeat with the second piece of dough. Cut each log into eight pieces. Working in two batches, put the rolls in a large steamer and place over a wok or saucepan of boiling water, then cover and steam for 7–8 minutes.

Fill a wok one-third full of vegetable oil and heat to 180°C (350°F), or until a cube of bread dropped into the oil turns golden brown in 15 seconds. Fry the mantou in batches for 3–4 minutes, or until golden brown. Drain well on paper towel and serve with sweetened condensed milk for dipping.

Xi'an 'hamburgers'

Makes 8

Buns

1 teaspoon instant dried yeast

500 g (1 lb 2 oz/3⅓ cups) strong plain (all-purpose) flour

½ teaspoon salt

vegetable oil, for cooking

Filling

1 kg (2 lb 3 oz) lamb shoulder (a half shoulder), on the bone

1½ tablespoons sugar

1 tablespoon light soy sauce

1½ tablespoons dark soy sauce

2½ tablespoons shaoxing rice wine

1 star anise

1 piece cassia bark

1 piece dried tangerine peel

5 slices unpeeled ginger

chilli flakes, to serve (optional)

1 small handful coriander (cilantro) sprigs

To make the filling, put the lamb in a saucepan large enough to fit it snugly, then add enough water to just cover. Bring to a simmer, then cook over a low heat for 1½ hours, or until the meat is tender, adding a little more water if needed to keep the meat covered. Cool the meat in the liquid, then strain, reserving the liquid. Remove the meat from the bone in large pieces, then cut it across the grain into 5 mm (¼ inch) thick slices. Put the lamb in a saucepan, then add the sugar, soy sauces, rice wine, star anise, cassia, tangerine peel, ginger and enough of the cooking liquid to just cover the meat. Bring to a simmer and cook for 30–40 minutes, or until the liquid has reduced by about three-quarters. Discard the whole spices and tangerine peel.

Meanwhile, to make the buns, sprinkle the yeast over 125 ml (4 fl oz/½ cup) lukewarm water in a large bowl, then set aside in a draught-free place for 5–6 minutes, or until foamy. Add the flour, salt and 150 ml (5 fl oz) lukewarm water and stir to form a very firm dough. Add a little extra water if the dough is too firm to handle, but not too much. Turn the dough out onto a lightly floured surface and knead for 10 minutes, or until smooth and elastic (alternatively, knead using an electric mixer with a dough hook attachment). Form the dough into a ball, then place in a large, lightly oiled bowl, turning the dough to coat. Cover with plastic wrap and set aside in a draught-free place for 1 hour, or until the dough has doubled in size.

Knock back the dough, turn it out onto a lightly floured surface and roll it into a 30 cm (12 inch) log. Cut the log into eight even pieces, then use your hands to roll each piece into a thin sausage about 20 cm (8 inches) long. Using a rolling pin, roll out each sausage until it is about 36 cm (14 inches) long and 5.5 cm (2¼ inches) wide. With a narrow side facing you, tightly roll up each strip, then sit it flat on one end. Flatten it with your hand, then use the rolling pin to roll it out into a 10 cm (4 inch) round.

Place a large, non-stick frying pan over a low heat, brush the base with oil, then cook the buns in batches for 12–15 minutes on each side, or until cooked through and light golden. Cool slightly, then cut a horizontal opening in each bun, taking care not to cut all the way through. Divide the warm lamb mixture and some of the sauce among the buns and sprinkle with chilli flakes, if using. Add a few coriander sprigs and serve.

Xi'an 'hamburgers'; Pickled chillies (page 410)

Cabbage and pork dumplings

Makes 48

....

450 g (1 lb/3 cups) strong plain (all-purpose) flour

4 dried shiitake mushrooms

1 tablespoon vegetable oil

250 g (9 oz) Chinese cabbage (wombok), trimmed and finely chopped

500 g (1 lb 2 oz) minced (ground) pork

60 ml (2 fl oz/¼ cup) chicken stock (page 405)

1 tablespoon light soy sauce

3 teaspoons sesame oil

1 tablespoon shaoxing rice wine

2 teaspoons finely chopped ginger

60 g (2 oz/½ cup) chopped garlic chives or coriander (cilantro) leaves

sea salt and ground white pepper

125 ml (4 fl oz/½ cup) black rice vinegar

2 tablespoons finely chopped ginger

....

To make the dough, put the flour in a bowl and make a well in the centre. Add 275 ml (9½ fl oz) water to the well, then use a wooden spoon to gradually work the liquid into the flour to form a soft dough. Turn out onto a lightly floured surface and knead for about 8 minutes, or until smooth and elastic — the dough should be soft but not sticky. If the dough is too sticky, add a little extra flour, but not too much or the dumpling wrappers will be tough. Form the dough into a ball, cover with plastic wrap and set aside at room temperature while you make the filling.

To make the filling, put the shiitake mushrooms in a small heatproof bowl, cover with boiling water and soak for 30 minutes, or until softened. Drain well, squeeze dry, then finely chop. Meanwhile, heat the vegetable oil in a saucepan over a medium heat, then add the cabbage and cook, stirring occasionally, for 7–8 minutes, or until the cabbage is tender. Remove from the heat and set aside.

Put the pork and stock in a bowl, then use your hands to work the liquid into the pork to form a smooth paste. Using a spoon and stirring in the one direction, stir in the soy sauce, sesame oil, rice wine and ginger; stir for 4–5 minutes, or until the mixture is light in texture and smooth. Stir in the garlic chives, mushrooms and cabbage and season with sea salt and white pepper.

Place the dough on a lightly floured surface and cut into four even pieces. Place three pieces to one side and cover loosely with plastic wrap to prevent them drying out. Roll the remaining piece of dough into a log about 12 cm (4¾ inches) long. Cut the log into 12 even pieces, then roll each piece into a ball. Using a small rolling pin, roll a dough ball into a 7.5 cm (3 inch) circle, then repeat for the remaining 11 dough balls. Place 2 teaspoons of pork filling in the middle of the round, then bring the edges together over the filling, pressing them together and making a few pleats to secure the join. Place on a tray lined with baking paper. Repeat the process with the remaining three pieces of dough and filling.

Bring a large saucepan of water to the boil. Cook the dumplings in two or three batches, stirring them gently so they don't stick to the base of the pan, for 5–6 minutes, or until they float to the surface and are cooked through. Remove using a slotted spoon and transfer to warmed bowls or a platter. To make a dipping sauce, combine the vinegar and ginger in a small bowl and serve with the dumplings.

Cabbage and pork dumplings: Smashed radish (page 105)

Sesame buns

Makes 12

Shao bing *are sesame cakes or buns, found in many parts of China but particularly throughout the north, where wheat flour is a staple. They're often eaten as a morning snack, with the option of a salty or sweet version. This recipe is for savoury buns, which make a great accompaniment to gutsy northern-style lamb or beef dishes. To make a sweet version, just sprinkle each smear of sesame paste with a teaspoon or so of sugar as you roll them.*

1 tablespoon caster (superfine) sugar
3 teaspoons instant dried yeast
600 g (1 lb 5 oz/4 cups) plain (all-purpose) flour
2½ teaspoons salt

2½ tablespoons Chinese sesame paste
1 tablespoon vegetable oil, plus extra for cooking
100 g (3½ oz/⅔ cup) sesame seeds

Combine 125 ml (4 fl oz/½ cup) lukewarm water and a large pinch of the sugar in a bowl, then sprinkle over the yeast. Set aside in a draught-free place for 5–6 minutes, or until foamy. Add another 310 ml (10½ fl oz/1¼ cups) lukewarm water to the mixture.

Combine the flour, remaining sugar and 2 teaspoons of the salt in a large bowl, then add the yeast mixture and stir with a wooden spoon to just bring the dough together. Turn the dough out onto a lightly floured surface and knead for 8–10 minutes, or until smooth and elastic (alternatively, knead using an electric mixer with a dough hook attachment). Form the dough into a ball, then place in a large, lightly oiled bowl, turning the dough to coat. Cover the bowl with plastic wrap and set aside in a draught-free place for about 1½ hours, or until the dough has doubled in size.

Combine the sesame paste, oil and remaining salt in a small bowl. Knock back the dough, turn it out onto a lightly floured surface and roll it into a log about 40 cm (16 inches) long. Cut the log into 12 even pieces, then roll each piece into a ball. Working with one ball at a time and using a rolling pin, roll the dough ball into a 16 cm (6¼ inch) circle. Using the back of a teaspoon, smear about 1 teaspoon of sesame paste mixture over the circle. Roll up tightly to form a log, then form the log into a tight spiral, pinching the end to seal. Use your hand to flatten the spiral into a 9 cm (3½ inch) round. Repeat with the remaining dough balls and sesame paste mixture.

Put the sesame seeds on a plate. Lightly brush the buns on each side with water, then dip into the sesame seeds on both sides to coat. Lightly brush the base of a large, heavy-based frying pan with oil, then heat over a medium–low heat. Add the buns in batches, then cover the pan and cook for 10 minutes on each side, reducing the heat if the buns brown too quickly and rotating them in the pan to ensure even cooking if necessary. Serve as a light snack or accompaniment.

Photograph page 271

Spring onion pancakes

Makes 8

Another carb staple of the north, spring onion (scallion) pancakes aren't a pancake in the true sense because they are made from a dough, not a batter. There are countless regional variations, all of them delicious — some are thin and flaky, others are made using a yeasted dough and are fat and puffy. Sometimes sesame seeds or garlic chives are added; other times they're cooked with egg smeared over one side.

large pinch of caster (superfine) sugar

1 teaspoon instant dried yeast

260 g (9 oz/1¾ cups) plain (all-purpose) flour, plus a little extra if needed

1 teaspoon salt

60 ml (2 fl oz/¼ cup) melted lard or vegetable oil, plus extra for cooking

3 spring onions (scallions), chopped

Combine 125 ml (4 fl oz/½ cup) lukewarm water and the sugar in a small bowl, then sprinkle over the yeast. Set aside in a draught-free place for 5–6 minutes, or until foamy.

Divide the flour between two bowls. Combine the yeast mixture with one portion of flour, and stir with a wooden spoon to just bring the dough together. Add the salt to the other bowl of flour, then, stirring vigorously, slowly add 125 ml (4 fl oz/½ cup) boiling water and then 2 tablespoons of the melted lard; stir to bring the dough together.

Turn both doughs out onto a lightly floured surface, then knead them together for 5 minutes, or until the dough is soft and smooth — add a little more flour if the dough is very sticky, but do not add too much as the dough should be quite soft. Form the dough into a ball, then place in a lightly oiled bowl, turning the dough to coat. Cover the bowl with plastic wrap and set aside in a draught-free place for about 40 minutes, or until the dough has doubled in size.

Knock back the dough, turn it out onto a lightly floured surface and roll it into a log about 28 cm (11 inches) long. Cut the log into eight even pieces, then roll each piece into a ball. Working with one ball at a time and using a small rolling pin, roll the dough ball into a 15 cm (6 inch) circle. Brush the surface with some of the remaining lard, then sprinkle with 1 tablespoon of the spring onions. Roll the dough up into a tight sausage and pinch the ends to seal, then roll it into a tight spiral (this helps to create flaky layers when the pancakes are cooking), with the seam side in. Using the rolling pin or your hands, flatten each spiral into a 16 cm (6¼ inch) round. Repeat the process with the remaining dough balls and spring onions.

Place a large, heavy-based frying pan over a medium heat, brush the base with lard or oil, then cook the pancakes in batches for 6–7 minutes, turning once, or until deep golden and cooked through. Cool slightly and serve warm.

Photograph page 266

Steamed pumpkin dumplings

Makes 20

'Pumpkin dumplings!' shrieked our Taiwanese friend Sarah, who has lived all over the Mainland for years. 'That's not Chinese!' Unhappily we've never quite made it to Xinjiang, the sprawling Muslim region in the northwest, but we have eaten bucketloads of food from that area during our travels. These are based on a dish from that region, kawa mantisi, or pumpkin dumplings. So, technically, she's right; these aren't strictly Han Chinese, but Xinjiang counts as part of Greater China, as it's within the borders.

2 tablespoons vegetable oil

1.5 kg (3 lb 5 oz) jap or kent pumpkin (winter squash), peeled, seeded and chopped

1 tablespoon finely chopped ginger

1 teaspoon cumin seeds

sea salt and freshly ground black pepper

225 g (8 oz/1½ cups) plain (all-purpose) flour, plus extra for kneading

1½ teaspoons salt

black rice vinegar and chilli flakes, to serve

Heat half of the oil in a saucepan over a medium heat, then add the pumpkin, ginger and cumin seeds. Cover the pan and cook, stirring occasionally, for about 20 minutes, or until the pumpkin is tender, then remove the lid and cook, stirring often, for another 20 minutes, or until the liquid released from the pumpkin has evaporated and the mixture has thickened. Season to taste with sea salt and pepper, then cool.

Meanwhile, to make the dough, combine the flour and salt in a bowl. Add 185 ml (6 fl oz/¾ cup) water, then use your hands to mix to form a soft dough. Turn the dough out onto a lightly floured surface and knead for 5 minutes, or until smooth, adding a little extra flour if necessary; the dough should be a little soft. Form the dough into a ball, cover with plastic wrap and rest at room temperature for 30 minutes.

Place the dough on a lightly floured surface and divide it into 20 even pieces, then roll each piece into a ball. Using a small rolling pin, roll a dough ball into a 12 cm (4¾ inch) circle, rolling the edges so they are a little thinner than the middle. Place a slightly heaped tablespoon of cooled pumpkin mixture in the middle of the round, then lightly brush around the edge of the dough with water. Bring the dough edges up and over the pumpkin filling, pleating seven or eight times to enclose the filling, and twisting the ends together to seal. Place the completed dumplings on a tray lined with baking paper. Repeat with the remaining dough balls, rolling out a few each time and then filling them.

Put the dumplings in a steamer lined with perforated baking paper. Place the steamer over a wok or saucepan of boiling water, then cover and steam for 15 minutes, or until cooked through. Serve with small bowls of vinegar for dipping, and chilli flakes, to sprinkle over as desired.

Steam-fried pork buns

Makes 22

1½ teaspoons instant dried yeast

2 teaspoons caster (superfine) sugar

2 tablespoons vegetable oil, plus extra
for cooking

375 g (13 oz/2½ cups) strong plain (all-purpose)
flour

½ teaspoon salt

2 teaspoons baking powder

black rice vinegar, to serve

Filling

450 g (1 lb) minced (ground) pork or beef

80 ml (2½ fl oz/⅓ cup) jellied chicken stock
(page 405)

1½ tablespoons light soy sauce

3 teaspoons shaoxing rice wine

3 teaspoons sesame oil

25 g (1 oz/½ cup) chopped coriander (cilantro)
leaves

To make the dough, sprinkle the yeast over 250 ml (8½ fl oz/1 cup) lukewarm water in a large bowl, then set aside in a draught-free place for 5–6 minutes, or until foamy. Add the sugar, oil, flour and salt, then stir with a wooden spoon to just bring the dough together. Turn out onto a lightly floured surface and knead for 10 minutes, or until smooth and elastic. Form the dough into a ball, then place in a large, lightly oiled bowl, turning the dough to coat. Cover the bowl with plastic wrap and set aside in a draught-free place for about 45 minutes, or until the dough has doubled in size.

Meanwhile, put all the filling ingredients in a large bowl and stir to combine well, using a wooden spoon to break up the mince if necessary.

Knock back the dough and turn it out onto a lightly floured surface, then sprinkle with the baking powder and knead well to distribute it through the dough. Divide the dough into two even pieces. Working with one piece at a time, divide the dough into 11 even pieces, then roll each piece into a ball. Working with one ball at a time and using a small rolling pin, roll the dough ball on a lightly floured surface into a 13 cm (5 inch) circle. Place 1 tablespoon of the filling in the middle of the round, then lightly brush around the edge with water. Draw the dough up around one side of the filling, then fold and pinch the dough over the filling, working around the bun, making small pleats as you go. Gather the pleats together in the middle and twist firmly to seal. Repeat with all the remaining dough and filling.

Pour enough oil into a large, heavy-based frying pan to come about 5 mm (¼ inch) up the side of the pan and place over a medium–low heat. Add enough buns, pleated side up, to fill the pan, leaving a 1 cm (½ inch) space between each and also between the buns and the side of the pan. Cook for 4 minutes, or until deep golden on the base. Taking extreme care as the pan will steam, add 60 ml (2 fl oz/¼ cup) water to the pan, then immediately cover the pan loosely with a piece of foil; a little steam needs to be able to escape so condensation doesn't wet the top of the buns. Cook for 5–6 minutes, or until the water has evaporated, the pan is sizzling and the buns are cooked through (add a little extra water if necessary). Repeat the process with the remaining buns. Serve hot with vinegar, for dipping.

Steam-fried pork buns; Garlic chive packets (page 350); Taro and pork soup (page 224)

Garlic chive packets

Makes 6

These and the fried beef and dill flatbreads (page 365) have us yearning for Xi'an. There they make all manner of fried, filled bing (breads), which challenge many clichéd preconceptions about what Chinese food is. In Xi'an's Muslim Quarter, most shops and restaurants specialise in just one particular dish or snack, and our favourite shop on touristy Beiyuanmen Street makes the biggest, crispest, stuffed-est bing ever.

Filling
35 g (1¼ oz) bean thread (glass) vermicelli noodles
1½ tablespoons vegetable oil
2 eggs, lightly beaten
250 g (9 oz) garlic chives (2 bunches), chopped
3 spring onions (scallions), finely chopped
sea salt and freshly ground black pepper

Dough
260 g (9 oz/1¾ cups) plain (all-purpose) flour
1 egg, lightly beaten
2 tablespoons vegetable oil, plus extra for cooking

To make the filling, put the vermicelli noodles in a small heatproof bowl, cover with boiling water and soak for 15 minutes, or until softened, then drain. Finely chop the vermicelli and place in a large bowl.

Heat half of the oil in a wok over a medium–high heat, then add the eggs and cook, stirring, for 2 minutes, or until scrambled. Add to the noodles in the bowl. Heat the remaining oil in the wok, then add the garlic chives and spring onions and stir-fry for 2–3 minutes, or until wilted and bright green. Add to the noodle mixture and stir to combine well. Season to taste with sea salt and pepper.

To make the dough, put the flour in a bowl. Whisk together the egg, oil and 125 ml (4 fl oz/½ cup) water in a small bowl. Add to the flour, then stir with a wooden spoon to just bring the dough together. Tip the dough out onto a lightly floured surface and knead for 3–4 minutes, or until smooth. Form the dough into a ball, cover with plastic wrap and rest at room temperature for 30 minutes.

Divide the dough into six even pieces, then roll each piece into a ball. Working with one ball at a time and using a small rolling pin, roll the dough ball on a lightly floured surface into a 20 cm (8 inch) circle. Using about one-sixth of the filling, spread it over one half of the circle, leaving a 1 cm (½ inch) border around the lower edge. Lightly brush the border with water, then fold the unfilled half of the dough over the filling and press the edges together to seal. Repeat with the remaining dough balls and filling.

Place a large, heavy-based frying pan over a medium–low heat, brush the base with oil, then cook the chive packets in batches for 5 minutes on each side, or until deep golden, adding more oil as necessary. Serve hot.

Photograph page 349

Sweet baked lotus paste buns

Makes 12

We've never been quite sure why so many otherwise rational people, accomplished cooks among them, have such a terror of using yeast. People, listen up — it's simple to use! Particularly modern, instant yeast, which technically you don't even need to start in warm liquid — you can just throw it straight into the flour and mix and knead from there. The only thing that will kill yeast is if you mix it with liquid that's too hot, so make sure your water or milk is always at blood temperature.

2½ teaspoons instant dried yeast

170 ml (5½ fl oz/⅔ cup) warm milk

60 ml (2 fl oz/¼ cup) vegetable oil

2 eggs, beaten

1 tablespoon caster (superfine) sugar

485 g (1 lb 1 oz/3¼ cups) plain (all-purpose) flour, plus extra if needed

1 teaspoon salt

300 g (10½ oz) lotus seed paste

1 egg yolk

Sprinkle the yeast over 2 tablespoons lukewarm water in a small bowl, then set aside in a draught-free place for 6 minutes, or until foamy. Combine the yeast mixture, milk, oil, eggs and sugar in a large bowl and stir with a wooden spoon to combine well. Add the flour and salt and stir to just bring the dough together. Turn the dough out onto a lightly floured surface and knead for about 8 minutes, or until smooth and elastic, adding a little extra flour if the dough remains sticky — the dough should be soft. Cover the dough with a tea towel (dish towel).

Divide the lotus seed paste into 12 pieces and then roll each into a ball. Set aside. Divide the dough into 12 even pieces, then roll each piece into a ball. Working with one dough ball at a time, use your hand to flatten the ball to a 9 cm (3½ inch) circle. Place a ball of lotus paste in the middle of each circle, then bring the edges up and over the filling to meet in the middle. Pinch the edges together to seal. Place the bun on the work surface, seam side down, and shape it into a neat ball. As you fill and shape each bun, transfer it to a large baking tray lined with baking paper, leaving room between each for rising, and loosely cover with a tea towel. Leave in a draught-free place for 40 minutes, or until risen and puffy.

Meanwhile, preheat the oven to 180°C (350°F/Gas 4). Combine the egg yolk with 2–3 teaspoons water in a small bowl, then brush the mixture over the buns. Bake for 20–25 minutes, or until deep golden. Remove to a wire rack to cool. The buns are best served on the day they are made.

Potsticker dumplings

Makes 24

300 g (10½ oz/2 cups) plain (all-purpose) flour

½ teaspoon salt

1 tablespoon melted lard or vegetable oil

2 tablespoons vegetable oil, for frying

black rice vinegar and light soy sauce, to serve

Filling

300 g (10½ oz) boneless, skinless chicken thighs, trimmed and roughly chopped

1 carrot (about 100 g/3½ oz), grated

2 spring onions (scallions), finely sliced

1 teaspoon sugar

1 tablespoon light soy sauce

1 tablespoon shaoxing rice wine

1 small bunch coriander (cilantro), leaves picked and roughly chopped

1 tablespoon finely chopped ginger

2 garlic cloves, finely chopped

1 egg, lightly beaten

½ teaspoon salt

To make the dough, combine the flour, salt and lard in a bowl, then add 185 ml (6 fl oz/¾ cup) water. Stir with a wooden spoon to just bring the dough together, adding a little more water if needed, to form a soft dough. Turn the dough out onto a lightly floured surface and knead for 5 minutes, or until smooth and elastic. Form the dough into a ball, cover with plastic wrap and rest at room temperature for 20 minutes.

Meanwhile, to make the filling, put the chicken in a bowl with all the remaining ingredients and combine well. Refrigerate until required.

Place the dough on a lightly floured surface and roll it into a log about 30 cm (12 inches) long. Cut the log into 24 even pieces, then roll each piece into a small ball. Using a small, floured rolling pin, roll each dough ball into an 8 cm (3¼ inch) circle, about 5 mm (¼ inch) thick. Stack the rounds on a lightly floured tray and cover with a damp tea towel (dish towel) to prevent them from drying out.

Put about 1 tablespoon of the filling across the middle of one round, lightly brush around the edge with water, then fold the sides up and over the filling, to meet in the middle. Press the edges firmly to seal, leaving the ends open (you can add a few pleats along the seam if you like). The dumpling should have a flat base. As you fill each dumpling, place it on a tray lined with baking paper, seam side up, and keep covered with a damp tea towel.

Heat the oil in a large, heavy-based non-stick frying pan over a high heat. Working in batches, place the dumplings in the pan, flat side down and quite close together, then reduce the heat to medium and cook for 2–3 minutes, or until golden and crisp. Add 100 ml (3½ fl oz) water, cover the pan tightly and cook for about 12 minutes, or until most of the liquid has been absorbed and the dumplings are cooked through. Check the water halfway through cooking and add a little more if required. Remove the lid and cook for another 2–3 minutes, or until the liquid has been absorbed and the bottoms of the dumplings are golden brown. Repeat with the remaining dumplings. Serve with small bowls of vinegar and soy sauce, for dipping.

Mandarin pancakes

Makes 20

You've no doubt encountered these if you've ever ordered Peking duck or mu shu *pork in a Chinese restaurant. These thin, versatile pancakes are quite simple to make, requiring only flour, water and oil. We particularly love peeling them apart after they're cooked and smelling the unmistakable aroma of sesame oil. These freeze well too, if you want to make extra to have on hand.*

300 g (10½ oz/2 cups) plain (all-purpose) flour
1 tablespoon peanut oil

sesame oil, for brushing

Sift the flour into a mixing bowl, add 185 ml (6 fl oz/¾ cup) boiling water and the peanut oil and mix well with a wooden spoon or chopsticks. Turn the dough out onto a lightly floured surface and knead for about 8 minutes, or until the dough is smooth (take care, as the dough will be hot). Cover with a damp tea towel (dish towel) and leave to rest for 30 minutes.

Roll the dough into a log about 30 cm (12 inches) long. Cut the log into 20 even pieces, then roll each piece into a ball. Use your hand to press down on each dough ball, flattening it out into a 7 cm (2¾ inch) circle, about 5 mm (¼ inch) thick. Lightly brush one side of each circle with sesame oil, then sandwich two circles together with the sesame oil sides facing each other. Using a rolling pin, roll each pair of circles into 14 cm (5½ inch) pancakes, then cover with a damp tea towel.

Heat a large cast-iron or heavy-based frying pan over a medium heat. Add the pancakes in batches and cook each side for 1–2 minutes, or until they just start to bubble slightly and brown spots form on the cooked surface. Remove from the pan and pull the two pancakes apart, then stack with the cooked sides facing down. Cover with foil and keep warm in a low oven while you cook the remaining pancakes.

Photograph page 221

Sichuan dumplings in chilli

Makes about 30

An entire book could be devoted to the snack foods of Chengdu, a place granted City of Gastronomy status in 2010 by no less than UNESCO. When you go there, eat at a branch of Long Chao Shou restaurant for a free-for-all snack-fest that will be nothing short of revelatory. This dish, called zhong shui jiao, *involves crescent-shaped pork dumplings served in a glistening pool of viciously hot sauce. It's a masochistic wake-up call when eaten, as the locals do, first thing in the morning.*

400 g (14 oz) minced (ground) pork
1 egg, lightly beaten
2 teaspoons very finely chopped ginger
1½ tablespoons clear rice wine
sea salt and ground white pepper
about 30 round wheat dumpling wrappers

Chilli sauce
2 teaspoons sichuan peppercorns
80 ml (2½ fl oz/⅓ cup) light soy sauce
80 ml (2½ fl oz/⅓ cup) chilli oil (page 407), or ready-made
80 ml (2½ fl oz/⅓ cup) chicken stock (page 405)
1 tablespoon caster (superfine) sugar

To make the chilli sauce, first dry-roast the peppercorns in a small, heavy-based frying pan over a medium–low heat, shaking the pan often, for 3–4 minutes, or until fragrant. Cool, then transfer to a mortar (or an electric spice grinder) and pound with the pestle to form a coarse powder. Combine in a bowl with all the remaining ingredients, stirring to dissolve the sugar. Set aside.

Put the pork, egg, ginger and rice wine in a bowl, season with sea salt and white pepper, then use your hands to mix everything together. Lightly brush some water around the edge of one dumpling wrapper. Place a slightly heaped teaspoon of the pork mixture in the middle, then fold the wrapper over the filling to form a semicircle. Press the edges together to seal, pleating along the edge four or five times to secure. Repeat the process to fill all the dumplings.

Bring a large saucepan of water to the boil. Working in two batches, add the dumplings to the water, stirring gently to ensure they don't sink and stick to the base of the pan. Cook over a high heat for 5 minutes, or until the dumplings are cooked through. Remove with a slotted spoon and drain well. Stir the chilli sauce, then divide it among small warmed bowls. Divide the dumplings among the bowls and serve immediately.

Photograph page 357

From left to right: Black sesame tang yuan with ginger syrup (page 390); Stuffed sweet potato cakes (page 399); San da pao (page 393); Sichuan dumplings in chilli (page 355); Dan dan mian (page 317)

Curry puffs

Makes about 25

After rummaging through a fresh food market in Xiamen, truly one of the most enjoyable Chinese cities (and one with some remarkable food), we happened upon a street vendor frying curry puffs in a vat of oil. His pastries were the most beautiful study in crisp, delicate, puffy layers and perfect pleating — they looked way too good to eat. We demolished quite a few, waddled around the streets in a vain effort to walk them off, then simply turned around and went back for more. Ours are easier to make than his, but just as addictive.

Filling

1 small orange sweet potato (300 g/10½ oz), peeled and chopped

1½ tablespoons vegetable oil

1 onion, finely chopped

3 teaspoons finely chopped ginger

500 g (1 lb 2 oz) minced (ground) beef or pork

1 tablespoon mild curry powder

1½ tablespoons light soy sauce

2 teaspoons sugar

1 bunch coriander (cilantro), leaves picked and roughly chopped

sea salt and freshly ground black pepper

vegetable oil, for deep-drying

Pastry

400 g (14 oz/2⅔ cups) plain (all-purpose) flour

100 ml (3½ fl oz) vegetable oil

2 teaspoons sesame oil

To make the filling, cook the sweet potato in a saucepan of boiling salted water for 10 minutes, or until tender, then drain well and mash.

Meanwhile, heat the vegetable oil in a large frying pan over a medium heat, then add the onion and ginger and cook, stirring, for 3–4 minutes, or until the onion has softened slightly. Add the mince and cook, stirring with a wooden spoon to break up the meat, for 4–5 minutes, or until the meat has changed colour. Stir in the curry powder and cook for 1 minute, or until fragrant, then add the soy sauce and sugar and stir to combine well. Remove from the heat, stir in the sweet potato and coriander, season to taste with sea salt and pepper, then cool to room temperature.

To make the pastry, put the flour in a large bowl, then add the vegetable and sesame oils. Using your fingers, mix the oil through the flour. Add 200 ml (7 fl oz) warm water to the flour mixture, then stir using a flat-bladed knife to bring the dough together. Turn out onto a lightly floured surface and knead for 2 minutes, or until smooth.

Cut the dough into two even pieces. Use your hands to roll one piece into a ball. Using a rolling pin, roll out the other piece on a lightly floured surface into a 35 cm (14 inch) circle. Place the ball of dough in the middle of the circle of dough and bring the edges of the circle up to cover the ball, pinching to seal. Turn the ball over so the seam side is down. Loosely cover with a damp tea towel (dish towel) and rest at room temperature for 30 minutes.

Roll the dough out until it is about 3 mm (⅛ inch) thick. Using a 10 cm (4 inch) biscuit (cookie) cutter, cut out circles from the dough, reserving the scraps. Working with one round at a time, place about 1 tablespoon of the sweet potato filling in the middle of the round and lightly brush around the edge with water. Fold the pastry over to form a semicircle, then use your fingers to crimp the edges. Repeat with the remaining filling and dough, rerolling the scraps to use as well.

Fill a wok one-third full of oil and heat to 180°C (350°F), or until a cube of bread dropped into the oil turns deep golden in 15 seconds. Cook the pastries in batches for 4–5 minutes, or until golden and crisp. Drain well on paper towel and serve hot or at room temperature.

Abacus beads

Serves 4

From the Hakka culinary lexicon, which is marked by earthy, simple dishes, this dish is best described as 'Chinese gnocchi'. Taro is a starchy tuber very popular in Fujian and Guangdong Provinces, where it is used in everything from fillings in street snacks to an ingredient in desserts. Here its elastic texture makes for a delightfully chewy 'bead' and its gentle flavour provides a perfect foil for the strong, salty sauce.

550 g (1 lb 3 oz) taro (about ½ large taro), peeled

25 g (1 oz/¼ cup) dried shrimp

110 g (4 oz/¾ cup) tapioca flour

40 g (1½ oz/¼ cup) glutinous rice flour

60 ml (2 fl oz/¼ cup) vegetable oil

3 garlic cloves, finely chopped

250 g (9 oz) minced (ground) pork

340 ml (12 fl oz/1⅓ cups) chicken stock (page 405)

1 tablespoon soy paste

1 tablespoon oyster sauce

1 teaspoon sugar

1 teaspoon cornflour (cornstarch)

1 large red chilli, finely sliced

2 spring onions (scallions), finely sliced on the diagonal

1 handful coriander (cilantro) leaves, chopped

Cut the taro into pieces, place in a steamer over a wok or saucepan of boiling water, then cover and steam for 25 minutes, or until very tender. Set aside to cool. Meanwhile, put the dried shrimp in a heatproof bowl, cover with boiling water and soak for 30 minutes, or until softened, then drain.

Push the cooled taro through a mouli or a potato ricer into a large bowl. Add the tapioca and glutinous rice flours and 125 ml (4 fl oz/½ cup) water, stirring to combine, then slowly add another 2 or 3 tablespoons water, or enough to form a soft, pliable dough. Knead the mixture in the bowl with your hands until smooth. Take a heaped teaspoon of the mixture and roll it into a small ball, squashing the ball between your thumb and index finger to make a deep indentation. Repeat with the remaining dough. As you form each abacus bead, place it on a tray lined with baking paper.

Heat the oil in a large frying pan over a medium heat, then add the garlic and pork and cook, breaking the meat up with a wooden spoon, for 8 minutes, or until browned and cooked through. Add the shrimp, stock, soy paste, oyster sauce and sugar and stir to combine well. Combine the cornflour with just enough water in a small bowl to form a thin paste, then, stirring constantly, add to the simmering mixture in the pan; cook for about 30 seconds, or until the sauce thickens a little.

Bring a large saucepan of water to the boil, then add the abacus beads in two batches, stirring gently to keep them separated. Cook for 2–3 minutes, or until they float to the surface, then continue cooking for another 3 minutes, or until cooked through. Transfer to a colander and drain well, then add to the sauce in the frying pan, tossing to coat. Divide the abacus beads among four bowls, or place on a large platter, and spoon over the sauce. Scatter over the chilli, spring onions and coriander and serve immediately.

Our jian bing

Makes about 12

Sadly, it's impossible to make 'authentic' jian bing at home; it requires car noise, vehicle fumes and general kerbside clatter in order for them to really taste good — not to mention the skill needed. Versions of this breakfast-time pancake abound and it's particularly prevalent in Beijing. We've eaten our fill of them all over China, but our absolute favourite is made by the man who appears early each morning on Sichuan Middle Road in Shanghai, right near the budget Shijia Hotel. His has just the right balance of egg, chewiness, sweet hoisin, crisp lettuce and chilli.

110 g (4 oz/¾ cup) plain (all-purpose) flour
90 g (3 oz/¾ cup) millet flour
2 tablespoons cornflour (cornstarch)
1½ teaspoons salt
vegetable oil, for cooking
6 eggs, beaten
5 spring onions (scallions), finely sliced
chilli sauce, to serve
16–20 oakleaf or butter lettuce leaves

3 Chinese fried dough sticks, finely sliced on the diagonal (optional)
2 handfuls coriander (cilantro) leaves

Sauce
1 tablespoon vegetable oil
3 teaspoons very finely chopped ginger
2 garlic cloves, very finely chopped
125 ml (4 fl oz/½ cup) hoisin sauce

To make the sauce, heat the oil in a small saucepan over a medium heat, then add the ginger and garlic and cook, stirring, for 2 minutes, or until fragrant. Add the hoisin sauce and 2½ tablespoons water and stir to combine well. Remove from the heat.

Combine the flours and salt in a bowl, then add 375 ml (12½ fl oz/1½ cups) water. Whisk to combine well, adding 1 or 2 tablespoons water if the mixture is too thick — it should have a creamy consistency.

Brush a 16 cm (6¼ inch) heavy-based frying pan with oil and place over a medium heat. Pour about 60 ml (2 fl oz/¼ cup) of batter into the pan, spreading it as quickly as you can to the edge of the pan (a pastry scraper is the best thing to use for this). Pour a little of the egg over the top and spread it over the surface, allowing the egg to run into any holes or torn parts in the batter, to fill them. Scatter some of the spring onions over the egg, then cook for about 3 minutes, or until the egg just begins to set. Flip the pancake over and cook for another minute, then turn it out onto a plate. Cover loosely with foil and keep warm in a low oven. Repeat with the remaining batter, egg and spring onions.

Spread some of the sauce and chilli sauce over each pancake, to taste. Place a few lettuce leaves and some slices of fried dough sticks, if using, on the pancakes and scatter with some coriander, then roll up or fold loosely and serve.

Fried pork and coriander breads

Makes 8

Yet another inspiration from Xi'an, these meaty 'pies' come into their own on a punishing cold Shaanxi morning for breakfast. They are usually made with lamb or beef (not pork), but feel free to play around with the filling — however, don't, whatever you do, use meat that's too lean, as these really need a bit of juicy fat.

Dough

2½ teaspoons caster (superfine) sugar

¾ teaspoon instant dried yeast

1½ tablespoons melted lard or vegetable oil

300 g (10½ oz/2 cups) plain (all-purpose) flour

½ teaspoon salt

vegetable oil, for cooking

Filling

300 g (10½ oz) minced (ground) pork

2 teaspoons finely chopped ginger

1 garlic clove, crushed

1 bunch coriander (cilantro), chopped

2 teaspoons dark soy sauce

1 teaspoon sesame oil

2 teaspoons shaoxing rice wine

3 teaspoons cornflour (cornstarch)

sea salt and freshly ground black pepper

To make the dough, combine 125 ml (4 fl oz/½ cup) lukewarm water and a large pinch of the sugar in a small bowl, then sprinkle over the yeast. Set aside in a draught-free place for 5–6 minutes, or until foamy, then stir in the melted lard. Combine the flour, remaining sugar and salt in a large bowl, add the yeast mixture and an extra 60 ml (2 fl oz/¼ cup) warm water (or enough to form a soft dough) and stir with a wooden spoon to just bring the dough together. Turn out onto a lightly floured surface and knead for 4–5 minutes, or until smooth and elastic. Form the dough into a ball, then place in a lightly oiled bowl, turning the dough to coat. Cover the bowl with plastic wrap and set aside in a draught-free place for 40 minutes, or until risen.

Meanwhile, to make the filling, combine all the ingredients in a bowl and season with sea salt and pepper.

Knock back the dough, then turn it out onto a lightly floured surface. Cut the dough into eight even pieces, then roll each piece into a ball. Using a floured, small rolling pin, roll each dough ball into a 15 cm (6 inch) circle. Divide the filling mixture into eight even portions. Press a filling portion into the middle of each round, leaving a 2 cm (¾ inch) border around the edge. Lightly brush around the edge with water, then bring the edges together over the filling and press to seal. Shape the breads by placing them, seam side down, on the work surface and gently press them into a neat flat round, about 12 cm (4¾ inches) in diameter.

Liberally brush some oil over the base of a large, heavy-based frying pan, then place over a medium–low heat. Cook the breads in batches for 5 minutes on each side, or until the breads are deep golden and the filling is cooked, adding more oil as necessary. Serve hot or warm.

Fried beef and dill flatbreads

Makes 6

50 g (1¾ oz) bean thread (glass) vermicelli
  noodles
60 ml (2 fl oz/¼ cup) vegetable oil, plus extra
  for shallow-frying
250 g (9 oz) minced (ground) beef
3 large eggs, beaten well
2 garlic cloves, finely chopped

6 spring onions (scallions), sliced
3 bunches dill, chopped, including stems
sea salt and freshly ground black pepper

Dough
450 g (1 lb/3 cups) plain (all-purpose) flour
1½ teaspoons salt

To make the filling, put the vermicelli noodles in a small heatproof bowl, cover with boiling water and soak for 15 minutes, or until softened, then drain. Using kitchen scissors, cut the noodles into smaller pieces.

Meanwhile, heat 1 tablespoon of the oil in a wok over a medium–high heat, then add the beef and cook, breaking up the meat with a wooden spoon, for 5–6 minutes, or until browned and all the liquid has evaporated. Transfer to a large bowl, wipe the wok clean and return to a medium–high heat. Add another tablespoon of oil to the wok, then add the eggs, swirling to coat the base of the wok. Cook for 1–2 minutes, or until the egg has set on the base, then slide the omelette onto a plate, uncooked side up. Invert the omelette back into the wok and cook for another 30 seconds, or until just cooked. Turn out onto a chopping board, finely chop, then add to the beef in the bowl.

Return the wok to the heat, add the remaining oil and cook the garlic, spring onions and dill, stirring the mixture often, for 2–3 minutes, or until the spring onions have wilted. Add to the beef mixture along with the vermicelli and season to taste with sea salt and pepper. Set aside to cool.

To make the dough, combine the flour and salt in a bowl. Add 250 ml (8½ fl oz/1 cup) boiling water and stir to combine, then add 125 ml (4 fl oz/½ cup) cold water and stir to bring the dough together. Turn out onto a lightly floured surface and knead for 5 minutes, or until smooth and elastic, adding a little extra water if the dough is too stiff — the dough should be a little soft. Form the dough into a ball, cover with plastic wrap and rest at room temperature for 30 minutes.

Place the dough on a lightly floured surface, divide it into 12 even pieces, then roll each piece into a ball. Using a rolling pin, roll a dough ball into a 20 cm (8 inch) circle, rolling the edges so they are a little thinner than the middle. Repeat with the remaining dough balls. Divide the filling mixture into six portions. Spread one portion of filling over one round, leaving a 2 cm (¾ inch) border. Place another dough round on top, then press together in the centre, then around the edges to seal. Repeat with the remaining dough rounds and filling.

Heat about 1 cm (½ inch) oil in a large, heavy-based frying pan over a medium–high heat and cook the breads, one at a time, for 5 minutes on each side, or until golden and crisp. Serve immediately.

Sweets

Dessert, as such, is a foreign concept to the Chinese. Their dining style sees sweet and savoury dishes served together, with fruit the preferred finale. Which isn't to say they are strangers to the sugar hit — far from it. While many of their cakes, fruit dishes, sweet dumplings and fritters are technically snacks or sides, they're perfect for serving last, as a separate course.

Watermelon in rosewater sauce

Serves 6 to 8

230 g (8 oz/1 cup) caster (superfine) sugar
2½ tablespoons cornflour (cornstarch)
2 tablespoons rosewater, or to taste
red food colouring (optional)

2 kg (4 lb 6 oz) seedless watermelon, peeled
peanut ice cream, to serve (optional)
(recipe below)

Combine 580 ml (19½ fl oz/2⅓ cups) water and the sugar in a saucepan and bring to a simmer over a medium heat. Combine the cornflour with 60 ml (2 fl oz/¼ cup) water in a small bowl. Whisking constantly, add the cornflour mixture to the simmering syrup, whisking until the mixture simmers and thickens. Remove from the heat, then add the rosewater and enough red food colouring, if using, to tint the mixture pink. Set aside to cool.

Meanwhile, cut the watermelon into neat 1 cm (½ inch) cubes and divide among small bowls. Spoon the rosewater sauce over the watermelon and serve with a scoop of peanut ice cream, if desired.

Peanut ice cream

Serves 6 to 8

500 ml (17 fl oz/2 cups) cream (35% fat)
375 ml (12½ fl oz/1½ cups) full-cream (whole)
  milk
6 large egg yolks

230 g (8 oz/1 cup firmly packed) soft brown sugar
90 g (3 oz/⅓ cup) smooth peanut butter
80 g (2¾ oz/½ cup) raw, skinned peanuts,
  roasted (page 413) and crushed

Combine the cream and milk in a saucepan and slowly bring just to a simmer, then remove from the heat. Using an electric mixer, whisk the egg yolks and sugar until thick and pale. Stirring constantly with a wooden spoon, pour the cream mixture into the egg yolk mixture and stir to combine well. Place the mixture in a clean saucepan, then, stirring constantly with a wooden spoon, cook over a medium–low heat for about 8 minutes, or until the mixture thickens enough to coat the back of the spoon. Do not let the mixture get too hot or it will curdle. Remove from the heat and cool slightly.

Put the peanut butter in a heatproof bowl, pour about 250 ml (8½ fl oz/1 cup) of the hot custard into the bowl and stir to combine well. Add this to the remaining custard mixture in the pan, then stir well. Strain, cool to room temperature, then refrigerate until well chilled. Stir in the crushed peanuts, then freeze in an ice-cream machine according to the manufacturer's instructions. Place in an airtight container and transfer to the freezer. The ice cream will keep, frozen and covered, for up to 1 week.

Sweet peanut rice flour dumplings

Makes 16

Light, chewy, sweet and crunchy with nuts, these are typical of the kinds of snacks we so love in the south. They're best served while still warm straight from the pot — they'll become rubbery if you keep them for any length of time, even a few hours. As if they'd hang around for that long!

120 g (4½ oz/¾ cup) raw, skinned peanuts, roasted (page 413)

145 g (5 oz/⅔ cup) caster (superfine) sugar

320 g (11½ oz/2 cups) glutinous rice flour, plus extra for rolling

Put the cooled, roasted peanuts in a food processor with the sugar and process until the peanuts are finely chopped but not too powdery — they should still have some texture. Set aside.

Put the rice flour in a bowl. Stirring constantly with a wooden spoon, add 250 ml (8½ fl oz/1 cup) boiling water and stir to form a rough dough. Cool slightly; when just cool enough to handle (the mixture will still be hot) knead to form a soft dough, adding a little more boiling water if necessary if the mixture is too firm. Knead for 2–3 minutes, or until smooth.

Turn the dough out onto a lightly floured surface. Using your hands, roll the warm dough into a log about 20 cm (8 inches) long. Cut the log into 16 even pieces, then roll each piece into a ball. Working with one dough ball at a time, and taking care as the dough is soft, use a small, floured rolling pin to roll the dough into a 9 cm (3½ inch) circle. Place 1 heaped teaspoon of peanut mixture in the middle of the round, then carefully bring the edges of the round together above the filling and pinch to seal. Place the dumpling, seam side down, on a tray lined with baking paper. Repeat with the remaining dough balls and peanut mixture, reserving any left-over peanut mixture.

Fill a large saucepan with water and bring to the boil, then add the dumplings in batches and cook over a medium–high heat for 2–3 minutes, or until they float to the top. Carefully remove using a slotted spoon and place on a warmed serving platter. Sprinkle the dumplings with the remaining peanut mixture and serve immediately.

Pineapple cakes

Makes 14

Pineapple cakes are popular in Taiwan and in Fujian Province where tropical fruits are plentiful. We buy our cakes in Xiamen on Zhongshan Road, which is a fun place to head for a quick primer on the various local snacks and specialties: oolong tea, sweet peanut soup, popiah, oyster fritters, grilled squid and the like. We can but approximate the Xiamen original, which is a triumph of buttery pastry and sweet, sticky pineapple jam.

300 g (10½ oz) unsalted butter, softened
80 g (2¾ oz/⅓ cup) caster (superfine) sugar
1 egg
450 g (1 lb/3 cups) plain (all-purpose) flour, sifted

Filling
1 large ripe pineapple (1.2 kg/2 lb 10 oz), peeled, cored and chopped
100 g (3½ oz) caster (superfine) sugar
80 g (2¾ oz) liquid glucose

To make the filling, put the pineapple flesh in a food processor and, using the pulse button, process to form a coarse purée (you don't want it to be smooth). Combine the pineapple, sugar and glucose in a non-reactive saucepan and bring to a simmer over a medium heat. Cook, stirring often, for about 35 minutes, or until the mixture is very thick and jammy — the pineapple should reduce down to about 340 ml (12 fl oz/1⅓ cups). Remove from the heat and cool to room temperature.

Using electric beaters, cream the butter and sugar until light and fluffy, then add the egg and beat to combine well. Stir in the flour to form a soft dough. Turn out onto a lightly floured surface and use your hands to shape the dough into a disc. Cover with plastic wrap and refrigerate for 45 minutes.

Preheat the oven to 180°C (350°F/Gas 4). You will need two 12-hole non-stick square muffin tins (or cook the cakes in two batches).

Divide the dough into 14 even pieces, then roll each piece into a ball. Using your hands, flatten each ball to form a 12 cm (4¾ inch) circle; roll the edges with a small rolling pin so they are a little thinner than the middle. Place a heaped teaspoon of pineapple mixture in the middle of each round, then bring the edges of the dough together over the filling, pinching to seal. Place each pineapple cake, sealed side down, into a muffin hole, then use your hand to gently press down on the pastry so it fills the hole. Bake for 20 minutes, or until golden, then leave to cool in the tin for 20 minutes. Remove to a wire rack to cool completely. The pineapple cakes can be kept for up to 1 week in an airtight container at room temperature, or can be frozen for up to 8 weeks.

Pineapple cakes; Wife cakes (pages 374–5); Peanut brittle (page 401)

Wife cakes

Makes 14

The traditional method of making the Chinese flaky pastry for these — which separates as it cooks into the most delicate layers imaginable — is a true art. So we've suggested rough puff, which is by no means a shabby substitute. How these got their name isn't clear, although theories abound. One has it that a man fell into debt, hocked his wife to the landlord to make some cash, then promptly invented these cakes and sold them by the roadside in a bid to secure enough money to buy her back. Whatever their story, they are made from relatively humble ingredients: winter melon, sugar, flour and, traditionally, lard, which you can use instead of butter.

Pastry
250 g (9 oz/1⅔ cups) plain (all-purpose) flour
160 g (5½ oz) unsalted butter, slightly chilled and chopped
1 egg yolk mixed with 2 teaspoons water, for glazing

Filling
200 g (7 oz) candied winter melon, very finely chopped
50 g (1¾ oz/⅓ cup) sesame seeds, toasted (page 413), plus extra for sprinkling
30 g (1 oz/⅓ cup) desiccated coconut
40 g (1½ oz/¼ cup) cooked glutinous rice flour
2 tablespoons caster (superfine) sugar
2 teaspoons sesame oil

To make the pastry, put the flour in a bowl, add the butter and use your fingers to gently mix — do not rub the butter into the flour; it should be lumpy. Add 100 ml (3½ fl oz) ice-cold water, then, using a flat-bladed knife, mix to form a coarse, soft dough, adding about 1 tablespoon cold water, if necessary. Turn the dough out onto a lightly floured surface, knead very lightly until just smooth, then use your hands to shape it into a 15 x 10 cm (6 x 4 inch) rectangle. Cover with plastic wrap and refrigerate for 20 minutes.

Put the pastry on a lightly floured surface with a short end nearest to you, then use a rolling pin to roll the pastry away from you, without turning it, into a 30 x 12 cm (12 x 4¾ inch) rectangle. Keep the edges as straight as you can. Fold the bottom third of the pastry over, then fold the top third over that to form a square block. Turn the pastry block 90 degrees, then repeat the rolling and folding process. Cover with plastic wrap and refrigerate for 30 minutes. Put the pastry on a lightly floured surface and repeat the rolling and folding process again. Cover and refrigerate for another 30 minutes.

Meanwhile, to make the filling, put all the ingredients and 1 tablespoon cold water in a bowl and mix to combine well. Divide the filling into 14 even portions and roll each into a ball. Using your hands, flatten each ball so it is about 5 cm (2 inches) across.

Put the dough on a lightly floured surface and roll it into a 40 x 32 cm (16 x 12½ inch) rectangle. Using a 10 cm (4 inch) biscuit (cookie) cutter, cut out 12 circles from the dough, reserving the scraps. Working with one round at a time, use a small rolling pin or your fingers to roll or press the edges to thin them and make the round about 2 cm (¾ inch) larger. Place a flattened ball of filling in the middle of the dough, then bring the edges up and over the filling to enclose it, pleating the edge together to neatly seal. Place each finished pastry, seam side down, on a baking tray lined with baking paper. Repeat with the remaining dough circles and filling. Reroll the scraps and cut out another two circles, roll the edges to thin them, then fill with the remaining filling portions. Refrigerate the pastries for 30 minutes.

Preheat the oven to 180°C (350°F/Gas 4). Brush each pastry with a little of the egg yolk mixture. Using a small knife, make three small parallel cuts in the top of each pastry, then sprinkle with sesame seeds. Bake for 25 minutes, or until the pastry is light golden and cooked through. Transfer to a wire rack to cool. The cakes can be stored for up to 1 week in an airtight container.

Photograph page 373

Honeydew melon sago pudding

Serves 6

We know, we know ... many of us are scarred for life when it comes to sago through unhappy encounters with the stuff as children. In the south of China, they use it to great effect in creating light, refreshing desserts such as this one. Use rockmelon (cantaloupe) instead of honeydew if you like, but either way, make sure you get one with loads of sweet flavour or the pudding won't be as good.

195 g (7 oz/1 cup) sago

170 g (6 oz/¾ cup) caster (superfine) sugar

½ honeydew melon (about 1.2 kg/2 lb 10 oz), seeded

300 ml (10 fl oz) coconut milk

Put the sago in a saucepan, add 1.75 litres (60 fl oz/7 cups) water and slowly bring to a simmer, stirring often, over a medium–low heat. Cook, stirring often, for 25 minutes, or until the sago is translucent. Transfer to a sieve and rest it over a bowl or the sink for 20 minutes, stirring from time to time, to allow the excess thick liquid to drain off.

Meanwhile, combine the sugar with 125 ml (4 fl oz/½ cup) water in a small saucepan and slowly bring to a simmer, then cook, stirring occasionally, for 1–2 minutes, or until the sugar has dissolved.

Using a melon baller, cut about 24 small balls from the melon (alternatively, cut half of the melon into neat 1 cm/½ inch squares). Put the melon balls in a bowl, cover with plastic wrap and place in the fridge to chill. Peel and roughly chop the remaining melon, transfer to a food processor and process to form a smooth purée — you should have about 500 ml (17 fl oz/2 cups).

Transfer the sago to a large bowl, then stir in the sugar syrup, puréed melon and the coconut milk. Leave to cool to room temperature, then place in the fridge to chill. Divide the sago among six small bowls or glasses, top with some melon balls and serve.

Fried red bean pancakes

Serves 4 to 6

Typical of the snack foods of Beijing, where the harsh winters call for hefty fare, we find these are perfect with a cup of tea for breakfast. Red beans (hong dou) are an important food source in China, and mainly used in sweet guises, as here. The beans are thought to be native to an area near the foot of the Himalayas.

....

1 egg
1½ tablespoons vegetable oil, plus extra
   for cooking

150 g (5½ oz/1 cup) plain (all-purpose) flour,
   plus 2½ tablespoons extra
360 g (12½ oz) red bean paste (page 402), or
   ready-made

....

Whisk the egg and oil with 300 ml (10 fl oz) water in a bowl. Add the flour and whisk until smooth, adding a little extra water if the mixture is too thick — the batter should have a pouring consistency.

Brush a 20 cm (8 inch) non-stick frying pan with oil, then heat over a medium heat. Working quickly, add about 60 ml (2 fl oz/¼ cup) of batter to the pan, swirling the pan to thinly coat the base, and pouring any excess batter back into the bowl. Cook for about 3 minutes, or until the top surface is dry, then remove to a plate. Repeat the process with the remaining batter to make six pancakes.

Combine the extra 2½ tablespoons of flour in a small bowl with 60 ml (2 fl oz/¼ cup) water, or enough to form a thick paste. Place one pancake on the work surface, uncooked side up, and smear a little of the flour paste around the edge of the pancake. Place 2 tablespoons of red bean paste in the middle of the pancake, then spread it out to form a 12 x 8 cm (4¾ x 3¼ inch) rectangle. Fold the ends over the filling, then fold the sides over and press lightly to seal — do not fold too tightly or the pancakes may crack slightly. Repeat with the remaining pancakes and filling, folding them one at a time.

Add enough oil to cover the base of the frying pan, then return to a medium heat. Add two of the folded pancakes to the pan and cook, turning once, for 5–6 minutes, or until golden brown. Remove and drain on paper towel. Repeat with the remaining pancakes. Cut each pancake widthwise into three pieces and serve warm or at room temperature.

Almond 'tea'

Serves 4

This is what they call this starch-thickened dessert on the streets in Kaifeng, but it's not a 'tea' at all, it's more a … gloop. And, granted, it sounds unpromising, but once all the sweet, texturising bits and pieces are stirred in, with plenty of sugar added, it tastes amazing and is particularly warming, perfect for wintry nights.

....

60 g (2 oz/heaped ⅓ cup) lotus root powder

Garnishes

65 g (2¼ oz/⅔ cup) sweet southern apricot kernels (page 425)

115 g (4 oz/¾ cup) whole blanched almonds

110 g (4 oz/½ cup) sugar, or to taste

80 g (2¾ oz/½ cup) black sesame seeds, or to taste

85 g (3 oz/⅔ cup) large white raisins, coarsely chopped, or to taste

120 g (4½ oz/½ cup) coarsely chopped glacé cherries, or to taste

....

To prepare the garnishes, place the apricot kernels in a heatproof bowl, then add 500 ml (17 fl oz/2 cups) boiling water and soak for 1 hour, or until softened slightly. Drain well.

Meanwhile, preheat the oven to 180°C (350°F/Gas 4). Put the whole almonds on a baking tray and roast for 15 minutes, or until deep golden. Cool the almonds, then transfer to a small food processor and process until finely ground. Put the ground almonds, almond kernels and the remaining garnishes in individual bowls, ready to serve.

Put the lotus root powder and 200 ml (7 fl oz) cold water in a large heatproof bowl and stir until well combined. Stirring constantly and working quickly, add 800 ml (27 fl oz) boiling water to the lotus root mixture, then stir for 2–3 minutes, or until quite thick. Immediately divide the mixture among four 400 ml (13½ fl oz) serving bowls. At the table, each diner tops their bowl with 1½ tablespoons sugar or to taste, and the other garnishes to taste, then mixes the contents of the bowl together.

Almond jelly with poached kumquats

Serves 6

The bitter-edged almond taste here comes from apricot kernels, which the Chinese call 'sweet southern almond kernels'. In Chinese pharmacology, raw apricot kernels are considered more a drug than a foodstuff, purporting to combat cancer and blood disease, and to promote a general sense of well-being. Raw apricot kernels contain vitamin B17, which can cause nausea in high doses, so you do need to limit the amount you eat.

....

200 g (7 oz/1¼ cups) whole blanched almonds

75 g (2¾ oz/¾ cup) sweet southern apricot
  kernels (page 425)

500 ml (17 fl oz/2 cups) soy milk

170 g (6 oz/¾ cup) caster (superfine) sugar

9 teaspoons powdered gelatine

½ teaspoon almond extract

Poached kumquats

600 g (1 lb 5 oz) kumquats

400 g (14 oz/1¾ cups) caster (superfine) sugar

....

Combine the almonds and apricot kernels in a bowl, then add 750 ml (25½ fl oz/3 cups) boiling water and soak for 1 hour. Transfer the mixture in batches to a food processor and process until the solids are very finely ground. Transfer to a sieve lined with muslin (cheesecloth) and strain the liquid into a bowl. Gather the solids in the muslin and wring tightly to extract as much liquid as possible — the solids should be quite dry. Measure the liquid, then add enough water to make the liquid back up to 750 ml (25½ fl oz/3 cups).

Combine the soy milk, sugar and almond liquid in a saucepan and bring almost to the boil, then remove from the heat. Meanwhile, put 250 ml (8½ fl oz/1 cup) cold water in a small heatproof bowl or cup and sprinkle over the gelatine. Stand for 5 minutes, or until the gelatine has softened, then place the bowl in a saucepan of just simmering water for 5 minutes, or until the gelatine has completely dissolved. Add the gelatine and almond extract to the milk mixture and stir to combine. Pour into six 250 ml (8½ fl oz/1 cup) jelly moulds or two 750 ml (25½ fl oz/3 cup) moulds. Refrigerate for 8 hours or overnight, until firm.

To prepare the poached kumquats, prick the kumquats several times with a fine metal skewer. Place the kumquats in a saucepan of cold water and slowly bring to a simmer, then drain, cover with water again and repeat the process twice more. This helps to remove some of the bitterness in the skins. Combine the sugar with 310 ml (10½ fl oz/1¼ cups) water in a saucepan and bring to a simmer. Add the kumquats and cook over a medium–low heat for 15–20 minutes, or until tender. Remove from the heat and leave to cool in the liquid. The kumquats can be stored in the fridge in a sealed jar for up to 4 weeks.

To serve, dip each mould briefly in hot water to loosen the jelly, then turn out onto a plate and spoon over some of the kumquats and syrup.

Photograph page 384

Steamed coconut cakes

Makes 10

400 g (14 oz/2¼ cups) rice flour
1 tablespoon baking powder
400 ml (14 fl oz) coconut milk
3 teaspoons coconut essence

250 g (9 oz/heaped 1 cup) caster (superfine) sugar
food colouring (optional)

Line ten 150 ml (5 fl oz) dariole moulds, or similar, with baking paper or cupcake cases. If you don't have enough moulds, you will need to cook the cakes in batches.

Sift the rice flour and half of the baking powder into a large bowl. Whisk in the coconut milk and essence, then add 310 ml (10½ fl oz/1¼ cups) boiling water and whisk until smooth. Set aside until cool.

Stir the sugar and remaining baking powder into the cooled mixture. Divide the mixture in half or thirds, depending on the number of colours you want to make. Tint the mixture as desired using food colouring, then pour into the prepared moulds, filling them nearly to the top. Put the filled moulds into a steamer, place over a wok or saucepan of boiling water, then cover tightly and steam for 15 minutes. Remove from the steamer and remove the cakes from the moulds. If working in batches, re-line the moulds and cook the remaining mixture. Serve at room temperature.

Photograph page 385

Mung bean cakes

Makes about 11

200 g (7 oz/1 cup) peeled, dried mung beans
115 g (4 oz/½ cup) caster (superfine) sugar

1 tablespoon vegetable oil

Put the mung beans in a bowl, cover with water and soak for 3 hours or overnight, then drain. Put the mung beans in a steamer, place over a wok or saucepan of boiling water, then cover and steam for 15 minutes. Cool, then transfer to a food processor and process until very finely ground.

Combine the ground mung beans in a bowl with the sugar and oil. Use your hands to knead the mixture to form a smooth, stiff paste. Using a mooncake mould, or a similar shallow mould (with a 50 ml/1¾ fl oz capacity), shape the cakes by pressing the mixture firmly into the mould, then smooth the surface. Turn the mould over and tap sharply on the back to remove the cake, then place the cake on a small square of baking paper. Repeat with the remaining mixture. Working in batches, place the cakes on the baking paper in a steamer and steam for 5 minutes. Cool to room temperature, then serve.

Photograph page 384

From left to right: Almond jelly with poached kumquats (page 382); Mung bean cakes (page 383); Mango puddings (page 386); Steamed coconut cakes (page 383)

Mango puddings

Serves 6

The south of China is bursting with tropical fruits such as custard apples, dragonfruit, the 'dreaded' durian (smelly but delicious!) and mangoes. The Chinese don't really eat a dessert course, preferring fresh fruit instead, so this pudding would most likely end up on a yum cha cart or be sold as a snack — but it does make a glorious end to a meal.

....

3 large ripe mangoes

1 tablespoon powdered gelatine

80 g (2¾ oz/⅓ cup) caster (superfine) sugar

250 ml (8½ fl oz/1 cup) evaporated milk

....

Peel two of the mangoes, slice off the cheeks and remove the flesh. Put the mango flesh in a food processor and process to form a smooth purée. Measure the purée — you need 750 ml (25½ fl oz/3 cups). If you don't have quite enough, purée some of the third mango to make up the amount, reserving the remaining unpuréed flesh. Put the purée into a bowl and set aside.

Put 80 ml (2½ fl oz/⅓ cup) cold water in a small heatproof bowl or cup and sprinkle over the gelatine. Stand for 5 minutes, or until the gelatine has softened, then place the bowl in a small saucepan of just simmering water for 5 minutes, or until the gelatine has dissolved.

Meanwhile, combine the sugar with 170 ml (5½ fl oz/⅔ cup) water in a small saucepan and cook, stirring, over a low heat for 3–4 minutes, or until the sugar has dissolved. Cool slightly.

Add the gelatine mixture, sugar syrup and evaporated milk to the mango purée and stir to combine well. Divide the mixture among six 250 ml (8½ fl oz/1 cup) serving bowls, then refrigerate for 3 hours, or until set. Cut the reserved mango into 1 cm (½ inch) squares and divide among the puddings, then serve.

Photograph pages 384–5

Sweet ginger milk custard

Serves 4

Here's a sweet miracle of science. The name of this dessert, translated from the Chinese as 'ginger hits milk', originated in Shunde near Guangzhou, originally made using buffalo milk. Ginger contains an enzyme called protease, which coagulates the proteins in the milk and makes it into a wondrously soft, slippery curd. Do stir the sediment in the ginger as instructed (use old or young ginger; old has a stronger flavour) and don't jiggle the dessert for the first 30 minutes or it won't set.

200 g (7 oz) ginger, peeled and chopped

500 ml (17 fl oz/2 cups) full-cream (whole) milk

35 g (1¼ oz/⅓ cup) low-fat milk powder

115 g (4 oz/½ cup) caster (superfine) sugar

Put the ginger in a small food processor and process until finely chopped. Transfer the ginger to a clean piece of muslin (cheesecloth). Holding the ginger over a bowl to catch the juices, tightly twist the muslin around the ginger, pressing hard to extract as much juice as possible. Measure out 80 ml (2½ fl oz/⅓ cup) ginger juice, then pour 1 tablespoon into each of four 200 ml (7 fl oz) ceramic bowls.

Heat the milk in a saucepan until it is warm, then whisk in the milk powder and heat until bubbles just start to form around the side of the pan. Add the sugar, then remove from the heat and stir for about 1 minute, or until the sugar has dissolved. Stir the ginger juice in each bowl to redistribute any sediment. Holding the pan of milk about 15 cm (6 inches) above a bowl, pour the milk mixture onto the ginger juice in a single, steady stream — do not stir the mixture or disturb it in any way. Repeat until all the milk is used. Leave the ginger custard to rest for 30 minutes at room temperature, or until it has just set, then place in the fridge to chill for 3–4 hours before serving.

Sticky rice and black sesame cake with rosewater syrup

Makes about 20 pieces

This is our homage to Mrs Zhou. For thirty years she has been making feng mi liang gao *and selling them, cut into neat diamonds, from a mobile cart in Xi'an's Muslim Quarter. She's rather famous in Chinese food circles, and has been interviewed for television and other media. We've simplified her formula somewhat and while our sticky rice cakes are nowhere near as good as hers, they're still good!*

100 g (3½ oz/⅔ cup) sesame seeds, toasted (page 413)
450 g (1 lb/2¼ cups) glutinous rice, rinsed
170 g (6 oz/¾ cup) caster (superfine) sugar
1½ tablespoons lard
275 g (9½ oz) black sesame paste

Rosewater syrup
230 g (8 oz/1 cup) caster (superfine) sugar
3 teaspoons rosewater, or to taste

Lightly grease the base and sides of a 20 cm (8 inch) non-stick square cake tin with a removable base. Put the sesame seeds in a small food processor and process until coarsely ground. Sprinkle half evenly over the base of the tin.

Combine the rice and 750 ml (25½ fl oz/3 cups) water in a saucepan. Cover and bring to a simmer, then reduce the heat to very low (use a simmer pad if necessary — the rice should be only just simmering) and cook for 10–15 minutes, or until the water has been absorbed. Add the sugar and another 80 ml (2½ fl oz/⅓ cup) water, stir to combine well, then cover and cook over a low heat for 5 minutes, or until the mixture is very thick. Stir in the lard, then set the rice aside to cool.

When the rice is cool enough to handle, spread half of it over the base of the cake tin, working with one small handful of rice at a time and using lightly greased hands to flatten each handful as you add it to the tin, patching the rice together as you go. Smooth the surface using your hands. Add the black sesame paste and smooth it over the rice, using your hands to first flatten a small handful of the paste before patching it together over the rice. Use the remaining rice to form an even layer over the top of the sesame paste, using your hands to flatten and patch it. Smooth the surface with a lightly oiled spoon. Sprinkle the remaining ground sesame seeds over the top of the rice cake, pressing them lightly so they stick. Leave the rice cake to cool to room temperature.

To make the rosewater syrup, combine the sugar with 170 ml (5½ fl oz/⅔ cup) water in a small saucepan and slowly bring to a simmer. Simmer for 7–8 minutes, or until thickened slightly, then remove the pan from the heat and cool. Stir in the rosewater. Remove the rice cake from the tin and cut into slices or diamonds. Serve with the rosewater syrup spooned over the top.

Black sesame tang yuan with ginger syrup

Serves 6

We've eaten our fair share of tang yuan *over the years. The most famous were from Lai's Tang Yuan in Chengdu, an historic little shop that had been in business since the late 1880s, but now sadly bulldozed — and in Chaozhou, in Guangdong Province, we were served a bowl of five tiny dumplings, each with a different filling: sesame, peanut, and pastes of lotus, red bean and pumpkin (winter squash).*

320 g (11½ oz/2 cups) glutinous rice flour

Black sesame filling
150 g (5½ oz) black sesame paste
100 g (3½ oz/½ cup) soft brown sugar
110 g (4 oz/⅔ cup) salted peanuts, finely chopped

Ginger syrup
5 cm (2 inch) piece ginger, peeled and finely sliced
230 g (8 oz/1 cup firmly packed) soft brown sugar

To make the black sesame filling, put the sesame paste, sugar and peanuts in a bowl and stir with a wooden spoon to combine (or use your hands to combine everything if the mixture is too stiff). Cover and refrigerate for 30 minutes, or until firm. Divide the filling into 24 portions, then roll into balls and set aside.

Meanwhile, to make the ginger syrup, put 1 litre (34 fl oz/4 cups) water, the ginger and sugar in a saucepan and bring to the boil over a high heat, stirring occasionally to dissolve the sugar. Reduce the heat to medium and simmer for 15 minutes, then strain. Return the syrup to the saucepan and set aside.

To make the dough for the tang yuan, combine the rice flour and 200 ml (7 fl oz) water in a bowl and stir with a wooden spoon to make a soft, smooth and pliable dough — you may need to add extra water, a little at a time, to get the desired consistency.

Divide the dough into two even portions. Roll the dough into two logs, each about 25 cm (10 inches) long. Take one log and divide it into 12 even portions. Working with one piece of dough at a time (cover the remaining portions with a damp tea towel/dish towel to prevent them from drying out) and with floured hands, roll the dough into a ball, then use your hand to flatten the ball into a 5 cm (2 inch) circle. Place one ball of sesame filling in the middle of each round, and fold the dough around it to completely seal in the filling. With floured hands, gently shape and roll the dough into a ball. Place on a tray lined with baking paper and cover loosely with a damp tea towel. Repeat the process to make the remaining tang yuan.

Fill a large saucepan with water and bring to the boil. Add the tang yuan and cook for 3–4 minutes, or until they float to the surface, then cook for another 1–2 minutes. Remove with a slotted spoon and divide among six serving bowls. Reheat the ginger syrup in the saucepan, then ladle the syrup over the tang yuan.

Photograph page 357

Peanut biscuits

Makes about 42

Originally a Lunar New Year sweet treat, peanut biscuits (cookies) are ubiquitous year round, particularly in the south of China. They're really easy to make and a great thing to have on hand. Traditionally, a small indent is made in the top of each biscuit using a chopstick end, but we've gilded the lily by adding yet another layer of peanutty flavour. Here's a piece of peanut trivia: the Portuguese introduced the crop into China in the seventeenth century and now China is the world's largest producer, accounting for over 40 per cent of total supply.

320 g (11½ oz/2 cups) raw, skinned peanuts, plus extra for decorating

85 g (3 oz/⅔ cup) icing (confectioners') sugar

300 g (10½ oz/2 cups) plain (all-purpose) flour

1½ teaspoons salt

160 ml (5½ fl oz) peanut oil

Preheat the oven to 180°C (350°F/Gas 4). Spread the peanuts in a single layer on a baking tray and roast for 12–15 minutes, or until deep golden. Cool to room temperature, then transfer to a food processor, add the icing sugar and process until the peanuts are very finely ground. Reduce the oven to 170°C (340°F/Gas 3). Line two baking trays with baking paper.

Combine the ground peanuts, flour and salt in a large bowl, then add the oil. Use your hands to mix until a smooth, soft dough forms, adding a little more oil if the mixture is too dry.

Taking heaped teaspoonfuls of dough, form the mixture into balls and place on the prepared trays, spacing them a little apart. Gently press a peanut half into each biscuit, then bake for 20 minutes, or until light golden and firm, turning the trays in the oven once or twice so the biscuits cook evenly. Cool on the trays for 10 minutes, then transfer to a wire rack to cool completely. The peanut biscuits can be stored in a container for up to 1 week.

Polenta and red date shortcake

Makes 16 pieces

Bakeries in Beijing make cakes and slices of various shapes and sizes from these two simple ingredients: cornmeal (polenta) and red dates. Corn, a Chinese non-native, is seen all through China's north — great swathes of it grow all over the region. Grilled cobs are a popular street snack and corn congee (made from cornmeal) is eaten for breakfast. Red dates, more correctly called 'jujubes', can survive rather cold winters and are a popular northern Chinese fruit. They're eaten both fresh and dried, candied, in soups, teas and, as here, in baked goods.

200 g (7 oz/1⅓ cups) coarse polenta
200 g (7 oz/1⅓ cups) plain (all-purpose) flour
1 teaspoon baking powder
185 g (6½ oz) caster (superfine) sugar
175 g (6 oz) unsalted butter, chopped
2 eggs, lightly beaten

1 egg yolk mixed with 1 tablespoon water, for glazing
2 tablespoons sesame seeds

Red date filling
250 g (9 oz) dried large red dates (jujubes)
115 g (4 oz/½ cup) caster (superfine) sugar

To make the red date filling, put the dates in a heatproof bowl, then add enough boiling water to just cover, weighting down the dates with a plate to keep them submerged. Soak for 2–3 hours, then drain well, reserving the soaking liquid. Remove the stones from the dates. Combine the dates, reserved liquid and sugar in a saucepan, cover and bring to a simmer. Cook for 20 minutes over a low heat until very soft, then remove the lid and cook for another 15 minutes or so, until the liquid has mostly evaporated and the mixture is thick and jammy. Remove from the heat and cool.

Preheat the oven to 180°C (350°F/Gas 4). Grease and flour the base and sides of a 28 x 16 cm (11 x 6¼ inch) baking dish, then line the base with baking paper.

Combine the polenta, flour, baking powder and sugar in a bowl and stir to combine well. Using your fingertips, rub the butter into the flour mixture until it resembles coarse crumbs, then add the eggs and mix until a soft dough forms. Lightly knead the dough in the bowl until smooth, then divide in half. Working with one half at a time, place the dough on the work surface and use your hands to shape it into a rectangle, then roll it out to fit the base of the dish. Gently transfer the rolled dough to the dish, taking care as the dough is soft.

Spread the date mixture evenly over the dough, then shape and roll out the remaining piece of dough and place it over the top of the dates. Press the surface gently with your hands to make sure it is even. Brush the egg yolk mixture over the top and sprinkle with the sesame seeds. Bake for about 45 minutes, or until golden and firm. Cool in the dish, then cut into pieces to serve.

San da pao

Serves 4

The name of this dish translates as 'three cannon balls', referencing the sound the glutinous rice paste makes when pieces are smacked against a metal surface to form small balls, and the fact they are served in groups of three. This is another snack from the traditional repertoire in Chengdu. We love eating these when we visit the city's charming Renmin Park; there's a great snack restaurant there, plus one of the most atmospheric old tea houses left standing in town.

....

250 g (9 oz/1¼ cups) glutinous rice, soaked overnight, rinsed and drained

30 g (1 oz/⅓ cup) soybean powder

230 g (8 oz/1 cup firmly packed) soft brown sugar

....

Put the soaked, drained rice in a steamer lined with a tea towel (dish towel). Place the steamer over a wok or saucepan of boiling water, then cover tightly and steam for 20 minutes, or until the rice is tender.

Meanwhile, put the soybean powder in a large, heavy-based frying pan over a low heat and dry-fry for 8–10 minutes, shaking the pan often, until the powder turns a slightly darker colour and smells nutty. Transfer the powder to a large bowl.

Combine the sugar with 125 ml (4 fl oz/½ cup) water in a small saucepan and bring to a simmer. Cook over a medium–low heat for 5 minutes, or until the sugar has dissolved, adding a little more water if necessary to form a thin syrup.

When the rice is cooked, transfer it to a large mortar or bowl and pound it vigorously with the pestle to break down the grains and form a thick, coarse paste; you may need to add a little hot water. The mixture does not need to be completely smooth, so don't worry if not all the rice is broken down. Using damp hands, take tablespoonfuls of the rice mixture and form them into balls — they don't need to be perfectly symmetrical. Toss the balls through the soybean powder to coat well, then divide among four small bowls. Pour over the syrup and serve warm or at room temperature.

Photograph page 356

Rice-stuffed lotus root

Serves 6

If you go to Shanghai, take the train to Qibao, once a sleepy water town that has now been completely subsumed by urban creep. The street food there is legendary (read: 'you won't be having the place to yourself — it gets packed') and specialties such as this abound. We've included this in our dessert line-up as it's achingly sweet but, strictly speaking, the Chinese would eat this as a vegetable dish with a selection of meats and other mains.

800 g (1 lb 12 oz) lotus root (about 2 links)

250 g (9 oz/1¼ cups) glutinous rice, soaked overnight, rinsed and drained

575 g (1 lb 4 oz/2½ cups) caster (superfine) sugar

1 tablespoon honey

1 teaspoon cornflour (cornstarch)

dried osmanthus flowers, to serve (optional)

Peel the lotus roots and cut a 3 cm (1¼ inch) piece from one end of each link, reserving the cut ends. Divide the soaked, drained rice between the two links. Using a skewer, push the rice into the cavities in each link; each cavity should be about 75–80 per cent full of rice (you need to leave some room for the rice to expand when it cooks). You may not need all the rice; this will depend on the size of the lotus holes.

Replace the reserved ends on each link, securing them well with toothpicks. Place the stuffed lotus roots in a steamer, place over a wok or saucepan of boiling water, then cover tightly and steam for 3 hours, adding more water to the wok as necessary. Remove the lotus roots and set aside.

Combine 500 ml (17 fl oz/2 cups) water and 460 g (1 lb/2 cups) of the sugar in a saucepan (large enough to hold the lotus roots snugly) and slowly bring to a simmer, stirring occasionally to dissolve the sugar. Add the lotus roots and cook, turning occasionally, for 1 hour. Cool in the syrup.

Meanwhile, combine the remaining sugar, the honey and 250 ml (8½ fl oz/1 cup) water in a small saucepan and bring to a simmer, stirring to dissolve the sugar. Combine the cornflour with 3 teaspoons water in a small bowl and stir to form a smooth paste, then add the paste to the simmering syrup, stirring until the mixture has thickened slightly. Remove the pan from the heat and cool.

To serve, remove the toothpicks and trim the ends from the lotus root links to neaten them. Using a sharp knife, cut the roots into 1 cm (½ inch) thick slices and arrange them on a serving plate. Drizzle with the thickened honey syrup, sprinkle over a few osmanthus flowers, if using, and serve.

Peanut soup

Serves 6

---

160 g (5½ oz/1 cup) raw, skinned peanuts, roasted (page 413)

150 g (5½ oz/¾ cup) long-grain rice, soaked in water for 2–3 hours

large pinch of salt

165 g (6 oz/¾ cup firmly packed) soft brown sugar, or to taste

---

Put the peanuts in a food processor and process until very finely ground. Transfer to a large saucepan.

Drain the rice, then place in the food processor and process until very finely ground. Add 250 ml (8½ fl oz/ 1 cup) water and process until the mixture is as smooth as possible. Add the rice to the ground peanuts in the pan, along with 1 litre (34 fl oz/4 cups) water. Place the pan over a medium–low heat and, whisking constantly to prevent the solids sticking to the base of the pan, bring the mixture to a simmer. Cook for 7–8 minutes, whisking often, until the soup thickens and is smooth. Add the salt, sugar and enough water to thin the soup if desired, adjusting the thickness and sweetness to taste. Divide the soup among six bowls and serve hot or warm.

Black sesame soup

Serves 6

---

115 g (4 oz/¾ cup) black sesame seeds, toasted (page 413)

150 g (5½ oz/¾ cup) long-grain rice, soaked in water for 2–3 hours

large pinch of salt

170 g (6 oz/¾ cup) caster (superfine) sugar, or to taste

Put the sesame seeds in a food processor and process to form a fine powder. Transfer to a large saucepan.

Drain the rice, then place in the food processor and process until very finely ground. Add 250 ml (8½ fl oz/ 1 cup) water and process until the mixture is as smooth as possible. Add the rice to the ground sesame seeds in the pan, along with 1 litre (34 fl oz/4 cups) water. Place the pan over a medium–low heat and, whisking constantly to prevent the solids sticking to the base of the pan, bring the mixture to a simmer. Cook for 7–8 minutes, whisking often, until the soup thickens and is smooth. Add the salt, sugar and enough water to thin the soup if desired, adjusting the thickness and sweetness to taste. Divide the soup among six bowls and serve hot or warm.

Persimmon cakes

Makes 10

If there's one snack synonymous with the Xi'an Muslim Quarter it's shi zi bing, or persimmon cakes. The area is famous for its fire crystal persimmons, so named for the incredible clarity of their flesh and intense orange hue. On the streets, these cakes come stuffed with a variety of fillings, such as raisins, walnuts (another famous local product), red bean, red dates or sesame. They're fried in copious amounts of oil until golden and chewy on the outside and sweet and gooey within. We l-o-v-e them.

2 very ripe, large persimmons (the astringent type)

about 675 g (1½ lb/4½ cups) plain (all-purpose) flour

vegetable oil, for shallow-frying

Filling

145 g (5 oz/⅔ cup) caster (superfine) sugar

125 g (4½ oz/1 cup) walnut pieces, finely chopped

3 teaspoons rosewater

To make the filling, combine the sugar and walnuts in a bowl and stir to combine well. Add the rosewater and set aside.

Peel the persimmons, remove any stones, and put the flesh in a food processor. Process to form a smooth purée. Measure the purée — you will need 500 ml (17 fl oz/2 cups). Transfer the purée to a bowl, then add 600 g (1 lb 5 oz/4 cups) of the flour and stir to combine well, then add the remaining flour, a little at a time, until the dough can hold its shape — the dough will be rather sticky. With floured hands, knead the dough in the bowl for 3–4 minutes, or until smooth, then cover the bowl with plastic wrap and set aside at room temperature for 30 minutes.

Place the dough on a well-floured surface and divide into 10 even pieces. Working with one piece at a time, roll it into a ball, then use your hands to flatten the ball. Using a rolling pin, roll the ball into an 11–12 cm (4¼–4¾ inch) circle, rolling the edges so about 1 cm (½ inch) around the edge is thinner than the middle. Place some of the filling in the middle of one circle. Draw the edges up over the filling, pleating them as you go to enclose the filling, then pinch the edges together to seal. Repeat with the remaining dough balls and filling, rolling and filling them one at a time.

Pour enough oil into a large, heavy-based frying pan to come at least 1 cm (½ inch) up the side, then place the pan over a low heat. Cook the cakes in batches for 20 minutes, turning once, or until golden and cooked through. Drain on paper towel and serve warm.

Stuffed sweet potato cakes

Makes about 16

In China, sweet cakes or dishes made with vegetables are not uncommon: taro, sweet potato, peas, mung beans and pumpkin (winter squash) are all utilised this way. You can use pumpkin purée here if you want to change things up, and lotus seed or red bean paste as the filling if you want — this recipe is rather forgiving.

325 g (11½ oz) orange sweet potato (about 1 small), peeled
115 g (4 oz/½ cup) caster (superfine) sugar
240 g (8½ oz/1½ cups) glutinous rice flour
175 g (6 oz) black sesame paste
80 g (2¾ oz/½ cup) black sesame seeds

80 g (2¾ oz/½ cup) white sesame seeds
vegetable oil, for shallow-frying

Syrup
170 g (6 oz/¾ cup) caster (superfine) sugar
2½ tablespoons honey

To make the syrup, combine the sugar and honey with 80 ml (2½ fl oz/⅓ cup) water in a small saucepan. Bring to a simmer, stirring occasionally to dissolve the sugar, then cook for 2 minutes, or until thick and syrupy. Remove from the heat and cool slightly.

Cut the sweet potato into large pieces, then place in a saucepan, adding just enough water to come halfway up the pieces of sweet potato. Cover, then bring to the boil and cook for 20 minutes, or until the sweet potato is very tender. Drain well in a colander, then transfer to a large bowl. While still very hot, mash the sweet potato until smooth. Add the sugar, rice flour and 2–3 tablespoons boiling water, or enough to form a soft, smooth dough, then use your hands to knead the mixture, kneading in a little more water if it becomes too firm — it should be a soft dough.

Divide the sesame paste and dough into 16 even portions. With damp hands and working with one piece of dough at a time, roll the dough into a ball, then use your hands to flatten it out on an oiled surface to a 9 cm (3½ inch) circle; roll the edges with a small rolling pin so they are a little thinner than the middle. Place a portion of the sesame paste in the centre of the round, spreading it to cover about 3 cm (1¼ inches). Bring the edges together over the filling and seal them, then shape the cake by placing it, seam side down, on the work surface and gently pressing it into a neat flat round, about 10 cm (4 inches) in diameter. Repeat the process with the remaining dough and paste.

Combine the black and white sesame seeds in a bowl. Coat both sides of the cakes with the seeds, brushing each cake with a little water to help the seeds stick, if necessary. Pour enough oil for shallow-frying into a large, non-stick frying pan and place over a low heat. Cook the cakes in batches for 4–5 minutes on each side, or until golden and cooked through. Remove and drain on paper towel, then serve warm, drizzled with the syrup.

Photograph page 356

Kaifeng sweet potato dessert

Serves 4

This is another Kaifeng specialty that's sold on the street by vendors. It's a relatively pricey snack there, as an awful lot of work goes into laboriously straining the purée to rid it of every last bit of fibre, then carefully reducing it to a thick, unctuous paste over a slow, low heat. When you order a serve, a few spoonfuls of the purée go into the wok with an alarming amount of vegetable oil and a not insignificant heap of sugar. Serving it with peanut brittle is purely our idea — the Kaifengers would probably be horrified.

1.25 kg (2 lb 12 oz) orange sweet potatoes (about 2 large), washed

110 g (4 oz/½ cup) sugar, or to taste

60 ml (2 fl oz/¼ cup) peanut oil

peanut brittle (recipe opposite), coarsely chopped, to serve (optional)

Place the whole sweet potatoes in a steamer over a wok or saucepan of boiling water, then cover tightly and steam for about 40–50 minutes, or until very tender (you may need to top up the water in the wok occasionally). Remove from the steamer and cool slightly. When cool enough to handle, remove the skins. Using a potato ricer or mouli fitted with the finest blade, purée the sweet potatoes into a bowl, discarding any fibres left in the blade.

Place the purée in a saucepan with the sugar and oil and cook, stirring often, over a medium–low heat for 10–15 minutes, or until the sugar has dissolved. Continue cooking, stirring often, for another 20 minutes, or until the mixture has thickened slightly — it should fall heavily from a wooden spoon and retain its shape when dropped. Using a hand-held stick blender, process the mixture to refine the texture. Divide among four small bowls, sprinkle with some peanut brittle and serve hot.

Peanut brittle

Makes about 24 pieces

The Chinese propensity for sugar might surprise some, but sugar cultivating and refining came to China early — from India and in the seventh century. Wherever we go, it seems, there's some variety or other of a peanut or sesame candy being pulled or pounded on the street. In city parks, clever vendors fashion molten sugar into butterflies, dragons or puppies, then set them on sticks to sell to excited children.

100 g (3½ oz/⅔ cup) sesame seeds, toasted (page 413)

320 g (11½ oz/2 cups) raw, skinned peanuts, roasted (page 413)

515 g (1 lb 2 oz/2¼ cups) caster (superfine) sugar

2½ tablespoons clear rice vinegar

Grease the base and sides of a 26 x 14 cm (10¼ x 5½ inch) ceramic or glass baking dish, then line the base with baking paper. Sprinkle half of the sesame seeds over the base of the dish, then scatter all the peanuts evenly over the sesame seeds.

Combine the sugar, vinegar and 60 ml (2 fl oz/¼ cup) water in a saucepan and bring to a simmer over a low heat, then increase the heat to medium and bring to the boil; cook for 8–10 minutes, or until the mixture turns deep golden. Pour the caramel evenly over the sesame seeds and peanuts in the dish, taking care as the caramel is extremely hot. Cool for 5 minutes, then sprinkle the remaining sesame seeds over the top, gently pressing them into the caramel. Leave the peanut brittle to cool for 30–40 minutes, or until firm but not completely hard. Turn out onto a chopping board then, using a large oiled knife, cut the brittle into pieces and leave until cool and hard. Transfer to an airtight container. The peanut brittle can be stored in the container in a cool, dark place for up to 1 month.

Photograph page 373

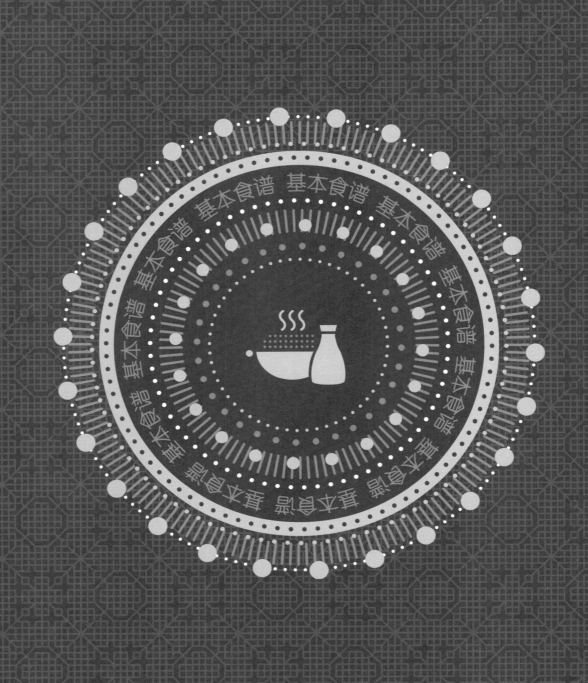

Basic Recipes

Not all essential sauce, paste and pickle recipes can be produced at home, but here are some that can be simply made — plus some other essentials such as stocks, how to roast peanuts or dry your own chillies. When time is short, buy these ready-made alternatives instead — they are readily available from your local Asian grocer. There's no contest with stocks, though. Homemade stocks are easy to prepare and taste way better than anything you'll ever buy.

Beef stock

Makes about 3 litres (101 fl oz/12 cups)

Brown beef stock isn't exactly Chinese, but as ex chefs we think there are occasions when nothing but a good homemade beef stock will do. Although the cooking time may seem daunting, the stock doesn't require much hands-on 'work' as such. Don't let it boil hard or it will go cloudy, and do skim all the fat off at the end. All stocks freeze well, so you can make a batch and have some on hand for when you need it.

3.5 kg (7 lb 12 oz) meaty beef bones
3 onions, coarsely chopped
2 carrots, coarsely chopped

2 heads garlic, halved crosswise
80 ml (2½ fl oz/⅓ cup) vegetable oil

Preheat the oven to 180°C (350°F/Gas 4). Put the bones, onions, carrots and garlic in a single layer, if possible, in a large roasting tin, then drizzle with the oil. Roast for about 1 hour and 10 minutes, turning the bones once, or until the bones and vegetables are browned.

Transfer to a stockpot and add about 4 litres (135 fl oz/16 cups) cold water, or enough to just cover. Bring slowly to a simmer, skimming off the impurities that rise to the surface. Reduce the heat to low and simmer gently for 8 hours, adding a little extra water if the level falls below the bones too much.

Strain the stock into a large container or bowl, discarding the solids. Leave to cool, then skim the fat from the top. The stock will keep, stored in an airtight container in the fridge, for 3–4 days, and up to 8 weeks in the freezer.

Chicken stock

Makes about 3 litres (101 fl oz/12 cups)

3 kg (6 lb 10 oz) chicken wings

5 garlic cloves, peeled and bruised by bashing with the side of a large knife

6 spring onions (scallions), trimmed and bruised

Put the chicken wings in a stockpot with the garlic cloves and spring onions, then add about 3.5 litres (118 fl oz/14 cups) cold water, or enough to just cover. Bring slowly to a simmer, skimming off any impurities that rise to the surface. Reduce the heat to low and simmer for 2 hours, adding a little extra water as required to keep the wings just covered, and skimming occasionally.

Strain the stock into a large container or bowl, discarding the solids. Leave to cool, then skim the fat from the surface. Once cooled, the stock will set naturally to a light jelly. The stock will keep, stored in an airtight container in the fridge, for 3–4 days, and up to 8 weeks in the freezer.

Note: Many of the recipes in this book require small amounts of chicken stock, so it's a good idea to pour some of the stock into ice cube trays and freeze them. When frozen, tip the blocks out of the trays and transfer to freezer bags or zip-lock bags.

Chicken and pork stock

Makes about 3 litres (101 fl oz/12 cups)

1 kg (2 lb 3 oz) chicken wings

1 kg (2 lb 3 oz) pork bones (ask your butcher to cut them into 5–7.5 cm/2–3 inch) pieces

2 pig's trotters, split lengthwise (ask your butcher to do this)

5 cm (2 inch) piece ginger, unpeeled and finely sliced

5 garlic cloves, peeled and bruised by bashing with the side of a large knife

6 spring onions (scallions), trimmed and bruised

Wash the chicken wings, pork bones and trotters under cold running water. Place in a stockpot with the ginger, garlic cloves and spring onions, then add enough cold water to cover. Bring slowly to the boil, skimming off the impurities that rise to the surface. Reduce the heat to low and simmer for 3–4 hours, topping up the water as required to keep the bones covered, and skimming every 30 minutes or so.

Strain the stock through a sieve into a large container or bowl, discarding the solids. Leave to cool, then skim the fat from the surface. The stock will keep, in an airtight container in the fridge, for 3–4 days, and up to 8 weeks in the freezer.

Fresh chilli paste

250 ml (8½ fl oz/1 cup)

....

250 g (9 oz) long red chillies, trimmed   1 teaspoon sea salt

60 ml (2 fl oz/¼ cup) black rice vinegar

....

If you prefer a milder paste, cut the chillies in half lengthwise and remove the seeds. Using a large knife, finely chop the chillies until they form a coarse paste, or alternatively use a small food processor.

Place the chillies in a non-reactive bowl, then add the vinegar and sea salt and combine well. The chilli paste will keep, stored in an airtight container in the fridge, for about 4 days.

Fresh chilli dip

Makes about 125 ml (4 fl oz/½ cup)

....

12 long red chillies, trimmed   pinch of caster (superfine) sugar

1 teaspoon sea salt   1 tablespoon black rice vinegar

....

If you prefer a milder paste, cut the chillies in half lengthwise and remove the seeds. Using a large knife, finely chop the chillies until they form a coarse paste, or alternatively use a small food processor.

Place the chillies in a non-reactive bowl, then add the sea salt, sugar, vinegar and 2–3 tablespoons water to thin it slightly. Stir to combine well. The chilli dip will keep, stored in an airtight container in the fridge, for about 4 days.

Chilli oil with sediment

Makes about 300 ml (10 fl oz)

3 tablespoons chilli flakes

250 ml (8½ fl oz/1 cup) vegetable oil

Put the chilli flakes in a heatproof jar. Heat the oil in a saucepan over a medium–high heat until the oil is almost smoking, then remove from the heat. Set aside to cool for 5 minutes, then pour the oil over the chilli flakes — the mixture should fizz slightly. Cool to room temperature, then seal the jar with the lid. The chilli oil will keep, stored at cool room temperature, for up to 2 weeks.

This oil, and the chilli–sesame variation below, can be served as a dip or condiment with noodles or dumplings, or any dish where you want an extra kick of chilli.

Chilli–sesame oil (variation)

Put 2 tablespoons sesame seeds and 3 tablespoons chilli flakes in a heatproof jar. Heat 250 ml (8½ fl oz/ 1 cup) vegetable oil in a saucepan (as above) and pour it over the seeds and flakes. Stir in 1 tablespoon sesame oil. Cool to room temperature, then seal the jar with the lid.

Chilli oil (strained)

Makes about 350 ml (12 fl oz)

20 g (¾ oz/¼ cup) chilli flakes

375 ml (12½ fl oz/1½ cups) vegetable oil

Put the chilli flakes in a heatproof bowl. Heat the oil in a saucepan over a medium–high heat until the oil is almost smoking, then remove from the heat. Leave to cool for 5 minutes, then pour the oil over the chilli flakes — the mixture should fizz slightly. Cover and leave the oil to infuse overnight, then strain into a jar, discarding the solids. Cool to room temperature, then seal the jar with the lid. The strained chilli oil will keep, stored at cool room temperature, for up to 2 weeks.

Sichuan pepper oil

Makes about 250 ml (8½ fl oz/1 cup)

15 g (½ oz/¼ cup) sichuan peppercorns

250 ml (8½ fl oz/1 cup) vegetable oil

Grind the peppercorns in an electric spice grinder until a coarse powder forms. Alternatively you can use a mortar and pestle. Combine the ground peppercorns and oil in a small saucepan over a medium heat. Cook for 5–6 minutes, or until fragrant, then remove the pan from the heat. Cool to room temperature, then stand for 6 hours or overnight for the flavours to infuse. Strain through a fine sieve into a jar, discarding the solids. The oil will keep, stored at cool room temperature, for up to 2 weeks.

Sa cha sauce

Makes about 625 ml (21 fl oz/2½ cups)

2½ tablespoons dried shrimp

2½ tablespoons dried scallops

12 dried red chillies

2 star anise

½ cinnamon stick

200 g (7 oz/1¼ cups) raw, skinned peanuts

2½ tablespoons sugar

1½ tablespoons mild curry powder

2 tablespoons sesame oil

60 ml (2 fl oz/¼ cup) clear rice wine

2½ tablespoons clear rice vinegar

80 ml (2½ fl oz/⅓ cup) dark soy sauce

80 ml (2½ fl oz/⅓ cup) sweet bean sauce

2 teaspoons shrimp paste (belacan)

80 ml (2½ fl oz/⅓ cup) peanut oil

1 onion, finely chopped

Put the dried shrimp, scallops and chillies in separate heatproof bowls, cover each with boiling water and soak for 30 minutes, or until softened. Drain well.

Using an electric spice grinder, grind the star anise and cinnamon to form a powder. Combine in a food processor with the shrimp, scallops and chillies and process until finely chopped. Add the peanuts, sugar, curry powder, sesame oil, rice wine, vinegar, soy sauce, sweet bean sauce and shrimp paste and process until a fine paste forms.

Heat the peanut oil in a saucepan over a medium heat, then add the onion and cook, stirring often, for about 7 minutes, or until soft. Add the paste in the processor and stir over a medium–low heat for 5–6 minutes, or until fragrant (stir often, so the sauce doesn't catch on the base of the pan and burn). Cool, then transfer to a container, seal and refrigerate. Sa cha sauce will keep, refrigerated, for up to 2 weeks.

Home-salted mustard greens

Makes about 600 g (1 lb 5 oz)

2 bunches (about 600 g/1 lb 5 oz) baby mustard greens

1½ tablespoons salt

Trim the very ends off the mustard greens, then wash the leaves and stalks well. Shake dry, removing as much water as possible. Place a single layer of mustard greens in a large glass or non-reactive dish and sprinkle with some of the salt. Repeat the layering and sprinkling with salt. Set aside for 20 minutes, then use your hands to toss the leaves well, making sure every leaf comes into contact with the salt. Set aside for another 20 minutes, then repeat the process twice more.

Transfer the greens, and any liquid, to a zip-lock bag, squeezing out as much air as possible, then seal. Refrigerate for up to 3 days. To use, rinse the greens well in plenty of cold water and press dry. Chop and use as required.

Pickled garlic

Makes about 400 g (14 oz)

500 ml (17 fl oz/2 cups) clear rice vinegar
8 heads garlic

220 g (8 oz/1 cup) sugar
2 teaspoons salt

Put the vinegar and 250 ml (8½ fl oz/1 cup) water in a saucepan and bring to the boil. Add the whole garlic heads and cook for 2 minutes, then remove the pan from the heat. Add the sugar and salt, stir to combine, then leave to cool to room temperature. Transfer the garlic heads and liquid to a clean jar, seal and refrigerate for 3–4 days before using.

Sichuan pickled vegetables

Makes about 2 litres (68 fl oz/8 cups)

325 g (11½ oz) carrots (about 3), peeled

1 bunch red radishes (about 300 g/10½ oz), trimmed

300 g (10½ oz) white turnip or daikon (white radish) (about ½ daikon), trimmed and peeled

Pickling brine

1 litre (34 fl oz/4 cups) water

80 g (2¾ oz/scant ⅔ cup) sea salt

6 dried red chillies

4 slices peeled ginger

1 garlic clove, peeled and bruised

1 teaspoon sichuan peppercorns

1 tablespoon clear rice wine

2 tablespoons sugar

To make the pickling brine, put all the ingredients in a large saucepan and slowly bring to a simmer over a medium–low heat. Remove from the heat and cool to room temperature.

Cut the carrots in half lengthwise, then cut into 5 mm (¼ inch) slices and place in a large bowl. Cut the radishes in half lengthwise, then cut into thin wedges and add to the bowl with the carrots. Cut the daikon in half lengthwise, then cut each half into three strips. Cut the strips into 5 mm (¼ inch) slices and add to the bowl. Toss to combine well. Transfer the vegetables to a cooled, sterilised 2 litre (68 fl oz/8 cup) jar or sterilised plastic container, then pour the brine over the vegetables. Seal, set aside at room temperature for 48 hours, then refrigerate. Sichuan pickled vegetables will keep, refrigerated, for up to 2 weeks.

Photograph page 253

Pickled chillies

Makes 200 g (7 oz)

200 g (7 oz) large red chillies

1½ tablespoons sea salt

2½ tablespoons clear rice wine

Remove and discard the stems from the chillies. Using a small, sharp knife, cut a slit in the side of each chilli, then pack them tightly into a sterilised jar.

Combine the salt, rice wine and 200 ml (7 fl oz) water in a small saucepan and bring to a simmer over a low heat, stirring to dissolve the salt. Pour the hot liquid over the chillies in the jar and leave to cool to room temperature. Seal the jar and refrigerate for 2–3 weeks before using.

Photograph page 341

Pickled radish

Makes about 600 g (10½ oz)

2 bunches red radishes (about 600 g/1 lb 5 oz), finely sliced

2 teaspoons sea salt

2 x 2 cm (¾ inch) wide strips orange peel, white pith removed

150 ml (5 fl oz) clear rice vinegar

55 g (2 oz/¼ cup) caster (superfine) sugar

5 slices peeled ginger

2 dried red chillies

Put the radishes in a colander with the sea salt and toss to combine well. Set aside for 1 hour to allow the excess moisture to sweat out. Using your hands, gently squeeze the radishes to get rid of the excess moisture, then pat dry with paper towel.

Meanwhile, combine the remaining ingredients with 80 ml (2½ fl oz/⅓ cup) water in a saucepan and bring to a simmer, stirring occasionally to dissolve the sugar. Remove the pan from the heat and set aside to cool to room temperature. Place the radishes in a sterilised jar, then pour the cooled liquid over them. Seal and refrigerate for 3–4 days before using. Pickled radish will keep, refrigerated, for up to 2 weeks.

Photograph page 229

Chilli pickled daikon

Makes 750 g (1 lb 11 oz)

1 daikon (white radish) (about 750 g/1 lb 11 oz), trimmed and peeled

1 teaspoon sea salt

150 ml (5 fl oz) clear rice vinegar

1 tablespoon caster (superfine) sugar

2½ tablespoons fresh chilli paste (page 406)

Cut the daikon widthwise into four even pieces, then finely slice each piece lengthwise. Cut the slices in half and place in a colander. Sprinkle with the sea salt and toss to combine well, set aside for 1 hour to allow the excess liquid to drain off, then rinse well under cold water. Drain, then transfer to a tea towel (dish towel) and gently press to remove as much liquid as possible. Transfer to a sterilised jar.

Meanwhile, combine the vinegar, sugar and chilli paste with 150 ml (5 fl oz) water in a saucepan and bring to a simmer over a medium heat, stirring to dissolve the sugar. Remove the pan from the heat and cool to room temperature. Pour the liquid over the daikon in the jar, seal, then store in a cool place overnight. The pickles are then ready to serve. Store in the refrigerator. Chilli pickled daikon will keep, refrigerated, for up to 2 weeks.

Photograph page 183

Red bean paste

Makes about 1 litre (34 fl oz/4 cups)

....

385 g (13½ oz/1¾ cups) dried adzuki beans
230 g (8 oz/1 cup) caster (superfine) sugar,
  or to taste

125 ml (4 fl oz/½ cup) vegetable oil

....

Put the adzuki beans in a bowl, cover with cold water and leave to soak overnight. Drain the beans and place in a saucepan, then add enough cold water to cover. Bring to a simmer and cook over a low heat for 30–40 minutes, or until very soft. Tip into a colander and drain well. Put the beans in a food processor and process to a smooth purée.

Transfer the bean purée to a saucepan with the sugar (if you like it sweeter, add 80 g/2¾ oz/⅓ cup extra sugar) and oil and bring to a simmer. Reduce the heat to low and cook, stirring often, for about 1½ hours, or until it has reduced and thickened to form a solid mass. The cooking time will vary a little depending on how much water is still in the beans and the size of your pan. Take care, as the mixture will become very thick as it nears the end of cooking and can easily burn — as the bean mixture starts to thicken, stir it frequently. Cool, then transfer to a container, cover and refrigerate. Red bean paste will keep, refrigerated, for up to 10 days.

Steamed rice

Serves 4 or 6

....

To serve 4
400 g (14 oz/2 cups) long-grain rice
750 ml (25½ fl oz/3 cups) water

To serve 6
600 g (1 lb 5 oz/3 cups) long-grain rice
1.125 litres (38 fl oz/4½ cups) water

....

Combine the rice and water in a medium-sized saucepan and bring to a simmer. Cover the pan tightly and cook over a medium heat for 12–15 minutes, or until the water has been absorbed. Remove the pan from the heat and set aside, covered, for 10 minutes, or until the rice is tender.

Home-dried chillies

Fresh chillies come in all shapes and sizes and with varying degrees of 'heat'; use the long red chillies here and not the smaller Thai bird's eye chillies, as they are too hot. As a guide, 500 g (1 lb 2 oz) fresh chillies yields about 150 g (5½ oz) dried chillies.

Preheat the oven to 80°C (175°F). Line a baking tray with foil. Trim the stems off the chillies, spread them evenly over the prepared tray and place in the oven for 4–6 hours — the drying time will vary depending on their size. After 3 hours, check the chillies every hour until they are dry and crisp (you should be able to crumble them with your fingers).

Remove from the oven and leave to cool. Depending on the recipe, you can then either use them whole, or crumble them as needed, using either your hands (wash your hands well afterwards) or an electric spice grinder to blitz them until you have even flakes. Store in a cool, dark place in an airtight container or jar.

Roasting peanuts

Preheat the oven to 180°C (350°F/Gas 4). Put the peanuts on a baking tray and roast for 15 minutes, or until golden, then remove the peanuts from the tray and cool.

Toasting sesame seeds

Preheat the oven to 180°C (350°F/Gas 4). Sprinkle the sesame seeds over a baking tray and toast for 8–10 minutes, or until golden. If toasting black sesame seeds, toast them for 7–8 minutes, or until they smell nutty. Remove the seeds from the tray and cool.

Rendering lard

Chop 500 g (1 lb 2 oz) fresh pork fat ('flare' fat or back fat are best: choose white, clear fat with no or few bits of flesh throughout) into small pieces. Add enough water to a heavy-based saucepan to come about 1 cm (½ inch) up the side of the pan, then add the fat and simmer over a low heat, stirring occasionally, for 40–50 minutes, or until all the fat has melted (the water will evaporate). Strain the rendered lard through a fine sieve or colander lined with muslin (cheesecloth) and store in a sealed container in the fridge.

GLOSSARY

Bamboo

Shoots There are over 200 types of bamboo grown in China, and the shoots of many of these are eaten as a vegetable. There are two periods of harvesting: spring and winter. Fresh bamboo must be peeled and blanched several times in boiling salted water before use, because they contain toxins that are only neutralised by boiling. Alternatively, you can buy peeled bamboo shoots in tins, stored in brine in vacuum-packs or frozen.

Preserved One of the most popular Chinese table condiments and a Sichuan must-have, bamboo shoots are preserved in chilli oil, retaining their crispness while taking on a kick of spice heat. A great accompaniment for congee and soups, preserved bamboo can also be added to stir-fries. Sold in either jars or vacuum-packed pouches in the condiment section of Asian grocers.

Dried leaves Steaming foods in leaves is a common technique in many parts of China. Bamboo leaves are essential for wrapping the famous sticky rice dumplings, called *zongzi*, and steamed meat dishes; the leaves keep the food moist and impart a distinctive, herbaceous flavour. The leaves are usually sold in dried bundles and are usually soaked overnight, then boiled briefly in water before they are used to wrap food.

Black cardamom

You may be familiar with green cardamom, but the species of black cardamom (*Amomum costatum*) used in Sichuan meat stews is a very different beast. It has larger pods than the more common black Indian cardamom, and its bold, smoky flavour comes from the traditional method of frying it over an open fire. When added to a long, slow braise, it imparts a deep, almost menthol note.

Candied winter melon

Winter melon (*dong gua*) looks like an elongated watermelon, but its flesh is snowy white. It is peeled and cut into batons, poached in a heavy sugar or glucose syrup, and then dried, giving it a texture similar to crystallised pineapple. Candied winter melon is a traditional Chinese New Year snack and is used as an ingredient in baking, notably in Wife cakes (pages 374–5).

Cassia

Also known as Chinese cinnamon or *rou gui*, cassia packs a bigger, more pungent and peppery flavour punch than cinnamon. Unlike the papery layers of cinnamon sticks, cassia bark sticks are thick and hard. It's one of the ingredients in five-spice, and is used in hotpots and Sichuan red braises. We suggest breaking larger pieces into smaller bits, 5 cm (2 inches) in length, and using one where a recipe calls for '1 piece cassia bark'.

Century eggs

Also known as thousand-year eggs or millennium eggs, these are traditionally made by curing whole eggs — usually duck eggs but sometimes chicken or quail — in an alkaline paste of salt and clay, ash, quicklime and rice hulls for several weeks. The solution penetrates the shell, changing the pH of the egg. This turns the egg white into a tea-coloured jelly and renders the yolk a dark greenish-grey and almost cheese-like in texture, with a strong whiff of ammonia. Modern methods achieve the same effect by soaking the eggs in a brine of calcium hydroxide, sodium carbonate and salt and wrapping them in plastic wrap. They're an acquired taste — the look and smell can be off-putting, but fans find them delicious on their own, with chilled tofu or in congee.

Chilli bean paste

Chilli bean paste is a Sichuanese product that's a specialty of Pixian, today a suburb of Chengdu. The best chilli bean pastes are ones based on broad (fava) beans but cheaper versions abound, using soybeans instead. Readily found in Asian grocers, this stuff is hot! Where specified in recipes, add less (or more) according to taste.

Chilli oil with sediment

A condiment from Sichuan province that's easy enough to make (page 407) but also readily available from Asian grocers. Essentially it's oil (peanut or vegetable) heated with chilli flakes, then cooled. Commercial types are red in colour and some are practically solid with the chilli sediment.

Chinese cured ham

There are regional variations in salting, seasoning, drying and/or smoking pork for ham in China. The most famous are the rich, smoky hams from southwest Yunnan and eastern Jinhua provinces — these are as sought after as artisan prosciutto in European cultures. These hams are not commonly exported; the nearest thing is cured salted pork, available in vacuum-packs in the refrigerated section of Asian grocers. If unavailable, prosciutto is a reasonable substitute. Some recipes also call for Chinese-style cured (dried) pork, a drier and more heavily smoked meat, which is sold vacuum-packed in long, thin lengths (you'll find it in the dried food section) — European speck would also do the trick.

Chinese olives

The fruit of the *Canarium album* tree, these look like Mediterranean olives but the similarity ends there. They are eaten most widely in the south of China, notably in Guangdong, and are used in hotpots, soups, stir-fries and even candied as unusual sweet treats. The fresh fruit is crisp, bitter, fragrant, sour and a little sweet all at the same time. The dried fruit and seeds are also eaten as a snack. Buy preserved Chinese olives in jars; they are usually labelled 'olive vegetable'.

Chinese pork sausage (lap cheong)

The Chinese make all manner of preserved and fermented sausage products, and many are regionally specific. The most common example in the West is *lap cheong*, a sweet fermented pork sausage that must be cooked before eating, despite its salami-like appearance. It is used in rice dishes, stir-fries, in soups and in sauces such as XO. *Lap cheong* is sold loose or in vacuum-packs. They keep well in the fridge once opened (for about 1 month), or for 10 weeks in the freezer.

Chrysanthemum leaves

Also called chrysanthemum greens or *tong hao*, the leaves and stalks, which come from the same family as the popular flower, are used as a vegetable in many Asian cuisines. Small, young leaves have a grassy, herbaceous and slightly sweet flavour and are a great raw ingredient for a salad. Mature leaves are more bitter and are best served steamed or in soups, hotpots and stir-fries, but require minimal cooking — more than 30 seconds of simmering or steaming and they'll turn mushy.

Chu hou sauce

Also known as *chee hou* sauce or paste, this dark-brown sauce is mainly used in braised dishes. It is a Cantonese specialty from the Foshan region. With hoisin sauce as its base, it features other aromatics such as star anise, garlic, fermented tofu and sesame oil. It keeps well in the fridge.

Claypot

When using your claypot for the first time, it needs to be soaked in cold water for 30 minutes, then left to dry at room temperature. Take care when using your pot; they can take high heat but not sudden fluctuations of heat, so always start cooking over a low heat and slowly increase the heat as needed. A sand pot is a type of claypot with a glazed interior and a rough, unglazed exterior. The 'sand' refers to the coarse texture of the pot, rather than it being made from sand. Claypots are porous, so hot air and moisture circulate constantly, promoting slow, even moist cooking, not unlike that done in a steam oven.

Dahurian angelica root

Known as DAR, Chinese angelica or *bai zhi*, dahurian roots are primarily produced in Sichuan province. The roots are harvested, finely sliced lengthwise and dried in the sun. Aromatic with a pungent taste, it's used extensively in Chinese medicine for cold and pain relief and as an anti-inflammatory. In cooking, it's used in soups and the dried root can be ground into a powder for desserts.

Dough sticks

Called *youtiao* or Chinese doughnuts, these are bought fresh each morning by the bag full to eat with congee or even just a simple mug of warm soy milk. They appear at yum cha wrapped in fresh rice noodles or inside fat, rolled *jian bing*, breakfast pancakes (page 362). Like croissants or puff pastry, these aren't the sort of thing people routinely make at home — buy them in packs from Asian grocers. Alternatively find a local dim sum or other casual Chinese eatery and see if they will sell you some, freshly cooked.

Dried salted fish

The Chinese have a long history of preserving fresh fish by sun-drying and salting it — the sight of fish hanging to dry is common in coastal and riverside villages. Saltwater and freshwater fish from anchovy-sized and up can be bought loose by weight at regional markets in China, but you'll find them packaged in the dried goods section of Asian grocers. Small fish can be deep-fried until crisp and eaten as snacks, while larger species, softened in hot water, are chopped up for frying or steaming.

Dried scallops

Also called conpoy, these come in all sizes and grades and can be very pricey. They are valued for their medicinal benefits, as well as being a tasty ingredient in sauces, stir-fries and rice dishes. They are very hard and need to be soaked in hot water before use. They are usually shredded into fine pieces for cooking.

Dried shrimp

These very small prawns (shrimp), which have been peeled and sun- or air-dried, have a salty, intense flavour with an odour to match. They are a protein source, a textural hit and a potent seasoning, used in soups, sauces and stir-fries — cooking mellows the flavour. The shrimp need to be soaked in warm water for about 30 minutes before use.

Fermented black beans

Made by fermenting and salting soybeans, which gives them a dry, crumbly, soft texture and a pungent, deeply savoury and salty flavour. Often they have been infused with orange peel. Always rinse well before use.

Fermented tofu, red and white

This preserved tofu is sometimes called 'Chinese cheese' for its surprisingly cheese-like texture — the result of fermentation breaking down the proteins in the curd. The red version has been cured in a brine with red yeast rice, shaoxing rice wine and chilli. The white tofu is cured in wine and/or brine, and can have seasonings added, such as chilli oil, sesame oil, star anise or dried shrimp. It is often served as a condiment with breakfast rice or congee, but also adds a sweet, intense edge to vegetable stir-fries and braises. You'll find it among the condiments at Asian grocers. Once opened, store in the fridge.

Garlic stems

Also called scapes, these are the flowering stems of certain types of garlic. Thick, long and bright green, they smell rather garlicky in their raw state, but when cooked (generally they are lightly stir-fried) they have a sweet, fresh flavour and crunchy texture that is rather unique.

Gingko nuts

These are found inside the seed of the *Ginkgo biloba* (maidenhair) tree and are held in high esteem by the Chinese as a cooking ingredient — in desserts, congee, stir-fries, braises and soups — and for their many health benefits (as an antioxidant, memory aid and to treat asthma, to name a few). The nuts (which can be spelled as either ginkgo or gingko) are potentially toxic if eaten uncooked and you're not supposed to eat too many of them. Small, yellow and a little mealy in texture, they're available in vacuum-packs.

Glutinous rice flour, cooked *See* Rice flour; glutinous rice flour

Glutinous rice wine

A sweet wine made from steamed glutinous rice that has been fermented using a special 'pill' that activates fermentation. You can buy the pills from Asian grocers, but the wine is readily available as well — look for large glass jars of it (filled with liquid and soft white rice grains) in the cooking wine section. Freshly made, the rice wine is quite thick and is eaten like a rice pudding although it is also used as a general cooking ingredient.

Goji berries

Also called wolf berries, goji berries come mainly from the northwestern province of Ningxia and are related to potatoes, tomatoes and eggplants (aubergines). They are packed with antioxidants and attributed with all kinds of health-giving properties. Goji berries are always cooked before they are eaten and are added to congee, tonic soups, chicken and pork dishes, or brewed into teas.

Guilin chilli sauce

Considered one of the 'three treasures' of the scenic city of Guilin (the others are a strong rice liquor and pickled tofu), this mixture of chillies, garlic and fermented black beans is widely used there and in other parts of Guangxi province. Readily available from Asian grocers.

Hoisin sauce *See* Sweet bean sauce

Honey dates

Also known as golden thread dates because of their ridged, thread-like appearance, or Shui Dong dates in honour of the area that produces them. The dried fruit is used in desserts, tonics, sweet soups and congee.

Lard

Lard is the fat of choice in Chinese cuisine, specifically pork lard. Yes, fat — natural, flavourful saturated fat. It's used for frying (it has a high smoking point and gives a nutty flavour), as shortening in pastries and doughs, and as an oil in various pastes. Many butcher shops render their own lard for home cooks, but it's easy to make your own (page 413).

Lily buds, dried

Sometimes labelled as 'daylily buds' or 'golden needles', the unopened flowers of the common daylily (*Hemerocallis fulva*) have been used in China as both a food and medicine for centuries. If you're lucky enough to find them fresh, they're a great addition to a stir-fry — they are something of a cross between a zucchini (courgette) flower and a green bean. The best dried buds are yellow-gold in colour and have a musky flavour; avoid ones that are brown and rubbery, as they're older and can be sour. Reconstituted in boiling water, they are used in pork and egg dishes and in hot and sour soups.

Liquorice root, dried

Liquorice may be considered a European sweet, but Chinese cuisine uses dried liquorice root as a spice in savoury dishes, such as broths and braises. In Chinese medicine, it's prized for its soothing properties. Indigenous to northern China, the liquorice plant is a member of the legume family. The woody root has a bittersweet, flavourful note similar to star anise. It's sold in dried and powdered form.

Longans, dried

Similar to lychees, longans are small, round fruits with peel-away skins, soft, almost translucent sweet flesh and a large seed. To use dried longans, rinse the fruit briefly before adding it to your dish — there's no need to reconstitute them if they will be cooked for 30 minutes or more. Longans are used for sweetening soups and desserts. Chinese medicine recommends dried longan fruit for its calming properties.

Lotus

Lotus root The knobbly under-water rhizome of the lotus plant. The root looks similar to a sausage and usually comes in a string of links of three. When peeled and cut crosswise, it reveals a lace-like pattern of symmetrical air holes. Young, smaller rhizomes, eaten raw, have a light, crisp texture and the flavour is sweet yet delicate; more mature ones can be bitter and are best cooked. Blanched lotus root can be used in cold dishes or stir-fries, added to soups and stews and even deep-fried. Store it in the fridge in a brown paper bag and use while fresh. It also comes peeled and vacuum-packed in salted water; look for it in the refrigerated section of Asian grocers.

Lotus root powder Made from finely ground, dried lotus root. The powder can be mixed with boiling water to make a gelatinous, porridge-like paste (often given to children as nursery food), and, like cornflour (cornstarch), it can be used as a thickener. Lotus root powder is a specialty of Hangzhou.

Lotus leaves, dried Used in much the same way as dried bamboo leaves as a wrap for steaming foods. They are prized in Chinese medicine for heart and liver health and even weight loss.

Lotus seeds Fresh lotus seeds are regarded as a seasonal delicacy, sold as a street-side snack during summer months. At other times, tinned or dried lotus seeds are used. Lotus seeds can be boiled and added to dessert soups, or sweetened and mashed to make a red-brown lotus seed paste, a popular filling for sweets like mooncakes.

Lotus seed paste Like red bean paste, this is made by blending cooked beans with sugar and a fat (either vegetable oil or lard). It has a golden-honey hue and good-quality commercial versions — sold in either jars, tins or plastic packs — have a silky texture. It's an alternative to using red bean paste in mooncakes, and also appears in sweet breads, buns and flaky pastries.

Maltose

This thick syrup is made from malted barley or wheat starches. Dense and sweet, it's the magic ingredient that gives *char siu* (barbecued pork) its moreish stickiness and Peking duck its burnished colour and flavour. The ancient Chinese preserved foods in maltose, and it still has a reputation as a tonic and a beauty aid to improve complexion. Maltose can be found in Asian grocers and major supermarkets.

Millet

Millet is a type of grass and its seeds are an important crop in northern China (its cultivation is said to pre-date rice crops). It is non-glutinous and highly nutritious, with a slightly nutty flavour. The seeds are cooked into congee and stews, while the flour is used to make noodles, steamed breads and baked goods. Both the grain and flour are available from health food shops and some supermarkets.

Mung bean starch

This is a highly refined gluten-free flour made by grinding dried mung beans. It is used in desserts, noodles, dumplings and certain pastries. Misleadingly, it is sometimes called green pea flour.

Osmanthus flowers, dried

While fresh osmanthus flowers (*gui hua*) have a heady fragrance, when dried, the tiny, delicate, golden-yellow blooms lend tones of apricot and peach to teas, infusions, savoury dishes and desserts. Popular in Jiangsu, Zhejiang and Shanghai cuisines, dried osmanthus also boosts the sweetness of tubers and roots, such as lotus and taro. Some Asian grocers may also stock osmanthus sugar for dessert decoration.

Pickled mustard greens

Also known as gai choy, this strongly flavoured, bitter plant (related to cabbage) is usually pickled in brine alone — hence a salty, sour tang — or with vinegar and sugar added. Most Asian grocers sell pickled mustard greens in vacuum-packs — look for a good yellow-green colour. Fresh versions are sometimes sold in tubs in the refrigerated section. Rinse first, then add to soups, stews or stir-fries, or serve as condiment.

Potato flour

Made from cooked, dried potatoes and used in baking, as a thickener and to coat foods for deep-frying. It contains no gluten. Potato starch flour is made using only potato proteins and it's slightly heavier when cooked, while potato flour tends to lighten (particularly) baked goods. Sweet potato flour is similar to potato starch flour (also called potato starch) but, as the name suggests, it's made from sweet potatoes.

Preserved mustard leaf

In a complex process, fresh mustard leaves are sun-dried, salted, fermented, steamed and dried again. The resulting dried clumps have a sweet tobacco-like smell, with a savoury funkiness. They're popular in Shaoxing cooking, adding a touch of umami to tofu and meat braises — rehydrate in water before adding to the pot. You'll find them in the dried goods aisle of Asian grocers where they might be labelled 'potherb mustard'.

Red bean paste

Adzuki beans are grown in the Yangtze River Valley and southern China. The small, slightly sweet, reddish beans can be made into a paste by blending the cooked beans with sugar and often lard or vegetable oil, which is then used as a filling for sweet cakes, steamed breads and dumplings. It's not difficult to make your own (page 412), and you can then regulate the sugar and fat content to taste, but commercial versions in jars and tins are readily available from Asian grocers; these have a firmer texture and are better for desserts.

Red dates

Also known as jujubes or Chinese dates, these don't grow on date palms but are the fruit of a deciduous tree in the buckthorn family. About the size of an olive, the dates dry on the tree before harvest. The result is a sweet-smelling fruit that's soft on the outside with a moist interior. Red dates are used in sweet soups and porridges, but also add a sweet note to slow-cooked beef and pork dishes.

Red yeast rice

A special rice product that has been fermented, a process that turns the grain from white to deep red. It is sold as hard grains and used as a natural colouring agent. Buy it from Asian grocers, and grind it as you need it using an electric spice grinder.

Rice flour; glutinous rice flour

These look identical but are not interchangeable so take care when purchasing. Confusingly, glutinous rice flour doesn't contain gluten (it's made from sticky or 'glutinous' rice) and is often sold as 'sweet' rice flour (it isn't sweet either). These fine, white, refined powders are widely used in Chinese cuisine, in various doughs, in desserts, to make noodles, breads and cakes and as thickening agents.

Cooked glutinous rice flour Also known as *koh fun*, commercially prepared cooked (or fried) glutinous rice flour is used in Chinese pastries and sweets, particularly mooncakes.

Roasted/fried broad beans

A moreish Chinese savoury snack made by deep-frying soaked, split dried broad (fava) beans in oil. They can be found skin on or off — the skin of the beans splits open in the heat and the bean itself becomes crisp and crunchy. Sold in the snack aisle of most Asian grocers and usually seasoned with salt, garlic and/or chilli.

Rock sugar

Rock sugar has a more subtle flavour than regular sugar. It is sold as hard lumps in either white or light brown ('yellow') forms. While the two types are interchangeable, use the pale sugar for dishes where ingredients are light in colour and the darker one (which does have a slightly stronger taste) where the finished dish is darker.

Sa cha sauce

We've included our own recipe for this sauce (page 408) but when you need some in a hurry, store-bought *sa cha* will do — it's often called 'barbecue' sauce on the bottle (look for Jimmy's brand). It is a feature of Taiwanese, Fujian and Teochew cooking and is a dark, sticky, complex, fragrant brew that includes dried shrimp, sugar, garlic, soybean oil and spices. For the *sa cha* noodle recipe, it's worth making your own; for the grilled squid (page 174), stir-fried pipis (page 165) or use on other barbecues, the ready-made one is fine if you are short on time.

Salted duck eggs

Soaking fresh duck eggs in salted brine is a traditional Chinese preserving technique. Like century eggs, the salt penetrates the porous eggshell and cures the white and yolk. If you open the egg without cooking, you'll find a very watery egg white and a firm-textured yolk that's turned from its normal yellow to bright orange-red. The eggs are normally boiled or steamed before being peeled and eaten — the white is intensely salty and some recipes call for it to be discarded. The yolk is less salty with a rich, buttery mouthfeel. Salted duck eggs are a popular condiment for congee. They're usually sold in packs of six.

Salted jellyfish

This is one of many odd, yet delicious, Chinese ingredients that is used more for its gelatinous crunch than its taste. The jellyfish is cured in salt, either in sheets or roughly shredded, and sealed in plastic. To prepare it, blanch in boiling water, then rinse repeatedly in cold water until the saltiness is removed. It is often eaten cold in salad-style dishes and has a texture similar to rubbery cooked squid.

Salted mackerel

Hold on to your nose — this fish is a stink bomb! Salted mackerel is not dried before packaging in plastic, so the flesh continues to 'ripen' during storage. Once you open the seal, the potent odour escapes in one, gasp-for-breath hit. Mainly it's used in recipes sparingly, as a flavouring agent for pork, rice or noodle dishes, adding a umami depth that's similar to anchovies.

Salted radish

Perhaps labelled as 'Chinese preserved radish', this is a daikon-style radish or turnip that has been heavily salted to preserve it. It's sold sealed in plastic in either whole, flattened pieces or shredded finely; some varieties have sweetening added. It gives dishes a crunch and savoury flavour.

Sesame seed paste

Chinese sesame paste Not to be confused with tahini, Chinese sesame seed paste is fragrant, thick and deeply flavoured. Made from roasted, finely pounded sesame seeds and oil, it has the consistency of peanut butter. Mainly used as an ingredient in savoury sauces (for noodles, tofu and chicken, for example), but also used in some breads. It keeps well, but store it in the fridge once opened.

Black sesame paste This paste is a daunting tar-black colour and has a rich, sweet, toasty flavour. If you can't find it in an Asian grocery store, try a Japanese one as it's popular in Japanese desserts, too.

Shaoxing rice wine/clear rice wine

The most famous Chinese cooking wine comes from Shaoxing, not far from Shanghai. It's often labelled as 'shaoxing wine'. Made using brewing techniques and from rice, there are various grades, from cooking wines to quality drinking ones, the latter of which are deep reddish-brown in colour and not unlike sherry in taste. In cooking, the wine is used in countless ways: in soups, stews, dumpling fillings, marinades and stir-fries, for example. A number of dishes, such as 'Drunken chicken' and 'Drunken prawns', make a feature of shaoxing wine and demand a good-quality drinking example.

Sichuan chilli bean sauce *See* Chilli bean paste

Sichuan pepper oil

This is essentially vegetable or peanut oil infused with the unmistakable fragrance and mouth-numbing properties of sichuan peppercorns. For an extra hit of flavour, it can be added at the last moment to stir-fries or dipping sauces or sprinkled over any of the rugged, Sichuanese-inspired recipes in this book. Buy it ready-made or make your own (page 408).

Sichuan peppercorns

A member of the citrus family, these are actually the husks of seeds from the prickly ash tree and not peppercorns at all. They have a unique, lemony aroma, which a light dry-roasting further enhances. Their main property, though, is their mouth-numbing ability, a sensation referred to in dishes called *ma la*, or 'numbing and spicy' in Chinese, applied when the peppercorns are used in tandem with chilli.

Sichuan preserved vegetables

Of the many preserved vegetables in Chinese cuisine, Sichuanese *zha cai* stands above the rest. A specialty of southern Sichuan, it's a pungent fusion of mustard green stems rubbed with salt and chilli powder, left to ferment to piquant perfection. Usually sold in jars, tins or foil/plastic sachets, this pantry staple has a salty, crunchy, spicy zing and adds a umami hit to tofu, noodle and rice dishes.

Southern apricot kernels

There's an important distinction between apricot kernels in Chinese cuisine. The northern kernels are small and carry traces of cyanide, which gives them a distinctive bitterness and calls for sparing use. Southern apricot kernels are larger, heart-shaped and distinctly sweeter. Both are used in traditional Chinese medicine to soothe the throat or cure coughs. In cooking, the southern apricot kernels are added to soups and desserts. Look for them in Asian grocers (they may be labelled as 'almond kernels') or try a Chinese herbalist.

Soy sauce

Soy sauce is made when soybeans, roasted grains and a specific type of micro-organism (*Aspergillus*), are left to ferment. The resulting mass is pressed and the liquid that is extracted is soy sauce. In the past, this process occurred naturally over some months, but these days most soy sauce is made on an industrial scale and faster methods are used.

Light soy sauce Made using steamed wheat, soybeans and *Aspergillus*, as mentioned above. The mixture is left to ferment in brine and results in a thinner, more opaque, lighter-bodied sauce than dark soy.

Dark soy sauce Uses no wheat, just the beans and culture. The beans are treated with rock salt and have a longer fermentation than for light soy. Because of this, the flavour is saltier and stronger and the sauce is thicker than light. Mushroom soy sauce is a dark soy that has been infused with dried Chinese mushrooms.

Soy paste Also called thick soy sauce, soy paste is a Taiwanese and Fujianese ingredient, made from soy sauce, thickeners and sugar or molasses. It's often used in cooking for extra colour as well as flavour.

Soybean powder

Sometimes called roasted soybean powder or soybean flour, this high-protein, high-fibre food is made from roasting and grinding dried soybeans. Use it in baking and as a thickener for soups.

Sweet bean sauce; hoisin sauce

Sweet bean sauce Variously called sweet bean paste, sweet flour sauce and sweet soybean paste. It exists in a few regional permutations, but essentially the ingredients include flour, sugar, soybean lees and salt. Sweet bean sauce is most famously used as an accompaniment to Peking duck. Yellow soybean sauce or paste is a Beijing ingredient and similar except that it's not so sweet.

Hoisin sauce Similar to sweet bean sauce, but contains extra ingredients, such as sesame, vinegar, garlic, a dash of chilli and other spices. Its name literally translates as 'seafood' but it is never really used with fish. It is an essential ingredient in the Cantonese *char siu* (barbecued pork).

Sweet potato starch noodles

This Sichuanese 'fast food' is sold by street vendors, who pass a thickish batter of sweet potato starch through a sieve and let the fresh noodles drop straight into boiling water before cooking it up with a zingy sauce. Lighter than wheat noodles but with more body than rice noodles, they have a chewy, elastic texture. Sold dried in Chinese and Korean grocery stores, they are a brownish-grey colour — not to be confused with the white or clear bean thread (glass) vermicelli noodles. Check the label to ensure they contain potato starch.

Tangerine peel, dried

Sometimes referred to as dried orange peel, the sun-dried skins of tangerines are used as a seasoning. Their slightly bitter, citrusy edge flavours dishes such as red bean congee, and various hearty stews and braises.

Tapioca flour

Also called tapioca starch, this is the very finely ground root of the cassava plant. It is used to thicken sauces, in some dumpling wrappers and to dust foods before deep-frying.

Tianjin preserved vegetable

Known as *dong cai* in Chinese, this may be variously labelled as Tianjin winter vegetable, Tianjin preserved vegetable or preserved cabbage. It's made by a simple process of salting and pickling finely chopped Tianjin cabbage, often with the addition of garlic, in earthenware crocks. Sold in jars or vacuum-packs, this odorous pickle adds zest to soups, stir-fries or stewed dishes.

Tofu

A high-protein food made from soy milk, which is coagulated using natural gypsum or seawater-based nigari. Tofu goes by many monikers — including bean cake and bean curd — and comes in many forms. It has a neutral flavour, so carries robust sauces and seasoning well; it can be stir-fried, steamed, braised and deep-fried; and it's an ideal meat substitute in vegetarian dishes. Most of the following are available at supermarkets or Asian grocers (fresh tofu is located in the refrigerated food section). Use within 2–3 days of opening.

Silken tofu A soft, creamy tofu with an almost blancmange-like texture. It is often set in the container it comes in — coagulant is added to hot soy milk and it's hygienically sealed, requiring no refrigeration until opening. Silken tofu can be served cold, warm or hot, in sweet or savoury dishes, but doesn't lend itself to stir-fries as the curds scramble. It forms the basis of the classic spicy Sichuan braised dish, *mapo doufu*.

Firm tofu This is drained and pressed, yet still holds a great deal of water. It has a firm skin, with an inner texture like a firm custard, and acts like a sponge to soak up flavours. You may want to press it to remove some of the moisture: set it between sheets of paper towel and top with a plate and a heavy tin for weight.

Hard tofu Also known as dry tofu, because most of the liquid has been pressed out of it. While it will crumble like feta cheese when sliced thinly, it generally retains its shape and meaty texture. Thanks to its high fat content, it crisps up well when fried.

Pressed tofu sheets/shreds These resemble sheets of fresh lasagne and have a similar (albeit tougher) texture to pasta. They are ideal for filled rolls or packages, dim sum style. They are sold in frozen packs at good Asian grocery stores. Tofu shreds are simply sheets cut into thin matchsticks, and used in salads and stir-fries. They are generally sold fresh in vacuum-packs.

Five-spice tofu The curd is pressed until firm, then braised in soy sauce, five-spice and other ingredients to produce a golden-coloured, rich-flavoured tofu. Just slice and stir-fry or add to soups or salads.

Egg tofu (tube tofu) A pale-golden tofu that takes its colour from the eggs in it or, sometimes, from added colouring. Beaten eggs are strained and mixed into the soy milk, coagulant is added, then the mixture is poured into plastic tubes to curdle — it's pre-cooked in that packaging ready for sale. It's creamy with a richer mouthfeel than silken tofu.

Tofu puffs A texture sensation. Hard tofu, with its lower moisture content, is cut into bite-sized cubes or triangles and deep-fried until golden-brown and crisp, yet still chewy — the frying makes the tofu even more flavour-absorbent. They make a moreish snack cold or hot, served in a light sauce, or can be added to hotpots.

Tofu skin (yuba) Technically, this isn't tofu, as it's not made with a coagulant. Rather, it's the skin that forms on the surface of soy milk when it's boiled. The skin is skimmed off the surface and dried into yellowish sheets. In cooking, the sheets are rehydrated and commonly used to wrap dim sum. Tofu skin can also be dried in bunches to resemble meat — it's often fried or steamed in this form as a replacement for chicken or duck.

Rice vinegar – clear, red, black

Compared to Western vinegar, the Chinese equivalent is mild with only 3–4 per cent acid. It is made by the action of acetic acid on rice wine (the wine in turn is made from fermented glutinous rice). In China, there are broadly three different types of vinegar: clear (white), black and red.

Clear The sharpest flavoured and used mainly in pickles and cold dishes.

Red Slightly sweeter than clear and gets its hue from the addition of red yeast rice, and is added to fish and seafood dishes.

Black Most black vinegar is produced in the city of Zhenjiang (Chinkiang of old), and is highly prized for its smooth mellowness, not unlike Italian balsamic. It is widely added to stews, stir-fries and noodle dishes and is often used as a dip for dumplings and the like. Black vinegar is also produced in Shanxi province, notably in the capital Taiyuan, where aged (mature) black vinegar is appreciated for its rich, smoky sweetness and extra body. The Pun Chun brand of black vinegar is a highly sweetened vinegar product that is used for cooking pork hocks with ginger (page 225).

Velveting

Velveting is a Chinese technique that protects foods (chicken, fish and meat) from becoming tough when cooked. The food is first usually cut into small pieces (for stir-frying, simmering or frying), then coated in a mixture of egg white, cornflour, wine and seasonings such as soy sauce or garlic, which protects the surface of the food as it cooks. Another velveting method calls for passing meat or chicken through a deep-fryer set to a relatively low heat to gently par-cook it; it is then finished at a higher temperature, generally in a wok as part of a stir-fry.

Wheat gluten

Used as a meat substitute, wheat gluten is made from washing wheat flour dough until everything has washed away except the elastic-like gluten. It looks like a sponge and it can be purchased in either a dried block or frozen form. Like tofu — usually its shelf-mate in Asian grocers — it's low in fat and high in protein and is prized for its ability to absorb flavours. Its texture passes easily as meat and is used as the base of 'mock' pork, duck and in other vegetarian dishes. A marinated version, often with peanuts or mushrooms added, makes a good condiment for congee.

Wood ear fungus

From the poetic 'cloud ear' to the prosaic 'black fungus', this edible fungus is known by many names. Sold fresh at many greengrocers, it comes in alien-looking furls of velvety brown-black that feel almost rubbery to touch. There's also a white cloud ear, which differs only in colour. Served raw in salads, wood ear fungus has a refreshing crunch; when cooked, it becomes gelatinous and slippery. If you can't find fresh wood ear, it's readily available in dried form — simply reconstitute it in boiling water for 30 minutes.

Yam bean

Also called jicama, this versatile root vegetable is a Chinese staple, variously termed potato bean, cool potato (*liang shu*) or earth melon (*tu gua*). The tubers look like squashed balls, pale cream-beige in colour with a thin skin. Once peeled, they can be eaten raw (young, less fibrous roots are best for this) and are sweet to taste with a pleasing crunch. Often used as a substitute for water chestnuts, it appears in western China in many forms: grated and added to soups and stir-fries; raw and shredded, mixed with chilli sauce to serve as a side dish; or processed as a starch and used as a gluten-free flour.

Yu zhu

This is the dried, edible rhizome of a member of the lily family called Solomon's Seal. It is sweet with a marked fragrant edge and is used extensively in soups. Its place in Chinese cooking is due to its potent medicinal properties — it's believed to be good for the lungs and stomach. Buy lightly golden-coloured *yu zhu* — the very white specimens have probably been bleached.

INDEX